First published 2011 by Ashgate Publishing

2 Park Square, Milton Park, Abingdon, Oxon OX14 4RN
711 Third Avenue, New York, NY 10017, USA

Routledge is an imprint of the Taylor & Francis Group, an informa business

First issued in paperback 2016

British Library Cataloguing in Publication Data
Caudill, David Stanley.
Stories about science in law : literary and historical images of acquired expertise. -- (Law, language and communication)
1. Science and law. 2. Literature and science. 3. Law and literature. 4. Law in literature. 5. Trials in motion pictures.
I. Title II. Series
340.1'1-dc22

Library of Congress Cataloging-in-Publication Data
Caudill, David Stanley.
Stories about science in law : literary and historical images of acquired expertise / by David S. Caudill.
p. cm. -- (Law, language and communication)
Includes bibliographical references and index.
ISBN 978-1-4094-2680-6 (hardback) 1. Science and law. 2. Literature and science. I. Title.
K487.S3C38 2011
344'.095--dc22

2011005816

ISBN 978-1-4094-2680-6 (hbk)
ISBN 978-1-138-26136-5 (pbk)

Stories About Science in Law

Literary and Historical Images of Acquired Expertise

DAVID S. CAUDILL
Villanova University School of Law, USA

Routledge
Taylor & Francis Group
LONDON AND NEW YORK

Contents

For Penny and Chris

Preface and Acknowledgements

Much of the material for this book originated in a series of conference papers and law journal publications over the past decade. Chapters 2 and 3 are based upon and include substantially revised portions of my articles entitled (i) "Scientific Narratives in Law: An Introduction [to a special issue on law, literature, and science]," in *Law and Literature* vol. 14, no. 2, pp. 253–74 (© 2002 by The Cardozo School of Law, Yeshiva University; published by the University of California Press), and (ii) "Law-and-Literature, Literature-and-Science, and Enhancing the Discourse of Law/Science Relations," in *Journal of the Legal Profession* vol. 27, no. 1, pp. 1–22 (2003). Chapter 4 is based upon a CLE presentation given at a Washington and Lee University Law School Fall Alumni Law-and-Literature Weekend, and includes a substantially revised version of my article entitled "Ibsen's *An Enemy of the People* and the Public Understanding of Science in Law," in *Georgetown International Environmental Law Review* vol. 16, no. 1, pp. 1–19 (2003) (reprinted with permission of the publisher, Georgetown International Environmental Law Review © 2003). Chapter 5 is based upon a law-and-literature conference paper delivered at the University of Melbourne Law School, and includes a substantially revised version of my article entitled "Idealized Images of Science in Law: The Expert Witness in Trial Movies," in *St. John's Law Review* vol. 16, no. 1, pp. 1–19 (2008). Chapter 6 is based upon a CLE presentation given at a Washington and Lee University School of Law Fall Alumni Law-and-Literature Weekend, and includes a substantially revised portions of my article entitled "The Year of Truman Capote: Legal Ethics and *In Cold Blood*," in *Oregon Law Review* vol. 86, no. 2, pp. 295–328 (2008). Finally, Chapter 7 is based on my research as the 2007/2008 Société de Chimie Industrielle (American Section) Fellow at the Chemical Heritage Foundation in Philadelphia, and includes a substantially revised version of my article entitled "Arsenic and Old Chemistry: Images of Mad Alchemists, Experts Attacking Experts, and the Crisis in Forensic Science," in *Boston University Journal of Science and Technology Law* vol. 15, no. 1, pp. 1–33 (2009). I appreciate the permissions granted by the foregoing journals to use revised and updated portions of my earlier articles in this book.

I am grateful for the research support over many summers from the Law Center at Washington and Lee University and from Villanova University Law School, and I would especially like to thank Dean David Partlett, Dean Mark Sargent, and Dean Doris Brogan for their encouragement and guidance. Over the last decade, in developing the themes of this book, I have benefitted greatly from interactions with Professors Gary Edmond (UNSW), David Mercer (Univ. Wollongong), Simon Cole (Univ. Calif.-Irvine), Hugh Crawford (Georgia Tech), Barbara Allen

(Virginia Tech), L.H. LaRue (Washington & Lee), Joseph Sanders (Univ. Houston), Michael Risinger (Seton Hall Univ.), Carl Cranor (Univ. Calif.-Riverside), Keith Warner (Santa Clara Univ.), and Jeremy Gans (Melbourne Univ.), as well as with Jody Roberts and Ron Brashear (Chemical Heritage Foundation). In addition, I want to thank Anne Wagner and Vijay Kumar Bhatia, the editors of the series on Law, Language and Communication, for including this book in that series. I am also grateful to Maria Natale for her tireless effort in preparing the manuscript for publication. Finally, I want to thank the editors and staff at Ashgate Publishing Ltd, and especially publisher Alison Kirk, for this opportunity.

David Caudill
Villanova, Pennsylvania

Chapter 1
Introduction

Near the end of 2010, at the mid-point of the (first?) Obama Administration, a *Wall Street Journal* editorial opinion entitled "Ag Department Uproots Science" warned of a "jaw-dropping" move on the part of U.S. Agriculture Secretary Tom Vilsack:

> [He] has invited activists and biotech critics to shape the agency's regulatory decision on a biotech product. If the precedent stands, it could permanently politicize a system that is supposed to be based on science (*Wall Street Journal* 2010).

Even though "Roundup Ready," an alfalfa variety produced by Monsanto to withstand a popular herbicide, recently endured an environmental impact review that judged the product as "substantially equivalent to other varieties without red flags for regulators," Vilsack suggested "that science itself is subjective, and that he could have three different groups bring him three different supposedly scientific opinions" on the risks of Roundup Ready (*Wall Street Journal* 2010). Such "antics," granting governmental imprimatur to "vintage antibiotech activist fare" of a type seen "in trade disputes with the European Union," compelled the editorialist to conclude:

> If nonscience criteria are introduced as considerations for allowing the sale of biotech crops, the effect would be disastrous for the [U.S. Dept. of Agriculture's] regulatory reputation. We hope Secretary Vilsack makes his decision based on science, not politics (*Wall Street Journal* 2010).

Plain and simple, black and white, science versus politics.

The editorial is a microcosm of sorts for the world of law/science relations. Its author unwittingly revived the decades-old "science wars," which oversimplistically divided those who believe in the esoteric and decisive authority of objective science, from those who saw science as a cultural activity betraying social, institutional, rhetorical, and even political aspects in the construction of its authority. The former resisted what they saw as an attack on science (Collins and Evans 2002:276), while the latter resisted caricature as complete relativists with no appreciation for scientific progress. In academic terms, the former view was associated with a positivistic or idealized view of science as rising above politics and culture, while the latter view, associated with "science studies" or the sociology of scientific knowledge, variously emphasized:

> that it is necessary to draw on "extra-scientific factors" to bring about the closure of scientific and technical debates—scientific method, experiments, observation, and theories are not enough (Collins and Evans 2002:239).

Finally, while adherents of the former view might have seen the need for elite scientists alone to make political and legal decisions on matters involving science and technology, the latter view's adherents "[a]lmost invariably … call[ed] for greater dialogue between science and the public, and for increased participation in decision-making about science and technology" (Collins and Evans 2002:272).

These positions can easily be identified in the brief *Wall Street Journal* editorial—in the implied criticism of Vilsack's suggestion that science is subjective, in the reference to the European Union (where greater dialogue between science and the public has been normalized), and in the clean divisions between science and politics, between scientific data and nonscience criteria, and between seemingly rational actors and "activists." The notion that there might be three credible but contradictory scientific opinions on any regulatory matter is dismissed as virtually impossible—hence the adjective "supposedly" when discussing different scientific opinions. The editorial therefore represents a particular view of expertise in law/science relations, namely one that eclipses genuine scientific controversy. That is, the environmental impact review (conducted by the Department of Agriculture's Animal and Plant Health Inspection Service branch) is assumed to be "science," while critics are marginalized as pseudo-scientific activitists, and Vilsack's acknowledged doubt is dismissed as politically-driven.

Of course, the fact that the editorial appeared in the *Wall Street Journal* could lead one to discredit the argument as pro-agri-business, and its status as an editorial opinion rather than a news report reduces its significance. For my purposes, however, the editorial highlights the significance of one's images of science and scientific expertise and their role in legal contexts, whether in administrative decision-making involving science and technology or in the courtroom when a lawsuit involves scientific issues. Clearly, law relies on science, but how do we picture that relationship? One resource for exploring our understanding of science and its place in law is popular culture, including the literary representatives of law and science in novels, plays, and movies, as well as in historical narratives. My question in this book, without exhaustively surveying the field but by offering some examples, is what do we learn about the place of science in law when we consider the popular culture images of that relationship? A preliminary question for the reader, however, may be why those sources—stories about science in law—are promising for the study of law/science relations. My answer is that popular culture images of law, on the one hand, and popular culture images of science, on the other, have proved to be fruitful for understanding law, and science, respectively.

For example, the law-and-literature movement is based in part upon the notion, controversial in some critics' eyes, that literary representations of law and lawyers can offer insights into contemporary legal processes and institutions. While a fictionalized account of a legal proceeding may in some respects be inferior to an historical or scholarly legal account, fiction about law and lawyers can nevertheless function to raise ethical issues, demonstrate how established law might reflect social bias, or provide models for reform. Indeed, Richard Weisberg refers to literature as a "source of law," providing "unique insights into law's underpinnings" that can be "richer and certainly more accessible" than philosophy of law texts (Weisberg 1992:3). The notion that literature is a *source* of law sounds controversial—law is usually found in statutes, judicial opinions, reputable commentaries—but Weisberg means to make a strong point that literature about lawyers is not dispensable. From another vantage, Cynthia Bond argues that cinema participates in the constitution of race and racial classifications, such that audiences viewing a law film actually *construct* legally significant categories as part of their spectatorship (Bond 2010). While that too may sound counter-intuitive, the capacity of visual media to construct culture, and the way that law reflects culture in its operation and interpretation, grants to popular culture an oft-hidden power to create social realities. Thus William MacNeil coins the term *lex populi* (people's law or pop law) in turning to literary, televisual, and cinematic sources for jurisprudential insights (MacNeil 2008:1). Such sources "not only reach a much larger audience than standard legal texts, but potentially ... help restore topics of jurisprudential import—justice, rights, ethics—to where they belong: ... with the community at large" (MacNeil 2007:1–2). Historical accuracy, which some might see as the primary value of literary representations of law and legal processes, is somewhat beside the point in light of the capacity of fictional images of law to direct sympathies, encourage moral judgments, or create hero-figures, which effects can in turn influence how law students, lawyers, and judges respectively learn, practice, and apply the law.

Similarly, literature-and-science studies are based in part on the notion, likewise controversial, that popular culture images of science and scientists have the power to change public perceptions of the scientific enterprise, influence government policy, inspire (or discourage) future scientists, affect research support and funding, and even create public consensus concerning a particular scientific theory. For example, there is a literary tradition of negative portrayals of science and scientists, documented by Haynes (1994) and suggesting that science is dangerous, or that scientists are amoral; likewise, Tudor (1989) documented the persistent image of the mad scientist in the history of horror movies. Both traditions can be linked to cultural awareness of the risks of science and the need for ethical or other regulatory controls. But there is also a contemporary backlash among scientists interested in (or writing) science fiction. Jennifer Rohn, the author of two laboratory novels (and editor of the website LabLit.com) coined the term "Lab Lit" in 2001 "to describe realistic novels that contain scientists as central characters plying their trade" (Rohn 2010a). Like those who distinguish *hard* science fiction (or [plausible] science *in* fiction) from science *fantasy*, Rohn distinguishes "Lab Lit" from "science fiction, in which the action takes place in speculative worlds and may not involve scientist characters" (Rohn 2010a).

Rohn describes the stereotypes in science fiction—"arrogance, asexuality, semi-autism, out-of-control experiments and concomitant downfall"—as clichéd, and seems to prefer positive portrayals (albeit in a "culture [that] is a complex web of urgent human passions and behaviors") to help science's image and to reduce public distrust of science (Rohn 2006). There is, nevertheless, a critical edge in Lab Lit; Rohn says of biotech that "what constitutes truth is just as ephemeral here as in the academic world, no matter how shiny its packaging" (2010b). Allegra Goodman's *Intuition* (2006), an unflattering example of Lab Lit, involves scientific fraud—"one of the guilty secrets of the scientific world," the prevalence of which "policymakers seriously underestimate" (Cookson 2009).

> *Intuition* ... is a brilliant fictional account of what might drive a scientist to manipulate data—and [it] captures the sheer uncertainty and ambiguity over research misconduct .... Fraud proves itself an excellent theme for bringing out the human side of science[:] ... every "proof" and every "truth" is brought to us by humans, who are far from infallible (Cookson 2009).

Scientists, in Goodman's novel, rely on luck, "charm money from NIH," crave recognition, and suppress data in a feudal institution of jealousy and politics (Goodman 2006:18, 31, 127, 182, 211, 230). Thus the pursuit of realism in Lab Lit, albeit escaping the negative portrayals of *Frankenstein*-genre clichés, actually enhances the critical potential for offering the public a modest, rather than idealized, view of science. While one might not be able, in hard science fiction studies, to replicate Weisberg's form of argument—literature is not a *source* of scientific knowledge—it is arguably a source of knowledge *about* science, and certainly a source of popular culture images of science.

My own effort is aimed at combining (1) law-and-literature studies (wherein literature offers insights into legal processes and institutions) with (2) literature-and-science studies (wherein literature offers insights into scientific practice and progress) to enrich the discourse of (3) law/science relations (which is itself a field of study that focuses on contemporary rules of evidence and regulatory frameworks, and seldom relies on literary or historical sources). In such an enterprise, we do learn something about law, especially the ways in which law relies on science and sometimes idealizes the capacity of science to settle legal disputes; we also learn something about science, especially the ways in which science is like law—institutional, rhetorical, cultural, and even political. But my primary goal is to focus on stories that explore the relationship between law and science, and especially the cultural images of science that prevail in legal contexts.

The particular approach in this book contrasts with but parallels other methods of exploring the ways that expertise is transferred to or constructed within legal contexts. Sociologists of scientific knowledge might proceed by conducting ethnographic studies—visiting laboratories, interviewing scientists—to understand how credibility and expertise are established, and then observe what happens to science in law—how experts function in regulatory or litigation contexts, and how controversies are settled. Likewise,

> [p]olitical scientists study expertise [and its role in public decision making], and more often than not they have important things to say ... Economists of various persuasion, but in particular the new economics of science ..., are [also] rediscovering the phenomena analyzed by sociology of scientific knowledge ... (Rip 2003: 421, 428).

And of course, historians and philosophers of science attend to questions concerning the origins and development of, as well as criteria for judging, scientific expertise.

By contrast, the subject of inquiry for this book, literary and historical images of scientific expertise in law, lies at the intersection of the three aforementioned interdisciplinary projects: law and science, law and literature, and literature and science. The first two projects are primarily associated with legal scholarship—i.e., "law" is typically "the privileged element" or object of interdisciplinary inquiry in the two dyads (law and science, law and literature), insofar as the inquiry is typically concerned with what literature (both its texts that represent law and lawyers and its critical methodologies) or scientific knowledge can tell us about or *do* for law (Pether 2009:318 n.7). The third project (literature and science), conversely, is not typically viewed as a field of science, but is rather associated with literature (both its texts that represent science or scientists, and its critical methodologies, including language and rhetoric studies) or science studies, including historical, philosophical, or sociological studies of science. My own focus on literary and historical images of expertise (appropriated into legal contexts) simultaneously harnesses elements from all three projects to create a hybrid enterprise of sorts.

The law and science project is not so much a unified field of inquiry as it is a general recognition that the understanding of science and technology is crucial for numerous areas of law, including not only scientific expertise to offer insights in the courtroom and in regulatory contexts, but also patent law, bio-ethics, and regulation of science and technology (including pollution abatement, genetically-modified food safety, pre-market drug testing, and restrictions on synthetic biology, to name but a few). The relationship of law and science is therefore the subject of conferences, journals, associations (e.g., the ABA section on science and technology), and law school courses. Nevertheless, the "project" of law and science can be variously defined, and because its perceived elements are part of numerous other sub-disciplines (evidence law, administrative law, environmental law, health law, cyberlaw), its boundaries are vague. In any event, since this book is about scientific expertise in law, albeit focused on literary and historical images, my inquiry can be located within the "law and science" project.

As to the law and literature, and literature and science, projects, and the potential for a hybrid law, literature, and science project, they are the subject of Chapter 2. Acknowledging the difficulty of identifying law-lit and lit-sci as "movements" or clearly bounded subdisciplines, I explore the twin inquires in law *and* literature studies (i.e., law *in* literature, and law *as* literature) and the twin inquires in literature *and* science studies (i.e., science *in* literature, and science *as* literature). I characterize my approach as a hybrid because, for example, a fictional text about a scientist testifying in court is not only a literary representation of law (law *in* literature), as well as literary representation of a scientist (science *in* literature), but the testimony of the scientist is both a legally significant text (law *as* literature) and a scientific text (science *as* literature) that can be analyzed using literary critical or rhetorical tools.

The chapters that follow provide examples of my hybrid approach in various literary and historical contexts. Chapter 3 considers several exemplary "literature and science" short stories (by Ramón y Cajal) that not only reveal the ethical, rhetorical, and reputational (or public relations) aspects of the scientific enterprise, but frequently contrast law and lawyers with science and scientists. My goal is to compare Cajal's literary descriptions of science and scientists with an idealized view that often dominates legal discourse. Chapter 4, focusing on Arthur Miller's adaptation of Ibsen's *An Enemy of the People*, explores the recent interest in the public understanding of science and the argument that the public should play a role in scientific controversies. I then identify judges as belonging to the public (i.e., not on the "side" of science) with respect to courtroom experts and admissibility determinations, and distinguish between two judicial images of science. In Chapter 5, I turn to trial movies involving experts, and identify there the same two views of science—an idealized view and a modest or pragmatic view—that correspond to the two views of science in the post-*Daubert* U.S. courtroom. Judicial and public idealizations of science, I argue, have adverse consequences in law. Chapter 6 re-visits Capote's *In Cold Blood* to reflect on the ethical obligations of lawyers with respect to expert evidence. Notwithstanding Capote's claim that his "true" novel has no authorial message, I show that Capote implicitly condemns legal processes as potentially detrimental to both scientific progress and the goal of justice in law. Finally, in Chapter 7, I consider the ethical obligations of scientific experts, with reference to an early nineteenth-century episode of alleged arsenic poisoning. The medical journal article on the affair by Dr Samuel Jackson, published in 1829, not only reveals the discursive and literary aspects of scientific texts, but demonstrates the modesty required of experts in the courtroom. Moreover, I show that the history of arsenic poisoning expertise in the nineteenth-century parallels in some important respects the crisis in forensic science nowadays.

I conclude in Chapter 8 that the foregoing stories reveal important aspects of science and its interaction with legal processes and institutions. Challenging the idealized view of science as a catalog of stabilizing truths to be appropriated into law, the literary materials selected for this book reveal science to be a social enterprise involving public relations, cultural authority, contradictory self-images, ethical dimensions, and rhetorical strategies that together determine the place of science in law.

I consider this book to be introductory and suggestive, rather than comprehensive, with respect to the potential value, for law, of reflecting on stories of appropriated scientific expertise. Following the U.S. Supreme Court's opinion in *Daubert v. Merrill Dow Pharmaceuticals* (*Daubert* 1993), there was a barrage of scholarly interest and publication concerning the appropriate standards for judicial assessment of the scientific validity of expert testimony. Questions about the nature of science and scientific methodology, and whether the image(s) of science developed by courts hearing cases involving scientific expertise were accurate or realistic, sustained numerous legal debates in the decade following *Daubert* (1993). And then, just as those debates might have died down, the so-called forensic sciences, especially identification techniques (other than DNA technologies) associated with police crime laboratories, began to come under a severe scrutiny that continues today. Questions about the nature of science and scientific methodology, and whether some forensic "sciences" are science at all, have therefore been revived in legal contexts. This book, in an indirect fashion due to its attention to presumably marginal (from a scientific perspective) literary and historical sources, focuses on and questions some of the contemporary images of science in law.

The project described in this book intersects with, benefits from, and sometimes builds upon the work of numerous scholars in law, literature, and/or science. First, in the wake of *Daubert*, Beyea and Berger identified two competing visions of science or "schools of thought" that judges alternatively draw upon in their judgments of scientific validity: (i) Science as Logical Reasoning, wherein science is viewed as an accessible catalog of truths, comporting "with the popular concept of a scientist doggedly collecting irrefutable facts" and moving "from observations or data to general laws of nature"; and (ii) Science as Process, wherein science is viewed as a contentious process of "intuition, conjecture, inference, professional judgment, and repeated testing," involving subjective elements in each step of the production of scientific knowledge (Beyea and Berger 2001:328–30). While one might criticize Beyea and Berger for setting up a superficial contrast between the so-called positivist tradition and a fairly conventional process account which they associate with Karl Popper and Thomas Kuhn, thereby appearing to be oblivious to decades of scholarship in science studies (or the sociology of scientific knowledge) that moves well beyond Popper and Kuhn by identifying the role(s) of social, rhetorical, and institutional aspects of the production of scientific knowledge, it is nevertheless helpful to identify visions of science that matter in law and influence legal decisions. Moreover, the judiciary may well be limited, in its understanding of science, to a narrow set of conventional perspectives, and one of the purposes of this book is to try to broaden that horizon in mainstream legal discourse.

Second, in the debates over environmental protection, some have raised the notion of opposing "worldviews" concerning technological progress.

> The precautionary worldview approaches the uncertainties associated with any new technology with caution, placing substantial burden of proof on its

> proponents ... The opposite ... is [the] Promethean [worldview, reflecting] faith in the capacity of humans to manipulate complex systems for their own advantage ... (Levidow 2001:866).

While these views probably reflect extremes of a continuum, and not clearly bounded positions (Levidow 2001:866), the dualism highlights the importance of cultural conceptions of scientific dangers and opportunities in making legal judgments. Recent work in the cultural cognition of risks indicate, for example, that individuals with an egalitarian or communitarian worldview seem to be skeptical concerning the risks associated with synthetic biology, but quite sensitive to the risks associated with global warming or nuclear power; conversely, those with hierarchical and individualistic worldviews seem to be skeptical about global warming or nuclear power risks, but quite sensitive concerning synthetic biology risks (Mandel et al. 2008). Similar research confirms that an image of nature as robust leads to greater tolerance of risk and more trust in science, whereas an image of nature as vulnerable leads to more concerns about risk and less trust in science (Schwartz and Thompson 1990:2–4). Thus, in political and legal debates in the shadow of science,

> what are considered facts depends ultimately on an accepted framework of social (and therefore evaluative) premises. Even scientific knowledge, whilst perhaps not wholly fluid, is certainly plastic in the sense that it is socially negotiated (science being a social activity) and molded by values of various kinds (Schwartz and Thompson 1990:19).

Scientific authority and public trust in science are not given, but depend upon cultural images of science, thereby intertwining science with social frameworks.

Finally, the possibility of a law, literature, and science fiction enterprise was explored over a decade ago by Bruce Rockwood, who highlighted an unfortunate tendency in law and literature studies

> to focus on canonical literature, rather than literature more widely read. Science Fiction, while referred to in some law and literature collections and criticism, remains a largely unmined mother-[lode] for explaining our understandings of law through literature (Rockwood 1999:267–8).

In this perspective, science fiction (i) shapes "metaphors of everyday life, including those we use to view law and society"; (ii) explores political, legal and ideological alternatives ... and possible futures"; and (iii) has the potential to "explore and develop jurisprudential concepts" (Rockwood 1999:269, 271–2). Examples include Jeffrey Nesteruk's analysis of corporate law and personhood in the story of the android Lieutenant Commander Data in *Star Trek: The Next Generation* (Nesteruk 1999:281), William Pencak's work on the Orpheus myth and technological subjugation in cyberpunk science fiction (Pencak 1999), Derrick

Bell's science fiction parable about race, entitled "The Space Traders' Solution" (Bell 1999:318–45), and the sustained argument by Kieran Tranter that attending to the works of science fiction is crucial for understanding the interaction of law and technology in numerous contexts, including the regulation of early automobiles (Tranter 2005), and the cloning and stem cell controversies in Australia (Tranter 2010). Tranter offers compelling examples of how we draw our images of the dangers and potential benefits of technology from popular science fiction books and films.

This book, by contrast, is concerned with literary accounts (including several historical narratives) of the use or appropriation of science in legal contexts, but I am convinced, as are the scholars discussed above, that popular culture images of science have consequences for law. Our images of scientific authority (discussed in Chapter 3), of public scientific controversies (discussed in Chapter 4), of scientific expertise in the courtroom (discussed in Chapter 5), of the potential for erroneous science in law (discussed in Chapter 6), and of the ethical obligations of experts (discussed in Chapter 7) have everything to do with how science is appropriated in law. The sources selected for analysis in this book have the potential to create, confirm, and, by providing a critical distance or point of reflection, challenge the various cultural images of science that matter in legal contexts.

Chapter 2
Law-and-Literature, Literature-and-Science, and a Hybrid Law-Literature-Science Field of Study

Two Parallel Movements

> For the first time since its creation, perhaps since Galileo, science—which has always been on the side of the good, on the side of technology and cures ... —begins to create real problems on the other side of the ethical universe.
>
> ... [We must] question the rapports between law and science, [because] the natural sciences, without the law, become inhuman (Serres and Latour 1990:17, 142).

French philosopher Michel Serres identifies a certain collusion between science and law in contemporary culture, which is due to the failure of the legal system to provide a *check* on, or to be critical of, science. The failure is understandable, since science "finds itself in a dominant position," with "all the power, all the knowledge, all the rationality, ... all plausibility or legitimacy," which is also "the reason for the sudden decline of all the surrounding areas of culture—the humanities, arts, religion, even the legal system" (Serres and Latour 1990:86–7). Indeed, the

> great problems of our era, since the dawn of Hiroshima, have to do with the whole set of relationships between the law and science. We must reinvent the place of these relations ... so that lawyers can invent a new system of laws, and perhaps scientists a new science (Serres and Latour 1990:137).

Serres clearly suggests, in albeit abstract generalizations, that law should take its place on the side of ethics—critical of science—and that science needs ethics—a sense of responsibility. Post-*Daubert* jurisprudence on law/science relations seems to confirm Serres' worries—some hope for and celebrate the integration of "a sophisticated understanding of science into legal decisionmaking" (Faigman et al. 2002:v). In this view, the object of critique is not science but ignorance of science, and while the "law should not, nor could it, adopt the scientific perspective wholly and without qualification," the rapport, even submission as to all matters "scientific," is apparent (Faigman et al. 2002:vii).

Law and Literature

Ethical criticism of law's failures (e.g., the failure to regulate science in Serres' account) and of science's failures (e.g., the failure to be responsible in Serres' account) is sometimes based in literary traditions. The law-and-literature movement is, in part, based on the notion that the engagement of law students and lawyers with literature about law and lawyering can help develop or maintain ethical sensibilities. Examples include requiring that first-year law students read Harper Lee's *To Kill a Mockingbird,* (1960),[1] assigning Dickens' *Bleak House* in a course on law and literature,[2] requiring (as I do) that Professional Responsibility students view a video production of Shakespeare's *Henry V*, and studying the text of Faulkner's *Intruder in the Dust* (1948) with attorneys in a continuing legal education ethics program.[3] In each case, the goal is usually to use literary images of law and lawyers—usually negative images—as a point of reflection on legal ethics, professionalism, and moral responsibility. The strength of Atticus Finch's convictions in the face of social injustice, the picture of Chancery in *Bleak House* as sluggish (and of lawyers as cold and impersonal), the legalistic interpretation of Salic Law (i.e., you can make it say anything you want) in the opening scene of *Henry V*, and the enlightenment of Gavin Stevens (under the unlikely, for him, guidance of a woman, a child, and a person of color) at the end of *Intruder in the Dust* each raise ethical questions for lawyers. Richard Weisberg therefore refers to the analysis of law in fiction as "poethics," because of its "deeply ethical aspects" (1992:34). Obviously, there are no guarantees that reading novels and plays automatically ensures ethical practitioners, but law-and-literature studies do seem to provide an opportunity, albeit non-exclusive, to gain some critical distance from everyday legal discourse and practice.

Another project in the law-and-literature enterprise, seemingly quite distinct from analysis of fiction about law, is the study of law as textual—as narrative, story-telling, interpretation, discourse, and rhetoric. Judicial opinions can be analyzed as literary productions; statutory and constitutional construction each betray interpretive strategies; and rhetoric is everywhere—in expert scientific testimony and legal ethics opinions, not just in jury arguments and appellate briefs. Disclosing such structures is often a critical enterprise, revealing

1 *But see* Atkinson 1999 (acknowledging the popularity of *To Kill a Mockingbird* as an inspirational text for law students and lawyers, but recommending Faulkner's *Intruder in the Dust* (1948) as a replacement).

2 *See* Weisberg 1992: 117 (including *Bleak House* in a typical syllabus for a course in law and literature). Significantly, Weisberg does not limit the law and literature project to reading great books about law, but also includes the study of legal opinions, statutes, and lawyers' interpretive strategies as significant materials for reflecting on ethics in law (Weisberg 1992: 5–34, 127–75).

3 In November, 2001, Washington and Lee University School of Law sponsored an alumni CLE ethics program on Faulkner's *Intruder in the Dust* (1948).

alternative readings or interpretations that are hidden by convention, ideology, or prejudice. And while the law *in* literature project—reading fiction about law—is associated with ethical criticism, and the law *as* literature project is associated with understanding how law works (rhetorically, as story-telling, etc.), the latter project is also characterized as ethical by Weisberg:

> [T]here can be no dichotomy between craft and result in law ... [Such a dichotomy] implies that an outcome wrong on the law, and even unjust, can be rendered pleasing and fully acceptable by elegant rhetoric or close logic ... [T]his approach bifurcates the craft of law from law's purpose, the doing of justice (Weisberg 1992:8).

Theoretically, of course, it would be possible to read fiction about law to better understand law and its history (through its value as a doctrinal or historical source seems doubtful), and it would be possible to study rhetorical and narrative techniques not to criticize law but to construct "winning" arguments at trial, neither of which is an ethical enterprise. The law and literature movement, however, has emphasized the ethical aspect of both law *in* literature and law *as* literature.

The tremendous diversity of actual and potential conceptions of law-and-literature as a "movement" (or as two projects, law *in* literature and law *as* literature) leads some to conclude that there is no movement at all, a point to which I will return later in this chapter. For example, is every law school classroom discussion of the holding in a case as a judicial choice between two alternative narratives, one of which was more persuasive, an exercise in law *as* literature? Is every reading by a lawyer of a crime fiction novel an exercise in law *in* literature? Arguably, yes, but law-and-literature is obviously more than that, as evidenced by law-and-literature books and journal articles, bibliographies (even a "canon") and collections of essays, conferences and law school courses, and even continuing legal education programs, all of which suggest a somewhat focused enterprise notwithstanding the absence of firm boundaries.

Literature and Science

Paralleling law-and-literature, the field of literature-and-science has also grown in popularity over the last several decades, and is likewise evidenced by publications, conferences, and university courses, even though it is as diverse an enterprise as law-and-literature.

> Given its roots in philology and the history of ideas, the study of literature and science has all too often been, prior to the 1980s, a matter of "finding" scientific ideas "in" literature and literary ideas "in" science, in order to demonstrate, in the service of an ideal of cultural unity, that writers have not been hermetic, anachronistic curmudgeons on their part and that scientists have not been

> illiterate laboratory spooks hovering exclusively over their air pumps and galvanic piles for theirs (Peterfreund 1987:5).

For example, just as one might study nineteenth-century English law to better understand Dickens' *Bleak House*, "the science of an era [can be] studied for its ability to illuminate the literary productions of that era" (Gross 1990b:5). Indeed, that is how Alan Gross virtually defines "literature and science," before contrasting it with the "rhetoric of science" as an effort to increase "our understanding of science both in itself and as a component of an intellectual and social climate" (Gross 1990b:5).

Literature-and-science has since flourished beyond such narrow conceptions to include two projects that roughly correspond to the division in law-and-literature between law *in* literature and law *as* literature. First, literature about science and scientists can be used to reflect critically on the scientific profession. For example, in Mary Shelley's *Frankenstein* (1818), it is Dr Frankenstein himself—"the heir of Baconian optimism and Enlightenment confidence," and of mechanistic reductionism—who is the monster (Haynes 1994:94). Similar condemnations in the Romantic literary tradition include Hawthorne's "attack on scientific hubris and its consequences," couched in moral terms, in *Septimius Felton, or the Elixir of Life* (1871); Balzac's belief, expressed in *La Recherche de l'Absolu* (1834), "that preoccupation with science atrophies the normal emotions that sustain personal relations and social responsibilities"; and of course Goethe's *Faust* (Part 1, 1809; Part 2, 1832) (Haynes 1994:86, 90). Just as lawyers have been represented negatively in literature, stories about scientists as arrogant, Godless, inhuman, mad, dangerous, impersonal, and amoral abound in Western literature (Haynes 1994).

A contemporary example is Stephen Wright's *The Amalgamation Polka* (2006), which includes the chilling image of a Southern, Civil-War-era scientist committed to discovering how to transform African-Americans into white citizens by a "chemical process too intricate for lay understanding" (237). The protagonist of the novel, noticing "two black men [who] displayed upon their hands and faces a mottled network of strange, open sores", questions the project:

> "Please, go right ahead, assault me with your skepticism ... I'm quite accustomed to defending myself against honest objections ..."
>
> "Kind of touchy about these notions of yours."
>
> "Science, young man, not baseless conjecture. What do you know of natural history, of comparative anatomy, cranial capacities, facial angles?" (Wright 2006:226, 236).

The horrible disfigurement of the victims of the experiments is brushed aside by the scientist—"the march of knowledge, you know. Always a few casualties left hobbling about in the rear" (Wright 2006:237).

Apart from using literature as a humanistic critique of science, valuing literature as a humanizing force is evident in the sub-discipline (of literature-

and-science) known as literature-and-medicine, "a legitimate, if modest, field, of study" (Anderson 1987:33).

> By providing physicians with symbolic experiences that draw them out of their own worlds and into those of the texts they read, literary discourse teaches doctors ... to overcome their reluctance to engage in the messy, painful reality-building that absorbs their patients (Anderson 1987:33).

Such hopes are echoed in the law-and-literature movement, since stories

> like *Bleak House* evoke the need for great sensitivity to those vulnerable enough to need legal counsel, a comprehensive understanding that is both technical and humane and that can only be conveyed through a language of pragmatic caring (Weisberg 1992:38).

Scientists, too, need to "face up to the warning" in the persistent folklore of "Dr Faustus, Dr Frankenstein, Dr Jekyll, ... Dr Caligari, Dr Strangelove":

> In these images of our popular culture resides a legitimate public fear of the scientist's stripped-down depersonalized conception of knowledge—a fear that our scientists, well-intentioned and decent men and women all, will go on being titans who create monsters (Roszak 1974:31).

In contemporary literature and film, public fear of science, impliedly a warning to scientists to be more careful and responsible with respect to both their potentially false confidence and their actual capabilities, continues to be expressed. David Lodge's recent novel *Thinks* (2001) includes a telling conversation between a scientist and a novelist:

> "Science is for real. It has made more changes to the condition of human life than all the preceding millennia of our history put together ... " ... "But aren't there areas of human experience where scientific method doesn't apply? ... I was thinking of happiness, unhappiness. The sense of the sublime. Love." "Of course that's an unsolved problem," he said. "How to connect brain states, which can be observed, to mind states which, at present, can only be reported. But if you're a scientist you must believe there's an answer to be found" (Lodge 2001:229).

The film *The Madness of King George* (1995) represents physicians (who bleed patients to cure ailments) as overly confident, while the newer film *AI* (2001) clearly condemns competent but irresponsible neuroscientists as they create disposable robots who can love. And rebellion against dehumanizing scientific progress is represented in Andrew Niccol's futuristic thriller *Gatacca* (1998) in which the characters played by "Ethan Hawke and Uma Thurman prove their love for each other by throwing away the hair offered by [each to the other, which hair was legally required] to be analyzed in order to establish his/her genetic quality. In this futuristic society, authority (the privileged elite) is established 'objectively,' through genetic analysis of the newborn ... " (Zizek 2002:306).

As with law-and-literature, one of the benefits of literature-and-science is to hold a mirror up to the professionals, to let them know that their cherished self-image of their work "as both reputable and socially beneficent" is generally not shared by the public (Haynes 1994:1). Contemporary surveys "indicate an almost wholly negative estimate" of scientists and their contributions to society, not unlike "literary representations of scientists, many of them centuries old and apparently irrelevant to their modern analogues" (Haynes 1994:1).

The second project in literature-and-science studies corresponds to the focus, in law-and-literature, on law as a discourse associated with particular narrative structures, rhetorical strategies, and linguistic conventions. Formal scientific discourse and texts, such as scientific reports and journal articles, are the subjects of analyses that reveal scientific knowledge to be a rhetorical achievement.

> [W]e can engage in a systematic examination of the most socially privileged communications in our society: the texts that are the chief vehicles through which scientific knowledge is created and disseminated. We can argue that scientific knowledge is not special, but social; the result not of revelation, but of persuasion (Gross 1990b:20).

In another formulation, there is in scientific writing no

> escape from informal argumentation, or from figures or tropes, or from the selective naming and framing of issues, or from appeals to communally-held values, or from the need to adapt arguments to ends, audiences, and circumstances (Simons 1993:150).

Some studies identify the agentless prose in scientific narratives, and the predominance of "discourse-oriented verbs like *indicate, suggest,* and *show,*" rather than "cognition verbs like *think, believe,* and *suspect*" (Hyland 1998:364–5). Others highlight the constitutive, and not merely stylistic, use of metaphor[4] or analogy in scientific articles—"rhetorical figures ... *enable* scientists to develop and extend their knowledge about scientific concepts ..." (Graves 1998:45). Popular scientific narratives are also the subject of rhetorical analyses—Jeanne Fahnestock's study of the rhetorical life of scientific facts, from formal publications to their accommodation in lay or popular publications, showed that the latter are characterized by greater claims of certainty and fewer qualifications (Fahnestock 1986:335–42). Apart from formal scientific discourse and even popular scientific

4 *See* Bradie 1998:311–12 ("metaphors are more than mere rhetorical devices and cannot be disposed with at will without seriously misrepresenting the way science works").

journalism, the effort to analyze less formal discourse among scientists is necessitated by the impression that in the formal literature,

> the versions of their acts which scientists give ... will always look as though they were legitimately constitutive of scientific knowledge; whilst the versions given *of the same acts* may, in other settings [e.g., informal discussion, gossip, personal allegations], look much more contingent (Mulkay et al. 1983:189).

That is, the "formal text of the published paper" may not be "a reliable guide to the actions involved in producing it and to other actions on which it reports" (Mulkay et al. 1983:178). This perspective helps explain why those who study scientific practices often appropriate, from anthropology, ethnographic methodology to produce transcripts of interviews with scientists/informants for analysis. In light of science's self-image as an effort to let nature speak, and its corresponding view of rhetoric as ornamental, the effort in literature-and-science to view science as a narrative can also be seen as "humanizing," insofar as science is revealed as social or institutional, and as involving persuasion, negotiation, and consensus-building. An ethical aspect of this project is also apparent, because the responsibility of human actors is brought to the fore. Scientists

> construct texts in which the physical world often seems literally to speak or act for itself. When the author is allowed to appear, he is presented either as being forced to undertake experiments, to reach theoretical conclusions, and so on, by the unequivocal demands of the natural phenomenon ... or as being rigidly constrained by rules of experimental procedure (Mulkay et al. 1983:197).

Literature-and-science studies therefore highlight the personal, social, historical, political, and economic aspects that accompany but are often concealed in scientific progress.

The Semiotic Turn in Science Studies

Even as I identify "literature and science" as a movement to designate the enormous interest nowadays in scientific discourse and rhetoric, identifying a unifying method or common approach is highly problematic. Locating "literature and science" within other, or alongside allied, movements is a bit easier. From the broadest perspective, if one considers that the last 50 years of reflection on the nature of science has seemingly produced a dualism between positivists and social constructivists, then the literature and science movement occupies the latter side.

> If positivists seek to remove the subjective, social, and political elements to the margin of their favorite genre (method and discovery stories), the constructivists dismiss method stories as fundamentally circular and whiggish and strive to reposition the subjective and sociopolitical at center stage ... Where positivists

> insist that nature (when properly interrogated by experiment or observation) settles all scientific disputes, constructivists are reluctant to give nature a speaking role at all—let alone an independent voice, since the "language of nature" is nothing more than the mundane, human, rhetorical language of social discourse (Harris 1998:135–6).

Such "Manichaean" fables of binary opposition help delineate tensions in the field of science studies, but are "no longer an adequate summation of current scholarship" (Harris 1998:136). For example, the "naturalist turn" taken by leading sociologists of scientific knowledge created a middle ground not captured by the dualistic account (Callebaut 1993). Similarly, if one considers the three leading disciplines in the field—the history, philosophy, and sociology of science—the study of scientific discourse and rhetoric is usually associated with social studies of science. Consider, however, the narratology debate among historians of science (Clark 1995).

> Can we free ourselves from the constraints imposed by off-the-shelf narrative formats, and can we compose big-picture or *longue durée* narratives other than those of "origin story," "story of progress," or "stories of heroic exploration and conquest" to give order and meaning to the available historical material? (Harris 1998:131).

Add to that the attention paid by philosophers of science to the argumentative form of scientific papers often ignored in standard philosophical accounts (Suppe 1992), and this association with sociology is also an oversimplification. Nevertheless, Sharon Traweek, in her 1993 overview of cultural and social studies of science and technology, includes (in her list of 20 "stunningly diverse" academic disciplines studying science) the field of "literature (medical, scientific, and engineering rhetoric; medical, scientific, and engineering writing; medicine, science, and technology in literary forms and themes; science fiction, including s/f, speculative fiction, and fantasy; and autobiography in medicine, science, and engineering)" (Traweek 1993:5). Traweek also identifies "cultural studies" of science and technology, some of which analyze "scientific, medical, and technological discourses, arguments, and debates (visual, verbal, and mathematical) for their diverse epistemological structures, ontological assumptions, and/or rhetorical techniques, including the creative and constraining uses of metaphor" (Traweek 1993:13).

> We interpretive anthropologists usually align ourselves with those literary theorists, art historians, classicists, economists, philosophers, historians, legal studies researchers, and so on who do "cultural studies": we all attend to patterned interactions, such as oral and written discourse, or any other "social text" such as a poem, an article, a scientist, a detector, a policy, a set of terms, or a conference, in which the form and the content reverberate to evoke significant strategic meaning to those who know the local patterns. Discursive, strategic, evocative practices are key terms in the lexicon (Traweek 1993:11).

Timothy Lenoir labeled this phenomenon the "semiotic turn" in science studies (Lenoir 1998), evidenced in part by the Society for Literature, Science and the Arts (founded in 1985), including its conferences and journal (*Configurations: A Journal of Literature, Science, and Technology*), and its annual bibliography, "Relations of Science to Literature and the Arts" (2276 entries for 1998) (Gwiasda 2000).

While considerations about language and science were not new, viewing science as a cultural production represented a

> move away from theory-dominated accounts of knowledge production in science and toward an account sensitive to actual scientific practice, in which theory was simply one of the many important games in town ... [C]oncerns about tacit knowledge and unarticulable skill, experimenter's regress, interpretive flexibility, and negotiated closure of debate all contributed to newer accounts of science as a disunified, heterogeneous congeries of activities (Lenoir 1998:2).

In another formulation, we recently witnessed "[a] turn—from the Kuhnian predilection for science as theory-driven (i.e., observation is theory-laden or biased by theoretical presuppositions) to post-Kuhnian engagement with science as experiment" (Rheinburger 1998:285). For Lenoir and others, such "considerations of science as practice" lead directly to science-as-culture studies (Lenoir 1999:291), since practitioners "of cultural studies typically explore the production or emergence of meaning within historically specific and localizable material settings" (Rouse 1999:442). For purposes of this brief historical overview, note the location of such efforts within the broader project of cultural studies of science as practice. Lenoir, for example, when he identified the "semiotic turn," did

> not mean to focus solely on the construction of language ... The emphasis on practice in recent science studies has included material as well as symbolic culture. We want to call attention to the materiality of the text and a materiality beyond it (Lenoir 1999:291).

Joseph Rouse went further to warn against reducing meaning to rhetorical force, and language to a technology of persuasion. Such a move is not unknown within science studies. Reducing "meaning or significance to rhetorical or material effects is nevertheless a fundamental mistake [that is avoidable] if we also conceive of power dynamically, not as a regularity of social life, a thing possessed or exercised by dominant agents, but as a situated and temporally extended relationship among agents and their surroundings" (Rouse 1999:450).

Rouse is here recommending a dynamic (i.e., not "reified") conception of power and language, as well as of scientific knowledge, which (like power) is also not "a thing possessed":

> Donald Davidson has argued against reifying languages (or linguistic conventions) as the background to linguistic understanding and communication. Thomas Wortenburg has also argued that social and political power relations are best understood if we avoid reifying either power itself or the social context in which power relations are situated. Neither model should be taken as merely analogous to criticism of the reification of scientific knowledge, for linguistic understanding and sociopolitical power are both integral to scientific practices. We should instead recognize that dynamic accounts of language, power, and knowledge function together in understanding scientific practices and their significance (Rouse 1996:179–80).[5]

For my purposes in this chapter, note that Rouse oscillated between viewing narrative as central to scientific practices and narrative as a mere "dimension" or "characteristic" of those practices. On the first account,

> the practices of scientific research and the knowledge that results from them acquire their intelligibility and significance from being situated within narratives ... I argue that [scientists'] practical understanding [of a research situation as a field of possible activities] takes on a narrative form, and that through their research activities, scientists attempt to fashion that narrative in a particular way (Rouse 1996:160–61).

However, even as scientific work is presented as an act of narrative reconstruction, Rouse's focus is on scientific practices, and his model of inquiry is cultural studies, focused "on the ways meaning emerges from agents' interaction with one another and their surroundings" (1996:177). This latter focus neither excludes "the ways in which the world materially resists or reinforces efforts to make sense of it," nor "consideration of cognitive or other psychological processes" (Rouse 1996:177–8). One might therefore conclude that "literature and science" studies is only a small part of a large project. However, considering that annual conferences of the Society for Literature, Science and the Arts attracts participants from history, sociology, anthropology, the cognitive sciences, philosophy of science, and all areas of science, technology, engineering and medicine, in addition to scholars in rhetoric, literary history and criticism, art history and media studies, it would be more accurate to conclude that "literature and science" is conceived broadly as concerned with cultural studies of scientific practices, knowledge, language, and power, including discursive and rhetorical practices.

Consider also Bruno Latour's warning against reductionism in science studies:

> Yes, the scientific facts are indeed constructed, but they cannot be reduced to the social dimension because this dimension is populated by objects mobilized to

---

5 *See also* Davidson 1986, Wortenburg 1990, and Rouse 1999:205–36 (chapter on Davidsonian semiotics), 177–204 (chapter on Wortenburg's discussion of power).

> construct it ... The ozone hole is too social and too narrated to be truly natural; the strategy of industrial firms and heads of state is too full of chemical reactions to be reduced to power and interest; the discourse of the exosphere is too real and too social to boil down to meaning effects. Is it our fault if the networks are simultaneously real, like nature, narrated, like discourse, and collective, like society? (Latour 1993:6).

That text is instructive, in several respects, for understanding the history of science studies. First, it breaks down the opposition (mentioned above) between the appeal to nature and the appeal to social interests by adding discourse and narrativity as a determinative aspect of the scientific enterprise. Such phrasing reflects the "semiotic turn" and confirms literature and science as a field of science studies. Second, Latour was as critical of social constructivism as he was of realism.

> What do we gain by substituting "social conditions" for what has been taken as "natural conditions" of scientific activity? If, in the perspective of social construction, we have lost the illusion of an ultimate reference called "nature," what do we gain by trying to compensate for this loss with the mirror image of "society" as a new and insurmountable reference? (Rheinberger 1987:285–6, citing Latour 1987:132–4).

Finally, Latour was introducing his notion that the objects of science—which cannot be reduced to natural causes, social interests, or discursive practices—are quasi-objects, Michel Serres' term for "what circulates in the collective and shapes it by its very circulation" (Latour 1999:284, 286, citing Serres 1987).

> We do not have, on the one hand, a history of contingent human events and, on the other, a science of necessary laws, but a common history of societies and of things. Pasteur's microbes are neither timeless entities discovered by Pasteur, nor the effect of political domination imposed on the laboratory by the social structure of the Second Empire, nor are they a careful mixture of "purely" social elements and "strictly" natural forces. They are a new social link that redefines at once what nature is made of and what society is made of (Latour 1999:284).

Refusing to reduce science to a purely social or to a purely natural activity might suggest that Latour was "talking just about discourse, representation, language, texts, and rhetoric," but Latour simply added those to the hybrid (Latour 1993:5). Rhetoric, textual strategies, and writing really are at stake, "but in a new form that has a simultaneous impact on the nature of things and on the social context" (Latour 1993:5). While Latour's work is controversial within science studies (Lenoir 1999, Cohen 1999:84–90, Fuller 2000), his "naturalist" turn to avoid the impasse of the realist/constructivist debates is common among contemporary sociologists of scientific knowledge (Caudill 2001:855–60).

In his introduction to *Essays in the Study of Scientific Discourse*, John Battalio credits Latour, among others, for laying the groundwork for contemporary scholars of scientific discourse (1998:vii). Battalio goes on to mention (i) Charles Bazerman's empirical methodology in *Shaping Written Knowledge* (1998), which has been a "model for numerous rhetoricians and historians of science," (ii) Lawrence Prelli's proposal in *A Rhetoric of Science* (1989) to link "rhetorical invention and the creation and progress of science," (iii) Alan Gross's *The Rhetoric of Science* (1990b), which demonstrated "the predominance of rhetoric in science," (iv) Greg Myers's *Writing Biology* (1990), which shows that "not only scientific narratives, but also popularizations of science create the cultural authority of scientists," and (v) Charles Alan Taylor's *Defining Science* (1996), which recommends "a study of the discursive, and thus rhetorical, practices contributing to the demarcation of science from other areas of endeavor" (Battalio 1998:vii–viii).

Taylor identified two perspectives in rhetorical studies of science—the first concerned with "hidden rhetorics inherent in knowledge claims," the second with "the ways in which various sets of claims are authorized as epistemically secure" (Taylor 1998b:90). An example of the first approach is provided in Herbert Simons' study of "drug-pushing" in a medical journal article (on the effectiveness of the cholesterol-lowering drug cholestryamine) (1993). Medical research articles do not, indeed cannot, simply "tell it like it is," even though "researchers typically conceal their rhetorical identities behind a mask of attempted objectivity" (Simons 1993:148–9). Simons mentions the controversy over how far to extend the claims of rhetoric—Gross tends to reduce science to rhetoric while Lyne maintains that "rhetoric alone ... cannot substitute for all the methods, plodding, tools, rationales, and (let us not forget) observables that the various sciences depend on"—and concludes that a rhetorical component is unavoidable but should be analyzed alongside the empirical component (Simons 1993:150). On that point, Taylor is suspicious of those who test rhetoric against "the facts" (i.e., lodging "agency for judgment in nature, which we must assume speaks clearly"), which are themselves "products of local judgments" (Taylor 1998a:287). In another formulation, principles "do not close down debates; principles, via selection and application of competing principles, do" (Taylor 1998a:287).

> [T]he empirical foundation ... is itself [therefore] pragmatically contingent on wider configurations of practices ...
>
> My point ... is not that all interpretations of the facts are of equal legitimacy [, but we should reject] the claim that the relative legitimacy of a given interpretation is a natural condition of the material to be interpreted, rather than a function of an audience's [e.g., the government's or a jury's] evaluations of the evidence adduced on its behalf before contextually authorized audiences (Taylor 1998a:289).

Taylor is not only taking a position in the debate over how far to "extend" the claims of rhetoric—he avoids "vicious relativism" as well as its "positivist alter ego," breaking down the boundary between the rhetorical component and the empirical component by viewing a successful interpretation of empirical facts as a "rhetorical accomplishment" (1998a:288–9)—but he also includes "community" alongside rhetoric and science, and their "interfaces," in his orientation:

> This view of "interdependent co-operation" (not always cooperation; indeed, usually agonistic) takes science to be a series of social and technical practices that stabilize in particular configurations at particular times, as a function of the symbolic mediation of multiple and competing constraints. This orientation gives presence to discourses conventionally considered nonscientific or, at best, peripheral to the conduct of science, such as those concerned within enrolling allies and funds, sustaining cultural authority, and the like (Taylor 1998a:285).

Taylor's configuration anticipates the rhetorical critique of technical discourses in law and policy contexts, where an "artificially inflated conception of scientific expertise" can lead to an "intellectual and communal feudalism," vesting a privileged few with literal "ownership" of knowledge claims (1998a:289). For Taylor, such "hierarchical configurations of practices are rhetorical constructions" (1998a:289).

Other examples of the first approach identified by Taylor—rhetorical analysis of knowledge claims—include Ken Hyland's study of hedges (e.g., possible, might, perhaps) and boosters (e.g., clearly, obviously, and of course) in academic writing, which confirms that scientific "knowledge is a cultural product, shaped by the practices of discourse communities and constituted, not just conveyed, by rhetoric … Writers ... must socially mediate their arguments, shaping their evidence, observations, data, and flashes of insight into the patterns of inquiry and knowledge valued by their community" (Hyland 1998:352–3).

Hedges, for example, "minimize the potential threat new claims make on other researchers by soliciting acceptance" and by pro-active self-criticism, while boosters "allow writers to strategically engage with colleagues, effecting interpersonal solidarity and membership [within a] disciplinary in-group" (Hyland 1998:353). Writers in the hard sciences, however, do not use hedges and boosters as often as those in other disciplines, which can be explained in part by "very different assumptions about the role of human actors in the construction of knowledge" (Hyland 1998:363). In the hard sciences,

> the authority of the individual is subordinate to the authority of the text ... Lab experiments ... and their textual representation are best designed to be faceless and agentless, claiming an appearance of objectivity and neutrality (Hyland 1998:364).

Dan Ding's historical study of the passive voice in scientific writing traces the rise of such agentless prose in the late nineteenth century: "by the time journals were established as the major forum, the passive voice and the impersonal active subjects had become dominant in scientific discourse" (1998:132). Paralleling the gradual disappearance of the active voice and personal subjects from scientific literature, "there has been a recurring backlash against figurative language in scientific discourse" (Johnson-Sheehan 1998:167).

> Since the Enlightenment, a cherished notion in Western culture has been that scientific discourse is ideally transparent and plain, devoid of the rhetorical and metaphorical maneuvers that are common in more humanistic forms of discourse (Johnson-Sheehan 1998:167).

Richard Johnson-Sheehan's study of metaphor in the rhetoric of science, on the other hand, attempts to demonstrate "not only the importance of metaphor to scientific discourse but also its centrality in the invention of scientific theories" (1998:167). Michael Bradie, likewise, argues that metaphors are an "indispensable element of scientific theorizing":

> The bottom line is that theories "connect up" with the world via metaphors. Each and every time a theoretical model gets applied a metaphor is involved. When the application is new, we are struck by it; when it becomes commonplace, we often fail to note the use of metaphor … These metaphors are more than mere rhetorical devices and cannot be dispensed with at will without seriously misrepresenting the way science works (Bradie 1998:311–12).

Responding to Marcello Pera's view that while science incorporates rhetoric, it is not rhetorical per se—which suggests that style is inessential to science—Heather Brodie Graves argues that it is "difficult to continue to conceive of style as 'ornamental' or reduced to surface features and separate from the thoughts being articulated" (1998:25). Graves, in her ethnographic study of a group of physicists, focused on the figure of analogy, which plays "a more active role in scientific inquiry than has been hitherto acknowledged" (1998:25–6).

> In fact, for the particular physicists that I observed, analogies assumed a reciprocal relationship with quantitative methods and experimental data ... If the data affect the analogy constructed and the analogy affects how the data [are] perceived, this reciprocal relationship can be viewed as rhetorical (Graves 1998:26).

Graves concludes that "style is epistemic in the scientific process"—"rhetorical figures such as analogy enable scientists to develop and extend their knowledge about scientific concepts ..." (1998:26, 45).

If the foregoing studies provide examples of Taylor's first perspective—revealing "the hidden rhetoric inherent in knowledge claims"—the second dominant view—exploring how claims are warranted or authorized as epistemically secure—is for Taylor exemplified by Lawrence Prelli's focus on how scientific knowledge claims are legitimized or delegitimized (Taylor 1998b:90). The deliberative activities of the "audience" of scientific practitioners, who judge the reasonableness and persuasiveness of science, thereby become the objects of rhetorical analysis (Taylor 1998b:90). Consider, for example, Frederick Suppe's description of the "credentialing process" that both precedes and follows publication of a scientific paper:

> The methods, data, interpretations, relevance, and replicability of observational claims are main dimensions of assessment in the credentialing process whereby knowledge claims are allowed into the scientific discipline's domain of shared putative knowledge ...
>
> The scientific paper is the vehicle whereby the scientist's private discourse and knowledge enters the intersubjective public discourse arena ... (Suppe 1998:384).

Taylor acknowledges the valuable contributions of those working within the two dominant perspectives he identifies, but wants to "move off in somewhat different theoretical and critical directions" (Taylor 1998b:90).

Taylor recommends that rhetoricians start viewing science as a series of cultural practices, the way sociologists of science do, because "what constructivist accounts of scientific practice lack is rhetorical consciousness, and awareness of the transformative capacity of human discourse" (1998b:91). Rhetorical studies of science should "move beyond the traditional exemplary texts of science ... to capture discourses that we have generally considered peripheral to 'real' science" (Taylor 1998b:91). Taylor's example of the peripheral, relevant to law, is the Congressional budget hearing to revive the ill-fated Super Collider project, which "can be understood as scientists' rhetorical practices intended to secure resources without which lab practice would be impossible" (1998b:91). "In retrospect it now seems apparent that the empirical 'fate' of the top quark was more dependent on what happened in Washington, D.C., than Waxahachie [where the project was located]" (Taylor 1998a:290). Taylor also highlights the "demands placed on jurors to make sense of increasingly technical testimony in legal proceedings," thereby suggesting that a more inclusive "rhetoric of science" might focus on law courts as consumers of technical discourses (Taylor 1998a:290). Recognizing that his inclusion of "what we have traditionally thought of as nonscientific rhetoric" in the cultural practices of science might leave "science (as any sort of practice) [without] any discrete identity," Taylor insists that the rhetoric of various discourses—"congressional hearings, funding deliberations, and even" journalists' accounts—converge to produce science in contemporary culture (1998b:97–8).

As to funding deliberations, the case study of three grant proposals by Professors Gay and Ted Gragson exemplifies the effort to broaden the study of the rhetoric of science: "the sponsored-research dialogue is critical because it determines which ideas will be allowed to become 'science" (1998:5). Scientific discourse, they conclude,

> must be persuasive, and is thus inseparable from the logos, ethos, and pathos of rhetoric. But it is rhetorical in a constitutive rather than ornamental fashion. Scientific claims are accepted only if they persuade the community within which they are put forward ... (Gragson and Gragson 1998:19).

Rhetorical studies of science as a network of relationships therefore cannot be limited to scientific research papers as objects of inquiry. First, "it is dangerous to base accounts of scientific work on published research reports which often do not correspond to actual thought processes that produced profound and seminal scientific work" (Suppe 1998:384). Second, if discourse analysts simply adopt a "participant's terminology, definitions, and interpretations as their own," they risk treating "characterizations of events as 'this is the way things really are' rather than as 'this is the way some actors made things appear'" (Mulkay et al. 1983:175, 187). Moreover,

> there is clear evidence that researchers can describe a given set of experiments in quite different terms, depending on the context. For instance, an experiment can be described in the published paper as a new method for measuring the known value of a well-established phenomenon, whilst being described in an interview as a moderately convincing test of a controversial theory (Mulkay et al. 1983:178).

While scientists might characterize the former context (formal discourse) as constitutive, and the latter (informal discourse) as contingent, those characterizations are themselves accounts, versions, segments of scientific discourse, and rhetorics of science (Mulkay et al. 1983:190–92). Whether a given set of actions constitutes "an experiment, an attempt indirectly to raise more research funds, an effort to secure professional credibility, [or] a bid for more students" depends "on the context in which the actor is talking or writing .." (Mulkay et al. 1983:190). Because "those advancing knowledge claims systematically exclude reference to contingent action from ... formal discourse," the discourse analyst cannot rely on formal discourse to demonstrate "a direct connection between contingent factors and the formal constitution of knowledge" (Mulkay et al. 1983:192, 195).

Leah Ceccarelli's *Shaping Science with Rhetoric* is also an effort to move beyond the rhetorical study of (i) scientific research texts, and (ii) their specific audiences, toward "some of the other ways in which scientists use persuasion to advance the scientific enterprise" (2001:3). Ceccarelli focuses on the genre of the "motivational" or "interdisciplinary inspirational" texts of Dobzhansky, Schrodinger, and Wilson, which functioned as catalysts for new research by way of "conceptual chiasmus" (her neologism for reversing disciplinary expectations) and polysemous textual construction (which produces an interdisciplinary alliance) (Ceccarelli 2001:5–6). Agreeing with Taylor that an exclusive focus on the prototypical scientific knowledge claim "does more to reify science as a purely cognitive enterprise than it does to open science to the illumination of rhetoric,"

Ceccarelli's expansion of the range of objects of analysis is aimed at developing a more complete picture of how science operates (2001:169).

"Third Wave" Science Studies: Expertise and Experience

Collins and Evans (2002) have recently presented a challenge to the type of science studies I have been describing, which they would identify as "Second Wave." Briefly, Collins and Evans associate the "First Wave" of science studies with those analysts who "aimed at understanding, explaining, and effectively reinforcing the success of the sciences, rather than questioning their basis" (Collins and Evans 2002:239). Examples include Mannheim's notion that "scientific knowledge evolves through the gradual accumulation of permanently valid conclusions about a stable physical world" (Mulkay 1979:11), Merton's "understanding of science as different from other kinds of knowledge-generating culture," and, to confirm that the first wave is still rolling on, contemporary "scientists concerned to resist what they see as an attack on science" in Wave Two of science studies (Collins and Evans 2002:275–6). Wave Two, running from the early 1970s to the present, is associated with "social constructivism" and the sociology of scientific knowledge:

> With science reconceptualized as a social activity, science studies has directed attention to the uses of scientific knowledge in social institutions such as courts of law, schools, and policy processes such as public inquiries. The emphasis on the 'social construction' of science has meant, however, that when expertise is discussed, the focus is often on the attribution of the label 'expert,' and in the way the locus of legitimated expertise is made to move between institutions (Collins and Evans 2002:239).

Unfortunately, by "emphasizing the ways in which scientific knowledge is like other forms of knowledge," it has become difficult to distinguish between experts and non-experts (Collins and Evans 2002:239). Instead of describing how scientific consensus is formed, Wave Three attempts to be prescriptive—how does one "make decisions based on scientific knowledge before there is an absolute scientific consensus?" (Collins and Evans 2002:241).[6] In an effort to answer that question, Collins and Evans propose conceiving of a field of science with three concentric circles: the inner circle (the "bull's eye") represents the "core"

6 "Proposals to intervene in public controversies over scientific issues have become so prevalent [in science and technology studies], and so central to programmatic c objectives ..., that it is fair to say that the field has undergone a *normative turn* ... [However,] the normative turn involves a possible contradiction between using [science and technology studies] to challenge extant claims to authoritative 'scientific' knowledge and treating [the field] as ... a positive source of epistemic authority ... [I]t seems fair to say that such a turn is not easily reconciled with constructionist, reflexivist, and relativistic conceptions of science and technology" (Lynch and Cole 2005:269–70).

of scientists involved in experimentation and theorization, the second circle represents the general scientific community, and the third the public (Collins and Evans 2002:242–5). Among the points made with the diagram are (i) that decisions concerning scientific knowledge should be made by the core scientists, without external or political interference, and (ii) that the non-expert public and general scientific community should not have a voice in scientific decision-making *unless* they acquire expertise in the field (either through formal training *or* by experience—in this way, Collins and Evans avoid the notion that convential scientific training and credentialing alone lead to expertise) (Collins and Evans 2002:249–50). Whereas Wave Two science studies was interested in deconstructing science (while remaining neutral or "relativistic") to reveal its social, institutional, rhetorical, and political aspects, thereby demonstrating how scientific authority is constructed (and along the way arguing for more public participation in scientific decision-making), Wave Three is interested in prescribing the criteria for reliable expertise (and along the way arguing for a decrease in public participation in some circumstances).

In response to Collins and Evans, Arie Rip has criticized their

> treatment of expertise as curiously decontextualized, as if the nature of expertise and the rights that might accrue [from expertise] can be discussed independent of the context in which they are shaped … Expertise is always about something that is relevant for an audience: the courts, policy makers, decision makers more generally (Rip 2003:420).

Collins and Evans, reacting against the tendency of sociologists of science to *over*-contextualize—to explain the closure of a scientific controversy as a social achievement—want to bracket institutional processes and ask about the grounds of knowledge (concededly "a rather old-fashioned approach") (Collins and Evans 2002:236). A court's or regulatory agency's judgment, relying on some experts but not others, is for Collins and Evans part of a political phase of decision making, in contrast to a technical phase concerning the content of science (Collins and Evans 2002:276). Rip, however, highlights the problem of privileging "core-set" expertise in the absence of an account of how that expertise is recognized, established, and maintained in practical settings:

> Core-sets become productive when (and because) a paradigm or dominant problem definition ... closes off foundational debates. One challenge, then, is how to evaluate such [social] closure ... If the black-boxing becomes absolute, the overall processes lose flexibility, particularly in their capacity to respond to the unexpected.

Thus there is a tension in contemporary science studies between the desire to provide useful insights in scientific controversies, and the desire to retain a critical stance concerning how scientific authority is socially constructed.

> ... [Core-set] achievements in the past are no guarantee for their being productive in the future (Rip 2003:423–4).

While Collins and Evans' approach is sociological, they reduce the socio-epistemic dimension "to a question of membership", and naively "take the existence of core-sets as given" without evaluating their contributions in practical settings (Rip 2003:427). A broader sociological account would inquire into the social, institutional, and particularly rhetorical framework that shapes and supports the authority of core-set scientists in various contexts, including legal and political processes and institutions.

Scientific Rhetoric in the Courtroom

Returning to Taylor's more inclusive rhetoric of science, an example which is particularly relevant to the analysis of scientific discourse in law is Jeanne Fahnestock's study of the accommodation of science in lay or popular publications (1986). Fahnestock compares several scientific papers with their respective accommodated versions, and highlights both the genre shift (from forensic to the epideictic or celebratory) and the changes in informational content that recur as scientific discourse is adapted for "noninitiated audiences" (1986:332–4). Because accommodations of scientific reports

> cannot rely on the audience to recognize the significance of information ... the work of epideictic rhetoric in science journalism requires the adjustment of new information to an audience's already held values and assumptions (Fahnestock 1986:333–4).

Journalists must appeal to the wonder of science—its "amazing powers and secrets of nature"—and/or its potential applications and benefits (Fahnestock 1986:334). "Under the pressure of this genre shift ..., it is not surprising that something happens to the information from one kind of discourse to the other" (Fahnestock 1986:334). Comparing original reports with their popularized versions, the latter are characterized by greater claims of certainty or "uniqueness," exaggeration for dramatic effect, selective inclusion of information, and fewer "hedges" and qualifications (Fahnestock 1986:335–42). Fahnestock concludes that her analytical technique could be employed in other contexts of discursive accommodation, such as

> the use of scientific and technology information by political factions and lobbying groups. What happens to technical specifications when they levitate from the engineering manual or report to the briefing memo, the white paper, the money-generating mailing? (1986:346–7).

The "rhetorical life" of scientific facts from laboratories to public policy disputes is analogous to the transformations of science in journalistic adaptations, even though the former context [i.e., public policy debates] is "frankly persuasive" rather than "fundamentally reportorial or archival" (Fahnestock 1986:347).

At first glance, the appropriation of science in the litigation context also seems to be an accommodation in Fahnestock's terminology, since the jury is an "uninitiated audience," and litigators, in their use of scientific evidence, arguably exaggerate certainty, select only helpful information, and avoid hedging and qualifications. That image of accommodation does not, however, accord with idealized accounts of the place and function of expert scientific testimony in trials. Recall the sense on the part of so many discourse analysts that unlike "the arts, humanities and professions," "the mathematical, natural, and technical sciences" betray "sheer oblivion to the rhetoricity of a field's own inquiries," and that even "the social sciences have insistently denied and ignored their own rhetoricity" (Nelson 1998:48). Paradoxically, however, while there can be no doubt that law is rhetorical, the discipline of law seems to be in denial about the rhetoricity of science in court. In fairness, there is likely no dispute that examining (and cross-examining) expert witnesses and making closing arguments are exercises in persuasion; but the context of the trial—in which jurors (or judges in a non-jury trial) weigh evidence and decide ultimate issues—must be distinguished from the context of judicial evaluations of admissibility—which will of course limit what the jury will hear. In the latter forum, the way rhetoricity is hidden mirrors formal scientific discourse.

Until 1993, in federal (and many state) courts, the *Frye* or "general acceptance" test functioned to admit scientific evidence if it was "sufficiently established to have gained general acceptance in the field to which it belongs" (*Frye* 1923:1014). That level of deference to the scientific community seemingly ended with *Daubert*, which gave a gatekeeping responsibility to federal judges, who now decide (typically prior to trial) whether evidence constitutes scientific knowledge (that is, whether the underlying methodology is scientifically valid) by inquiring into testability, error rates, peer-reviewed publications, and general acceptance (*Daubert* 1993). The federal rules of evidence have since been revised to confirm that courts should focus on methodology—sufficient data, reliable methods, and reliable application—as implied by *Daubert (Fed. R. Evid.* 702). Given the focus and structure of a pre-trial *Daubert* hearing, and in light of the various examples of rhetorical studies of scientific discourse identified in this chapter, how might a rhetorical analysis of scientific narratives in litigation proceed?

Even if, hypothetically (albeit mythically), rhetoric played no role on the part of lawyers and judges, the rhetoric of science is nevertheless imported into law, including its systematic exclusion of rhetoricity or at least its derogation of rhetoric as ornamental or nonepistemic. That is, if the testimony of scientific experts arrived unaltered, untranslated, and unaccommodated into court, the legal science-as-discourse analyst could nevertheless stay busy employing the techniques of "rhetoric of science" studies. Of course, the reliability of proffered scientific knowledge will be presented by a lawyer, and questioned by another lawyer, in both cases tracking *Daubert*, and then ruled on by an active, gate-keeping judge who must understand both lawyers and be persuaded by one. (Already, in preparing for trial, the lawyers will have worked with their scientific experts not only to understand their data, methodology, and conclusions, but to "shape" their testimony for relevance and persuasiveness.) Is this a scientific activity (scientists are likely present but not in control), a nonscientific forum (because it is not a laboratory or scientific conference proceeding), an accommodation in the rhetorical life of a scientific fact (but it is not popular culture or "public understanding of science"), an authoritative credentialing or warranting method (but members of a scientific discipline would not accept such credentials or warrants), or part of that new field of analyzable scientific discourse identified by Taylor (expanding the range of rhetoric of science, broadening our notions of what "counts" as scientific)? Among legal scholars, Charles Kester views the introduction of scientific discourse into legal discourse as a problem of translation—"the lawyer and the scientist literally speak different languages [, thus] scientific terms must be translated into terms that have meaning to legal professionals and lay persons" (1995:560). Brian Leiter, on the other hand, worries that judges are simply not equipped to make scientific judgments, and highlights "the serious epistemic limits of courts—intellectual, temporal, material" (1997:817).

> One might have a very high opinion of the intellectual caliber of the bench, and still worry that not only does *Daubert* ask too much, but also its doing so is an act of futility given the all-too-human limits of judges. Rather than making sure juries get an accurate picture of the world as seen by science, *Daubert* will ensure only that juries get an accurate picture of the world as seen through the often distorting lens of zealous and resourceful advocacy (Leiter 1997:817).

Such arguments suggest multiple narratives—the "real" scientific discourse that arrives in court, the (attempted) translation into legal discourse, the judge's (perhaps rushed and feeble) evaluative discourse (which may end up in a published opinion), each advocate's "scientific" (perhaps distorted) discourse, and the scientific expert's "legal" discourse—the analysis of which could help answer whether Kester's optimism concerning translation "into terms that have meaning" in law, or Leiter's implied optimism that science could make it into law if we returned to *Frye* and scientific (not judicial) gatekeepers, is warranted.

Despite such obvious opportunities, I have argued elsewhere that an idealized version of science predominates in judicial opinions and legal-scholarly discourse concerning admissibility of experts—science is frequently defined in cognitive terms, as if theory, experiment, and publication (including published criticism) are its constitutive elements (Caudill 2002b). That adoption of science's own self-image is a barrier to rhetorical inquiry, as well as to inquiry into science's other social and cultural aspects, since rhetorical and other social "factors" are either ignored or viewed as contingent, not as inherent or constitutive. Because we don't think of science as rhetorical, we tend not to think of scientific narratives in law as rhetorical; consequently, there is very little *legal* "rhetoric of science" discourse (Caudill 2002b). *Daubert* does not invite inquiries into the rhetorical and discursive features (including interpretation, negotiation and consensus-building techniques) of scientific knowledge, just as it does not invite inquiry into the contours of institutional authority (or training), the history of experimental conventions, economic and political interests, or values.

To claim that this book stages a rhetorical turn in studies of law/science relations risks overstatement, but the chapters that follow, on numerous fronts, begin to frame a new field of inquiry in law and literature scholarship. The result would hardly surprise literature and science scholars, but might seem a strikingly unfamiliar enterprise to the legal community.

Because of the significance of scientific knowledge for law, I am convinced that a merger of law-and-literature and literature-and-science, namely a hybrid law, literature, and science project, would be useful to our understanding of science, scientists, and scientific narratives in legal contexts. Before offering examples, however, I want to try to rescue the two enterprises in my proposed merger, law-and-literature and literature-and-science, from respective charges that they just aren't working.

In Defense of Law-and-Literature and Literature-and-Science

> Literature, *it is said*, sheds light on law's gaps, rhetoric, and moral stances. It elucidates law's limits and highlights law's exclusions. Interpretive methods conventionally applied to fictional texts can be applied productively to legal texts, and narrative techniques that draw readers into novels and plays can be employed in the service of legal arguments (Baron 1999:1060, emphasis added).

That being said, Professor Jane Baron doubts the current value, the influence, and even the existence of the law and literature enterprise. If there *is* a law and literature movement, despite its fractured state, then it has failed, Baron argues, to be interdisciplinary—it has paid attention to "literature," but not to "law" (as a category) or to the "and" (the connection between law and literature) in its name (1999:1061). Therefore, it "has failed to generate the excitement it is capable of generating" among academics and even among lawyers (Baron 1999:1060–61). Indeed, law-and-literature scholarship has seemingly "not questioned what the category 'law' consists of and has thus tended inadvertently to reinforce the notions of law as autonomous" (Baron 1999:1061).

As a law professor who self-identifies with (among other things) law-and-literature, who has taught law-and-literature both as a seminar and as part of professional responsibility courses, and who has used law-and-literature in continuing legal education of lawyers (who were at least "excited" enough to attend), I find Baron's assessment less than compelling. Moreover, I find her central claim—the failure of law-and-literature to come to terms with "law"—to be based on questionable assumptions and inconsistent directives for "reform" of the movement. Nevertheless, her critique will ultimately be important if it highlights a commonly-held perspective on law-and-literature and offers an opportunity for law-and-literature scholars to reflect on their "enterprise."

Baron begins her critique by acknowledging that everybody knows that law is not simply "rules," and that common sense reveals the social, cultural, linguistic, and normative aspects of law (1999:1059). Oddly, however, when law-and-literature scholars claim "literature" is useful to "law," they

> tend to treat both "law" and [literature] as bounded entities, [and] they do not explicitly consider how the boundaries are drawn ... [L]aw tends to be depicted as a more or less empty domain composed mainly of rules. [They have] not escaped the spell of Langdellian orthodoxy. More specifically, they have failed ... to examine how we categorize knowledge and why (Baron 1999:1061).

On the other hand, Baron concedes, the law-and-literature movement is a "multiplicity of approaches and concerns" (1999:1062), so it is difficult to see how all those working in law-and-literature could have both (i) missed what everyone else already knows—law is not a set of rules—and (ii) failed to consider how disciplinary boundaries are drawn. For example, if the *humanist* "law-and-lits" (in Baron's analysis) do view literary works as uniquely morality-productive items from one domain ("literature") that can be brought into the region of cold, abstract reason ("law") (1999:1064), they have committed both Baronian errors. But surely the *hermeneutic* and *narrative* law-and-lits, who see law as texts (to be interpreted) or persuasive stories (Baron 1999:1064–6) have made neither error—law neither consists of determinative rules nor is it bounded against culture (the latter *is* an explicit critique of how disciplinary boundaries are drawn).

Even Baron's critique of *humanist* law-and-lits, however, is unfair. Because there is no *guarantee* that literature aids in moral reflection, because even if it does it is not the *only* or *best* way, because even if it is the best way its proponents cannot agree on *which* books to read, and because even if they agree they cannot agree on interpretive methodology (Baron 1999:1066–8), the movement is in shambles? Law-and-economics, impliedly an exciting "law-and" project for Baron, surely suffers from theoretical disagreements. But it isn't merely the divisions among *humanist* law-and-lits that Baron finds *deeply* problematic—it is the "sameness [of] the *structure*": large claims supported by detailed reading of selected texts (1999:1066, 1068). "Are such claims true?," Baron asks (1999:1069). Who knows?

> But literary scholars rarely agree among themselves on anything like a single correct interpretation of an important work ... The certainty with which legal scholars assert what are actually quite contestable readings is ... incongruous (Baron 1999:1070).

Incongruous? The deep divisions over textual meanings is not unique to law-and-lits; if anything, it mirrors the disagreements among literary scholars, *each of whom asserts* "contestable readings," just like law-and-lits do! There is no disciplinary boundary problem here except in Baron's mind, wherein literary scholars are viewed as somehow different from legal scholars.

At the point in her article where Baron concludes that there can be no "movement" with such deep divisions, readers can certainly agree that she has "a cynic's eye," that she selectively ignored certain useful, rich, nuanced, creative, enlightening law-and-literature scholarship, and that she deliberately emphasized divergence to avoid presenting "the movement in its best possible light" (1999:1072–3). Even if she would have been more fair, however, she would not have found the lack of divisiveness that she associates with a movement. And that divisiveness is why she questions the movement's "potential as a source of enlightenment for law" (1999:1073). It's all or nothing for Baron, who even as she concedes that some law-and-literature scholarship is quite useful, concludes that "interest in law and literature does not a movement make" (1999:1072).

So ends her first critique—no movement—but since her second critique needs a target, Baron re-creates the law and literature "enterprise," which turns out to be a methodologically united "movement:" law-and-literature scholars "repeatedly" ask (i) how law is like/unlike literature and (ii) what can literature say to law? (1999:1075). Those questions (and their answers), Baron argues, posit two different disciplinary domains (1999:1075). The fact that James Boyd White does not see two opposed enterprises, and that Judge Posner does (Baron 1999:1075–6), is for Baron not evidence that law-and-lits *do* reflect on disciplinary boundaries, but is instead evidence that "ordinary" law-and-lits are not thoughtful:

> The debate calls into question what much ordinary law-and-literature scholarship assumes. One would think, then, that as a whole the law-and-literature enterprise would be very thoughtful about the delineation—or dare I say the construction—of disciplinary boundaries (Baron 1999:1076).

Law-and-lits, Baron argues, remarkably "lack self-consciousness about the use of the term 'law' [or even] 'literature'" (1999:1078). I would have thought that even if *humanist* law-and-lits can justifiably be accused of treating law as dehumanized and literature as humanizing, most other law-and-lits regularly break down disciplinary boundaries by suggesting that law is textual or narrative; but that's not good enough for Baron. If one suggests that *law's* textuality is not the same as *literature's*, or that new *stories* are needed in *law*, one has simply re-instated the boundaries (Baron 1999:1077–80). Even James Boyd White's collapse of law and the literary is not good enough, because it leaves law as an autonomous discipline, even though it now contains "nearly everything" (Baron 1999:1081). Thus, it seems, we cannot see law and literature as different, and we cannot see them as the same.

> I do not mean to call here for a new or different set of boundaries; quite the contrary. Fruitful exploration ... does not require the delineation of the "true" and "real" boundaries between law and literature. It cannot, for precisely the reason that "law" and "literature" are not natural categories .., preexisting and predefined ... [T]he interesting question is not whether any particular definition of the categories is true, but what it might tell us about our aspirations for law and for the place of law in our culture (Baron 1999:1082).

Why is that the interesting question? Baron is not, in the end, interested in reflection on disciplinary boundaries, which law-and-lits (other than her stereotypical *humanist* types) have clearly done, but in *reflecting on* that reflection on boundaries—in what existing reflection on boundaries tells us about our aspirations. That sounds like an interesting project, albeit complex, but I fail to see how that will make law-and-literature more popular among academics or more accessible or useful to lawyers. That is, I fail to see how defining "law," so that it reflects what we, as a culture, want law to be, will either recover the great promise of law-and-literature scholarship or lead to such a level of agreement as to constitute a movement. Moreover, I fail to see why law-and-literature as a whole—rather than a few misguided scholars—had to be trashed to make the point that law is not autonomous or rule-like, but reflects our aspirations. The argument that law-and-lits take law's boundaries for granted was just a ruse for saying that we should all think about what law is—but law-and-lits should be the last scholars accused of failing to do that. Law is a multiple narrative, a contested discourse, a set of linguistic conventions, an example of politics, a cultural phenomenon, a social practice, a place of stories—even though law *is* particularized each time it appears to us distinct from all other examples of those categories. Even stereotypical *humanist* law and lits read literature *about law*, convinced that fiction about law *reflects* our fear of and aspirations for law and lawyering, and in this way fiction becomes part of law's representations of itself.

With respect to literature-and-science, that movement or (inter)discipline has also been criticized for its "egregious lack of ideological, critical, and/or methodological self-consciousness" prior to the 1980s (Peterfreund 1987:5).

> [T]he discourse of literature and science, like any other discourse of a given culture, is language-bound ... language itself is the repositioning of ideological values and critical and methodological praxis ... (Peterfreund 1987:6).

Therefore, besides the projects of (i) finding science and scientific ideas in literature, and (ii) finding literary narratives in science, there is (iii) the project of reflecting on what assumptions are behind those projects, including assumptions about what literature is and what science is. As with law-and-literature, one does not have to look very long at the scholarship in the "field" of literature-and-science to realize that these assumptions vary, and that those who self-identify with the field are in disagreement about what they are doing and why. For example, Alan

Gross, who "does" rhetoric of science, *defines* literature-and-science as the study of "the science of an era ... for its ability to illuminate the literary productions of that era" (1990:5). That definition works for him, because he wants to distinguish the rhetoric of science as a field which increases our understanding of science (Gross 1990b:5), but the literature-and-science movement can be conceived of as including the rhetoric of science. Moreover, even among those who "privilege" literary texts about science (rather than scientific texts, as Gross does), the reason is often to disclose how nonscientists view science, or to warn scientists, or even to criticize scientists as impersonal, arrogant, amoral, or irresponsible. Similarly, those who study scientific discourse are not all doing the same thing for the same purpose—some want to reduce science to rhetoric, while others want to argue that scientific knowledge is a hybrid of rhetorical and empirical components (Simons 1993:150); others don't do "the rhetoric of scientific texts," preferring instead to analyze *informal* scientific discourse, and even they do not agree on how to proceed methodologically (Mulkay et al. 1983). Returning to Baron's indictment, does this mean that no literature-and-science movement exists? I don't think so, since literature-and-science, like law-and-literature, is more like a discipline—full of disagreements—than a "school of thought." More importantly, recalling Baron's skepticism, is the literature-and-science movement in trouble because it fails to generate excitement among scientists? Interestingly, there is some level of uniformity in contemporary literature-and-science scholarship insofar as it is generally neither useful to scientists in their daily work nor otherwise appreciated by scientists. There are exceptions; one could argue, for example, that Henrik Ibsen's play (and Arthur Miller's adaptation of) *An Enemy of the People,* discussed in Chapter 4 of this book, can teach scientists that Dr Stockman, upon discovering a scientific truth (pollution in the town's therapeutic baths), could have done a better job in his presentation to a hostile and economically-motivated citizenry—in his arrogance, expecting hero-worship, he was caught off-guard (Ibsen 1999, A. Miller 1950). Given that science nowadays has "to make its case at the bars of public opinion and administrative law as well as in the laboratory and the market ..." (Schuck 1993:45), that could be a valuable lesson. Likewise, one could argue that Mary Shelley's *Frankenstein* helps scientists understand how the public views science—with trepidation. On the other hand, *Frankenstein* is most often read as an indictment of science, or warning of what can come from an impersonal, power-hungry profession. Narrative and rhetorical studies of science are also typically critical, tending to debunk scientific pretensions rather than offering pragmatic advice to laboratory researchers.

Law-and-literature, like literature-and-science, is also a critical enterprise, which is not to suggest that its practitioners desire to be marginalized and silenced, but to confirm that their goal may not be to help maintain the status quo or to offer practical legal advice. Indeed, the law-and-literature studies that are most popular and accessible may be the least critically reflective about law, and about its disciplinary boundaries. (That is why Baron's critique of law-and-literature is a bit of a trap—there's no movement unless it is inspirational to lawyers; if one identifies inspirational studies, which are popular and accessible because they assume law is rule-bound and literature is humanizing, they are found to be lacking in reflections about disciplinary boundaries; if one identifies those who critically reflect on disciplinary boundaries, then unless there is both a profound level of agreement among them and some serious interest in their work by practicing lawyers, then there is no movement). There is a difference, of course, between the predominance of lawyers in law-and-literature (even though some non-lawyers join in) and the predominance of non-scientists in literature-and-science (even though some scientists join in): lawyers doing law-and-literature are insiders, and literary scholars doing literature-and-science are outsiders, with respect to the object of critique. Both enterprises, however, share the problems of interdisciplinarity, including (i) the problem of maintaining some level of expertise in two disciplines, and, as Baron usefully points out, (ii) the problem of defining each field and reflecting on their alleged relationship.

"Law," "Literature," and "Science" *are* hard to define, since they are fragmented professions and divided disciplines. Just as Peter Schuck conceded that describing law, science, and politics as distinctly different cultures is made difficult by the variations in each, but nevertheless concluded that each exhibits "enough normative coherence and behavioral regularity that one can fairly speak [of each] as a way of seeing, thinking, valuing, and acting that distinguishes it from other cultures" (1993:21), law-and-literature and literature-and-science have flourished in recent years despite such definitional challenges. Arguably, however, the prospect of a law, literature, and science enterprise exacerbates the problems of interdisciplinarity, requiring (in McCloskey's terms) a sort of tri-lingual capacity (McCloskey 1991:217). In the next chapter, I offer an example of an analysis that crosses three disciplinary boundaries in an attempt to understand and criticize the *discourse* of *science* in *law*.

Chapter 3
Ramón y Cajal: Hard SF for Lawyers

Introduction

> "... I enrolled ... in the legal college, [but] my education led me astray. Aside from his talent ... a smart lawyer is essentially an amoral being who couldn't care less about the ethical status of his defendants ... I lacked ... the theatrical touch needed to depict an outlaw as an angel of innocence and goodness ..."
>
> "You've been a victim," responded Jaime, "of the artificial nature of education. But luckily, there is a cure for your disease ... But before describing the regimen you need, I'm going to tell you about my own life ... I began [in my youth] to acquire an appreciation of Nature. I began to develop an ordered, logical memory, and with it a capacity for critical thinking ... [As my school teacher said,] 'With one voice, Nature and logic demand that knowledge be acquired in this order: first, the facts, the recording of perceptions so as to maintain the relations between them ... Then you can develop general empirical laws; and finally, hypotheses and theories'" (Cajal 2001:188–9, 195–6, 199, 202).

Because of his occasional references to law and lawyers, and especially their contrast with science and scientists, Santiago Ramón y Cajal's recently translated "science fiction tales" (first published in 1905)[1] offer a potential conjunction of literature-and-science, which Cajal's stories exemplify, and law-and-literature, the canon of which (literary works about law and lawyers) Cajal's stories enter quite by accident. Cajal (1852–1934), who won the Nobel Prize for medicine in 1906 for "showing that neurons were independent cells" and is considered the "Father

1 In her introduction to her translation of Cajal, Laura Otis writes:

> Originally, there were twelve *Vacation* Stories. Cajal wrote them early in his career, but he waited nearly twenty years to publish them. According to Cajal, the stories were unoriginal and stylistically defective. More probably, he feared that these "anti-religious, anti-establishment" tales would jeopardize his scientific funding ... Cajal waited to publish them until his reputation was well-established ... If these are the five stories he chose to publish, we can only wonder what the other seven were like. Sadly, we will never know, since they were lost in Madrid during the Spanish Civil War ... (Otis 2001:vii–viii).

Otis here cites O'Connor, D., Science, Literature, and Self-censorship: Ramón y Cajal's *Cuentos de Vacaciones*, *Ideologies and Literature*, 1(3), 98–122, and to Tzitsikas, H., 1965, *Santiago Ramón y Cajal: Obra literaria*, in Colección Studium No. 53.

of Neurobiology," was not only a successful scientist but an artist (specializing in scientific drawings) and a science fiction writer (even though his two novels have been lost) (Otis 2001:viii–xvii). Significantly, Cajal was more of an ambassador than a critic of the scientific establishment, though he was critical of ethically irresponsible science as well as popular "assumptions about the way science worked" (Otis 2001:vii, xviii). His stories tend, therefore, to impart a balanced view of science that is often missing from both idealized, internalist accounts of science (in scientific literature, including scientists' autobiographies) as well as literature-and-science criticism (by novelists or cultural theorists of science).

A Balanced, Albeit Not Modest, View of Science

In "For a Secret Offense, Secret Revenge," Cajal hoped "to expose some striking traits in the curious psychology of scientists, which is essentially amoral and profoundly egotistical (there are exceptions, of course)" (Cajal 2001:xxii). It is the story of Dr Max V. Forschung, a professor of bacteriology "accustomed to conveying the truth without veils or rhetorical artifices" (Cajal 2001:1) Suspecting that his wife was having an affair with his laboratory assistant, and wanting to know if it was true, Forschung turned "the unwitting lovers into guinea pigs[,] without ever compromising his scientific aims" to show that "tuberculosis was transmissible from animal to man" (Cajal 2001:11–12). Of course,

> no one had ever attempted the one decisive experiment: the production of tuberculosis in a healthy human being by inoculating him with microbes taken from other animals. Naturally, respectable feelings of humanity and scientific morality prohibited the performance of such a rash, radical experiment (Cajal 2001:11–12).

Nevertheless, Forschung, knowing that his laboratory assistant wrote and affixed labels to preparations and test tubes most evenings, "gathered up all the unused labels and amused himself by dextrously covering the gummy sides with a certain ... solution spiked with ... some extremely virulent bovine tuberculosis germs" (Cajal 2001:12). Twenty days later, "Forschung had the keen satisfaction (as a man of science, naturally) of spotting some tiny papules on" the assistant's lips—"the joy of conquering an important scientific truth" (Cajal 2001:12). When Forschung "spotted a painful-looking eruption upon" his wife's lips, the unknown, at last, "had become completely clear!" (Cajal 2001:13). Claiming that the bovine "culture was accidentally spilled onto a box of labels," Forschung announced his discovery in a scientific journal article, which only goes to show that:

> if we disregard the private, egotistical driving force that moves the investigative spirit and focus exclusively on the social impact of each discovery, the scientist's

> claim to altruism is affirmed. His inventions really do benefit humanity (Cajal 2001:8, 19–20).

Readers are, of course, left wondering whether they can so easily disregard "imbecilic pride and the vain desire for glory" simply because they are such "powerful forces for progress" (Cajal 2001:8). Nearly one hundred years after the tale of Forschung, the stem cell research debate pits (perhaps) overly anxious scientists, ready for progress, against worried bio-ethics proponents; the fact that the genome project was and is seemingly driven by greed leads some to wonder whether science is somehow infected, not simply moved along, by economic interests (e.g., patents); and the perennial concern over whether research sponsored by pharmaceutical companies is thereby biased calls into question the calm *division* between social contingencies and Nature itself. That is, can we assume, following Cajal's satirical distinction, indeed *disconnect*, between the genesis and the explanatory power of scientific knowledge, that science is only affected, but never constituted, by morality, funding, and opportunism?

The tale of Forschung's discovery is almost a paradigmatic or "classic" literature-and-science text—like Dr Frankenstein, Forschung is a monster—except for the fact that Cajal the scientist problematizes the ethical critique. Notwithstanding revengeful motives and unethical methods, the discovery is quite useful, "beneficial to humanity."

In another story, "The Fabricator of Honor," Cajal highlights the cultural *authority* of science. Dr Alejandro Mirahonda, on the basis of academic credentials and his *look* of "supreme authority," as well as his "substantial voice" and "colorful language," is able to convince the citizenry of Villabronca that he has discovered a serum,

> or rather antitoxin, [that] has the singular property of tempering the activity of nervous centers where the antisocial passions reside: idleness, rebelliousness, lasciviousness, criminal instincts, etc. ... (Cajal 2001:38–41, 43).

He even gave demonstrations, all staged, because strong minds are persuaded "only by irrefutable proof *de visu*, which cannot fail to be accepted" and he "signaled to his assistants, who led the people and animals who had undergone these experiments out of an adjacent chamber" (Cajal 2001:44). Because everyone was not in favor of the *moral vaccine*—"those who enjoyed having a good time once in a while," "the owners of gambling houses, taverns, and brothels," "impassioned anarchists ... fearing ... that the medicine would deaden the proletariat's rage," and arrogant, jealous spiritual leaders—Dr Mirahonda made substantial donations to the press, the anarchist's strike fund, and the church, all "clever maneuvers" by someone "who knew everything there was to know about certain matters" (Cajal 2001:45–7). All the while, Mirahonda bolstered his authority by giving advice to those who, calling him "the Christ,"

> rushed to him demanding illumination. They accepted his advice willingly, for our hero knew how to convince people of things without making them feel humiliated. To each one, he generously offered that portion of science and reason that was his due, skillfully avoiding any references to bad dealings or obvious ethical or intentional faults. Instead, he would attribute the injury to random chance, acts of God, the particular circumstances or the unconscious (Cajal 2001:42).

Thus the civic leaders of Villabronca required that the new vaccine "be obligatory for all persons between twelve and sixty years of age;" and it worked,

> surpassing even the most optimistic calculations. Criminality entirely ceased. All vices, greed, and dishonesty seemed to have disappeared forever (Cajal 2001:45, 55).

Eventually, after a year and a half, the authorities who had "respect for science and Mirahonda's prestige" asked for a new serum that would "restore [to the citizens] full enjoyment of their own free wills," and Mirahonda complied by producing a new serum based again on pure suggestibility (Cajal 2001:60). Interestingly, the fraud was justified by Mirahonda as a scientific experiment:

> Among the various ways of ... lulling the critical sense to sleep, there is none so effective as associating the suggestion with the banal act of taking some medicine ... If the doctor's scientific prestige is very great, the subject's reasoning facility is thrown off the scent ...
>
> From this one can infer that the most effective aid to the mental orthopedist is the common people's crass ignorance about the sovereign power of suggestion (Cajal 2001:52).

Again, Cajal problematizes a story about the social and rhetorical construction of scientific knowledge with the suggestion that in the hands of a scientific elite, "fabrication" can be beneficial to consumers of "science."

Cajal's apparent scientism is at the center of "The Accursed House," a story about a haunted house that brings misfortune to all of its occupants until a scientist, Julian, is able to explain "all the surprising phenomena ... by natural causes" (Cajal 2001:106). Even in the extended discussion or debate that follows among the scientist's neighbors—a surgeon, a spiritualist, "an old warship captain and distinguished naturalist," and others (Cajal 2001:101–17)—the future of scientific progress is never in doubt. Even though some "illustrious and distinguished" scientists were also spiritualists, and were "deceived by a great number of bamboozlers,"

> the day of [science's] reign is just dawning ... Science must broaden the sphere of the known at the expense of the unknown, a dark region where theoganies

> erect their heavens and raise up their gods. Science must reclaim the dominions of morality and philosophy for reason ... [S]cience will remove the spine of dogmatism (Cajal 2001:102, 107, 115).

And yet, the surgeon (quoted immediately above) is worried that religion may "disappear from people's hearts before science has progressed sufficiently to replace them," and the naturalist concedes that "the scientist, whose brain is adapted energetically, exclusively for a particular type of mental work, tends to be a child in everything else ..." (Cajal 2001:107, 115). Ascribing these scientific voices to Cajal, since he was both critical of organized religion and enamored of science's promise,[2] Cajal emerges as a particularly reflective ambassador of science. In his story "The Corrected Pessimist," for example, he highlights both the disagreements among scientists and the difficulty of introducing unconventional theories. The egotistical protagonist, Juan Fernández, was visited by "the spirit of science" who gave him amplified vision for a year. With his new powers, Fernández made amazing discoveries in both astronomy and bacteriology, and

> published the valuable fruits of this productive labor in singular, surprising, extremely lucid monographs, revealing the world of the great and of the very small. His researches reformed scientific thought and opened up splendid horizons for future investigation ...
>
> But ah! these admirable findings ran into one minor obstacle ... No one believed them (Cajal 2001:159).

Astronomers considered him a dreamer, and bacteriologists thought him a braggart (Cajal 2001:159–60). The "blind were judging the seer," the "one who should have felt pity was the one who was pitied," and genius "received only ignominy and ingratitude" (Cajal 2001:160). When "the term promised by the spirit came to an end," however, Fernández was cured of his arrogance—he was "fairer with his fellow men," "tolerant of errors," and "merciful and indulgent with his adversaries" (Cajal 2001:164–5). He won a hospital post, had more patients, was surrounded by friends, and married well—no "one remembered his old folly and madness" (Cajal 2001:166–7).

Cajal confirmed in his preface to his stories that he wanted his protagonists to "be more like real men than symbols, and that they offer the passions, defects, and limitations of real flesh-and-blood people" (Cajal 2001:xxiii). It is on this basis that I think that Cajal, never critical of the scientific enterprise *per se*, ends

2 Cajal mentions in his Preface that "he fails to disguise his sympathy for the moral figure" of the surgeon (Cajal 2001:xxiii). In her introduction to her translation of Cajal's stories, Otis notes that "*Vacation Stories* ... challenged ... organized religion," and states that "considering how quickly infectious diseases were being attributed to microorganisms, it seemed likely that someday all of them might be explained—and could—through microscopic studies" like Cajal's own (Otis 2001:vii).

up emphasizing the human side of science, including its social, institutional, and rhetorical aspects. It is revenge, as much as natural phenomena, that drives Forschung's research; Mirahonda's prestige is socially constructed, not established in the laboratory; religious prejudice and institutional conventions make rhetoric and consensus-building essential to the success of scientists like Julian and Fernández. And in Cajal's longest story, "The Natural Man and the Artificial Man," the conversation between a scientist and a lawyer focuses, in part, on how scientific knowledge is constructed in society.

> In a debate, as soon as your opponents discard revealed texts and reject traditions as a sure way of illuminating scientific problems, you, too, have to leave the ground of scholasticism and enter the arena of biological research. Scientific theses can only be fought with facts or scientific induction. If you'd [armed yourself] from the inexhaustible arsenal of paleontological, zoological, embryological, and physiological facts, you couldn't have helped but win. There one finds weapons for all arguments and tastes, to fit the most contradictory theories … (Cajal 2001:183).

There is the slightest critique—some would say realistic evaluation—in the concluding concession that scientific argument is a matter of style and rhetoric, but there is also the point that science in modernity overcomes revelation and tradition. The practice of law, on the other hand, seems to Cajal entirely a matter of fiction and theater—lawyers know how to "take advantage of all the ambiguities and contradictions in the experts' testimonies so that they will work in" their clients' favor; they see "shades of gray and complicate" their moral psychology (Cajal 2001:189–90). Of course, there

> is real glory and supreme pleasure in transferring error into proof through a stroke of genius, or casting deep shadows over the facts of a criminal case. There's even glory in disrupting the cautious prudence of judges and juries with showy plays on words (Cajal 2001:190).

The scientist, however, can "distinguish true, proven concepts from rhetorical disguises that [look] like the truth" (Cajal 2001:205). Nevertheless, the scientist Jaime (who is another moral figure in *Vacation Stories*, alongside the surgeon in "The Accused House," about whom Cajal cannot "fail to disguise his sympathy"), reminds his friend trained in law that

> in the city, fortune and power go to the one who speaks and writes the best. The respect we earn depends less on what we know than on our ability to persuade. You have to speak well to win people's confidence (Cajal 2001:xxiii, 203).

Not only is rhetoric important to science, but imagination is as well:

> [W]hen you're studying Nature, you find only what you're looking for. And *what you're looking for* is almost always an anticipated vision of the truth, a luminous image of your constructive imagination to which the facts end up adjusting themselves (Cajal 2001:232).

This striking statement, which (taken out of context) could have been written last year by a proponent of the social construction of scientific knowledge, is made by one who considers science "omnipotent" (Cajal 2001:242). For Jaime, as for Cajal, the world is not yet ready for justice, but they "let you use your common sense in the tranquil field of science [—] it's the only place they'll let us think freely" (Cajal 2001:242). Justice will come later, when science "has lit up all the caverns and dark corners of Nature ..." (Cajal 2001:242). This is neither amoral scientism nor an idealization of science as methodology in the absence of society and rhetoric. Science, for Cajal, is wonderfully beneficial but never disconnected from cultural contexts.

Cajal's stories are, in Charles Sheffield's terms, "hard sf"—*science* fiction (with a strong scientific content), not science *fiction* (or fantasy) (Sheffield 2002:4). Cajal says as much in his preface: "[T]hese stories are based on reasonable facts or hypotheses from the biological sciences and modern psychology" (Cajal 2001:xxii). Yet in contrast to scientific writing, which tends to erase the scientist's personality and to treat social context as irrelevant, and also in contrast to critical accounts of science that reduce science to social, institutional, and rhetorical accomplishments, Cajal offers a generous account of scientific progress while generously acknowledging its personal and cultural constitution—personality and culture are not mere contingencies. Ethics, rhetoric, cultural authority, and reputation are intertwined, in Cajal's stories, with the rigor of natural science.

The Idealization of Science in Law

When a recent study of judges concluded that judges do not generally understand how science works, the point of reference for a "genuine understanding" was the *Daubert* four-part test for valid scientific knowledge: testability, low-error rate, peer-reviewed publications, and general acceptance in the relevant field (Dobbin et al. 2002:247).

> [The] survey found that judges lacked the general scientific literacy required for full appreciation of the *Daubert* guidelines ... Indeed, many judges did not recognize their lack of understanding (Dobbin et al. 2002:247).

This emphasis on *Daubert* as the key to scientific literacy is understandable, since the U.S. Supreme Court decided to define and identify science in terms of the four factors (*Daubert* 1993:593–4). Perhaps the justices, or the *amici* on which they depended for their understanding of science, should have read Cajal's *Vacation*

Stories, or recommended them to all judges. There is as much idealization of science, as a stabilizing discourse on which law can depend, as anyone could want, but there is more—a picture of science as it really is, with active participants, rhetorical strategies, a non-scientific consumer citizenry, and a culture into which science is placed. Science is a matter of hypotheses, data, methodology, conclusions, *and* also the network described by Cajal.

In both policy/regulatory and litigation contexts, there is a tendency to idealize science as a disinterested arbiter of legal controversies. In the discourse concerning "junk science," its attackers assume that

> if scientists disagree in the face of the same empirical data ... there is a violation of scientific rationality. Such disagreement seems to illustrate ... that "experts on one side, or even both sides, are falling so much under the sway of 'interests' that they violate central norms of impartiality, emotional neutrality, universality ... and the like ... [T]heir behavior has been seen as the prostituting of science, as the selling of credibility ... (Mayo 1991:253, quoting Hamlin 1986:486).

But this perspective has been questioned, since "it is meaningless to think about disinterested science"—there is no separation of scientific from social issues, "but simply parties with different, more-or-less conflicting or compatible interests" (Hamlin 1986:487). A scientist, like Cajal, may have more credibility than sociological critics of science in his exploration of science as a social phenomenon. Moreover, "hard sf" as a genre has the capacity

> to entertain, certainly—otherwise it will not be read—but also to instruct, to stimulate, and to warn. No other branch of fiction satisfies so well those multiple objectives (Sheffield 2002:4).

While everyone, it seems, longs for the integration of "a sophisticated understanding of science into legal decisionmaking" (Faigman et al. 2002:viii), we should not forget the unique capacity of literary representations of law and science to educate in ways that official and conventional disciplinary texts and discourse do not.

Having said that, what have I (in light of Baron's critique, discussed in Chapter 2) done? Inevitably, I drew some boundaries by putting Cajal in the field of science, his "vacation stories" in the field of literature, and an idealized account of science in law; but I suggested that Cajal himself saw science as a cultural and rhetorical practice, that his stories are *science* fiction (not fantasy), and that the idealization of science in law is a tentative and changeable discourse, such that my initial boundaries variously shift, vanish and re-appear. Inevitably, I made a "large" claim—science is a cultural affair—based on a detailed reading of Cajal, but then I think Cajal's science fiction is particularly helpful to make that point, even though Cajal's stories are not the only way to justify that claim. My interest in Cajal "does not a movement make," and I suspect that such analyses may not appeal to those who idealize science in law. But those problems—building consensus and persuading others—are not unique to law-and-literature, literature-and-science, or the hybrid law, literature, and science enterprise. Indeed, they are the characteristics of scholarly discourse in any field, including both Baron's critique of law-and-literature and the study of science that is appropriated in law.

In the next chapter, I consider another story of a scientist who, like Cajal's Fernández, was unable to make the public understand his scientific insights.

Chapter 4
Ibsen's *An Enemy of the People*: The Public Understanding of Science in Law

Introduction

> I came to feel that I was trying to convince all parties concerned—the public, scientists and institutions—of the credibility of something that none of them wanted. All in all, not a bad version of hell (Stewart 1988:62).

Henrik Ibsen's play *An Enemy of the People* (1999), published in Norway in 1882 and first published in English in 1887,[1] is the story of a doctor who discovers that the public water supply in his village is contaminated. While Dr Stockmann expects to become a hero, he is instead viewed as an enemy, as his discovery threatens to destroy the village's spa tourism industry. Arguably, the central theme of the play concerns the "condemnation of a dissenter by the majority" (A. Miller 1989:74) —Dr Stockmann runs afoul of corporate and government interests, the press turns against him, and the citizenry fears higher taxes (to fix the problem of the poisonous water).

> It must be remembered ... that for Ibsen the poisoning of the public water supply by mendacious and greedy interests was only the occasion of *An Enemy of the People* and is not, strictly speaking, its theme. That, of course, concerns the crushing of the dissenting spirit by the majority, and the right and obligation of such a spirit to exist at all (A. Miller 1989:74).

Even though he holds the "truth," Dr Stockmann is condemned.

It is significant, however, that the "truth" that is rejected is a scientific truth. The play has therefore interested environmentalists, who see the play as a warning about how corporate interests and social ignorance can get in the way of public safety. Indeed, the "story of *Enemy* is far more applicable to our nature-despoiling societies than to even turn-of-the-century capitalism":

> The churning up of pristine forests, valleys and fields for minerals and the rights of way of the expanding rail systems is child's play compared to some of our

1 Quotations from the play and page numbers in this chapter, unless otherwise identified, will refer to Arthur Miller's popular 1950 adaptation of Ibsen's *An Enemy of the People*.

> vast depredations, our atomic contamination and oil spills, to say nothing of tainting our food supply by carcinogenic chemicals (A. Miller 1989:74).

Moreover, the play can also be associated with the "literature and science" movement, insofar as it is a literary work about science in society (Peterfreund 1990:3–13). Like "law and literature" studies, which often involves looking at literary representations of law and lawyers (usually bad) in order to reflect on the ethics of lawyering, literature and science studies often focus on literary representations of science and scientists (usually bad) in order to reflect on the lack of ethical consciousness in scientific practice (Haynes 1994:86–90). Ibsen's play, however, is interesting in two respects: first, the play is not a warning about science out of control (which is the theme of much science fiction) and in need of social regulation, but is rather a warning about social control *of* science; second, because of the importance of science in law, both in the regulatory and in the litigation contexts, *An Enemy of the People* is a relevant text for both law-and-literature and literature-and-science projects—indeed, the play can be seen as part of the canon of the hybrid project I have identified as law, literature, and science studies.

Among sociologists of science, interest in the "public understanding of science" has grown to a degree that "PUS"—its acronym—is now an identifiable sub-discipline, multi-discipline, or field of research (Michael 2002:357).

> There are three broad approaches that can be brought under the rubric of traditional [or "positivist"] PUS: survey analyses of the contents of PUS and of attitudes toward science, the study of mental models, and the theory of social representations.
>
> The alternative tradition in PUS is the critical strand primarily identified by its use of qualitative techniques. Crucially, the critical approach has a keen interest in the cultural context of the public understanding of science (Michael 2002:359–60).

Because Ibsen's *An Enemy of the People* is a convenient example of the interaction of science and society, Rachelle Hollander appropriates Ibsen's imagery in her study of collective moral responsibility with respect to risk identification and scientific evidence in policymaking (1991:160–62).

> Both the mayor and Dr Stockmann must recognize the limits of scientific understanding ... This does not mean that the [contamination of the water supply] does not exist or that one answer is as good as any other. But it does mean that the problem is not a scientific one and that science cannot solve it ... The risks to the townspeople and visitors are medical, social and economic; the solutions are similar, requiring consideration and negotiation. Times have not changed much, at least since 1882 (Hollander 1991:161–62).

In the legislative context, therefore, "scientific and value choices are intertwined":

> the questions of whether to use a test and what standards to use are not scientific questions, as they do not have scientific answers.
>
> The responsibility for answering them is social, that is, shared [by scientists and citizens] (Hollander 1991:164, 168).

In the litigation context, studying the "public understanding of science" has obvious implications for juries who must decide cases involving scientific expertise. Thus the study of how juries perceive and react to experts (Sundby 1997:1113–39) is exemplary of the growing research concerning public "uptake and understanding of scientific messages" (Wynne 1996:20).

My own focus in this chapter is on the less-than-obvious conception of trial judges as the "public" in "the public understanding of science." In the decade after the U.S. Supreme Court in *Daubert* (1993) attempted both to define scientific validity and to offer guidelines for judges who must evaluate scientific expertise for admissibility (*Daubert* 1993:589–90, 592–5), courts and commentators struggled to clarify the *Daubert* standard and the role of judges with respect to science (Caudill and Redding 2000). Judges, for example, must determine "whether the reasoning or methodology underlying [proffered expert scientific] testimony is scientifically valid," and in doing so they should ordinarily consider testability, error-rate, peer-reviewed publications, and general acceptance (*Daubert* 1993:593)—the so-called *Daubert* four factors or four-part test (*Kumho Tire* 1999:152). Federal Rule of Evidence 702, amended after *Daubert*, likewise confirms that admissible scientific testimony must be "based upon sufficient facts or data" and be "the product of reliable principles and methods" that have been applied "reliably to the facts of the case." Therefore, in the post-*Daubert* regime in federal and many state courts (Lustre 2001), judges have assumed the role of gatekeepers with respect to admissibility of scientific expertise; but because of their general lack of scientific training (Hans 2007), they function at trial like "public" consumers of science. Indeed, the survey (discussed in Chapter 3) decrying the sparse scientific literacy among judges (Gatowski et al. 2001:433) parallels the so-called deficit model in "public understanding of science" research, which is

> associated with the relatively well-established tradition of using survey instruments to measure knowledge of and attitudes to science. The term *deficit* reflects an expectation that members of the public are relatively ignorant of science and that these instruments help to establish the extent of their knowledge deficit (Locke 2002:87).

Like Dr Stockmann's fellow citizens, judges holding *Daubert* hearings (and making admissibility determinations) are generally non-scientists who are called upon to evaluate the reliability and credibility of proffered scientific expertise.

I discuss below the relevance of *An Enemy of the People* for judicial determinations of scientific validity. In particular, I identify the courtroom as a social context into which science is introduced. Then, in the remainder of this chapter, I draw upon fieldwork in the "public understanding of science" to explore my analogy of judges to the "public," and demonstrate that the same issues—trust, credibility, and suspicion of exaggerated certainty—that characterize public interaction with science are present in the courtroom. I conclude that an engagement with Ibsen and the growing tradition of PUS research enriches our understanding of the place of science in law.

Ibsen and the Social Aspects of Law-Science Relations

> [T]he cognitivist presumption that ... scientific knowledge [exists] independently as an object for measurable public attitudes or beliefs [is] at least two steps behind. The first step is the recognition that ... trustworthiness and credibility ... are basic to people's ... uptake of knowledge ... Thus 'understanding' science is a function of experience, judgment and understanding of science's institutional forms as much as its cognitive contents. However the second step is to recognize that trust and credibility are themselves analytically derivative of social relations and identity-negotiation; thus ... they too should not be treated as if they have an objective existence which can be unambiguously measured and manipulated (Wynne 1996:42).

Like any literary text, *An Enemy of the People* is susceptible of multiple readings—it is about majoritarian tyranny and a lone dissenter, it is about environmental risk and public safety, it is about science and society in conflict, and so forth. Even if one simply reflects on the play for insights into the place of science in the courtroom, however, multiple readings are nevertheless possible. For example, the play can be read as an indictment of "junk science," insofar as Dr Stockmann's true or genuine science is pitted against a false or popular scientific theory. The government, the press, business and economic interests, and a majority of the citizenry join together in denial of a scientific fact. In more traditional interpretations of the play, of course, the contamination of the healing springs becomes a metaphor for a poisoned and corrupt society (Ledger 1999:30).

> [T]he decontamination of the water supply [acts] as a metaphor for implicitly wider social reforms ... [T]he contaminating sewers, the cesspit on which, it is discovered, the spa town is built, acts in the play as a metaphor for *all* civil and political institutions (Ledger 1999:29–30).

The particular context for Ibsen's condemnation of majoritarian foolishness is, however, the discovery of a scientific fact that is kept hidden by political *bias* and economic *interests*.

Some might see an analogy in *Daubert's* recognition that novel science, which should be admissible if it is otherwise methodologically sound, is often out of step with generally accepted—"received" or majoritarian—science: some "propositions ... are too ... new ... to be published," even if they reflect the best science (*Daubert* 1993:593). Dr Stockmann, after all, speaks to the citizenry about "truths which are yet too new-born in the world on consciousness to have gained the adhesion of the plurality." (Boyeson 1973:240). The majority tends to follow "truths which are so aged that they are on the point of becoming decrepit" (Boyeson 1973:240). I think, however, that the analogy between Dr Stockmann and novel science is a weak one, because the conflict in Ibsen's play is between *good* science and contaminated or junk science, the latter being a production not of flawed laboratory tests but political expediency, financial interests, social bias, and a timid press.

Therefore the play functions well as a text about science (i.e., ignoring its primary theme as a moral indictment of majoritarianism), as a description of the social context of the scientific enterprise. Science cannot simply be viewed as the recording of natural facts on laboratory measurement devices, but always involves human scientists who must persuade each other and those in society that their findings are credible. The effectiveness of science therefore depends not only on rhetoric, but also on alliances with social and institutional interests (Kitcher 1998:36–7).

> The sciences depend upon their "context" not only for funding and material resources, recruits and auxiliary personnel; institutional location in universities, academies, corporations, bureaucracies, or foundations; social norms, cultural forms, and bodily disciplines; but also for much of what is ultimately at stake in scientific practices (Rouse 1999:445).

Ibsen's play is therefore particularly useful as an exploration of the rhetorical life of a scientific fact (Fahnestock 1998). The failure of Dr Stockmann's scientific crusade reveals a catalogue of social, institutional, and rhetorical *constraints* on science.

For example, Dr Stockmann himself is a barrier to scientific progress. He is self-righteous, spiteful, egotistical, stubborn, and inflexible. He demands attention, as "a doctor and a scientist"; he threatens to give those who won't listen "both barrels"; he says he cannot be bought, and asks whether the majority was right "when they stood by while Jesus was crucified"; and his brother the mayor said that his "hallucinations ... that we live in a pesthole" were "based on vindictiveness, on his hatred of authority" (A. Miller 1950:36, 56, 74, 94, 108). He is ignorant as to what he is up against, which of course affects the success of his scientific project. Thereafter, the political establishment, corporate interests, the press, and finally the "mob" interfere with Dr Stockmann's effort to clean up the water supply. While the ideal of genuine science, in the debate over "junk science" in the courtroom, implies that good science is not biased, motivated, or interested (*and* that "junk science" is) (Aron et al. 1990:151), all science is necessarily entangled in social structures. Values play a role at the outset of scientific research, as choices of problems to work on reflect social priorities; values are also implicated after a discovery like Dr Stockmann's, because risk evaluation reflects social priorities.

> Once science enters the policy making arena, ostensibly scientific decisions ... are not (or are not just) scientific. They are social, indeed moral decisions ... Testing for environmental toxicity might be [a] circumstance in which a risk-averse society would opt for [or "allow"] more false positives.
>
> That is, the best "science (in the sense of science that does not predict a toxic effect when there is none) is purchased at the cost of overlooking some toxicity. This kind of "good" science is also more likely to predict no toxic effect when there is one [i.e., a false negative] (Hollander 1991:167).

Nowadays, funding is available for certain projects and not others, which obviously affects science.

> [I]t is patently obvious that which questions get asked, taken seriously, investigated, funded, reported, analyzed, and so forth is the result of social processes, human interactions, and current interests. Very few detailed questions are asked about the most widespread tropical diseases because there is no money in it for drug companies (Hacking 2000:S69).

Institutional gatekeeping within the scientific community, as well as gatekeeping in administrative agency hearings and by judges, demonstrates that the social and the scientific are intertwined. Scientific authority is a social matter—as Mrs Stockmann says, "[w]ithout power, what good is the truth?" (A. Miller 1950:59). The power of scientific explanations is based on the rhetorical capacity to convince scientific colleagues, regulators and juries, and ultimately the public in a democratic society.

Late in the play, Dr Stockmann is "cross-examined" by his father-in-law ("Kiil"), who it turns out is responsible for the pollution and is thus interested in saving his reputation:

> KIIL: How do you know the day you made your tests there wasn't something unusual about the water? How do you know the rest of it wasn't pure?
> DR STOCKMANN: It's not probable. People were getting sick last summer.
> KIIL: They were sick when they came here [for the healing springs] or they wouldn't have come!
> DR STOCKMANN: Not intestinal diseases, skin diseases.
> KIIL: Maybe the food was bad. Did you ever think of the food?
> DR STOCKMANN: No, I didn't look into the food.
> KIIL: Admit it! You have some doubt.

> DR STOCKMANN: Well, there's always a possibility. Nothing is a hundred percent on this earth, but—
> KIIL: Then you have a perfect right to doubt the other way! You have a scientific right! (A. Miller 1950:113, 140).

In the fictional world of *An Enemy of the People*, the audience knows that the water is contaminated—it is a fact. Thus Ibsen is able to show how such facts get suppressed by social influences. On the other hand, "nothing is a hundred percent" in the real world, so scientific expertise in the courtroom is mediated by a social process that begins with a *Daubert* hearing on reliability. Because the standard for reliability is conventionally viewed as one belonging to science,[2] the gatekeeping judge could be conceptualized as being on the side of science—ensuring that scientific experts are living up to their own standards[3]—while the jury could be characterized as the "public," using science as an aid to its deliberations. I think, however, that the function of the judge in evaluating scientific evidence should also be characterized as a "public" role.

That is, the judge is on the same "side" as the parties and their lawyers in the courtroom, insofar as they are all non-scientists and not part of the scientific community to which scientific experts belong. The authoritative role of the judge in deciding whether an expert will be allowed to influence the jury is certainly unique, but the judge is part of the pre-established social context into which "science" is introduced. By analogy, the judge is in the position of the more powerful characters in Ibsen's play—the mayor, the newspaper publisher, the board of directors of the spa—who are capable of limiting Dr Stockmann's power as the figure of science. Moreover, just as Ibsen's village becomes a social context for science, the courtroom becomes a social or public context for science in cases involving scientific expertise. Scientific expertise "itself," however, is not simply an abstract "truth" that is dropped into a social context or community, but is the product of *another* context—the scientific community. Finally, these two social contexts or communities are never really isolated from each other because (i) the effectiveness of scientific knowledge depends on its reception by the public, and (ii) the production of scientific knowledge is affected, not only by availability of

2 Prior to *Daubert* 1993, the so-called *Frye* test (*Frye* 1923:1014) equated reliability with general acceptance in the relevant scientific community. The effort in *Daubert* to define science, which resulted in the four-part test (testability, low error-rate, peer-reviewed publication, and general acceptance), *see Daubert* 1993:593–4, is perhaps less deferential to scientists (because of judges' gatekeeping role regarding admissibility), but is clearly deferential to scientific methodology. *See* Faigman et al. 1998:1823 (judges are required under *Daubert* to come to terms with the scientific method) (Faigman et al. 1997:xi; ("legal culture must assimilate the scientific culture" after *Daubert*).

3 *See, e.g.*, Cooper 2000:1021 (under *Daubert*, methodology of a physician employing "the accepted diagnostic tool of examination accompanied by the physical history as related by the patient" was sufficient); Jahn 2000:391 (quoting *Kumho Tire* 1999:152) (expert testimony must reflect "the same level of intellectual rigor that characterizes" the expert's field)).

funding or ethical constraints, but by law—science is regulated by administrative rules and legislation, as well as by judicial decisions (e.g., patent protection). In this complex set of interactions, I think that a judge's evidentiary decision on admissibility, which may be seen as a legal constraint on (or regulation of) science, is also an example of the public reception of science. To explore that notion, I turn now to several recent studies of the public understanding of science.

Public Understanding of Science

> [T]he term public understanding of science has a degree of cultural/national specificity, being better established in the United Kingdom in comparison to other terms coined elsewhere, such as science literacy and public cultures of science (Locke 2002:88).

In the opening chapter of *Misunderstanding Science?: The Public Reconstruction of Science and Technology*, Professor Brian Wynne of Lancaster University presented "what is fast becoming the paradigm study of so-called 'lay expertise'" (Collins and Evans 2002:255). Wynne focused on

> one very specific example of public interaction with science—the case of the hill sheep farmers of the Lake District of northern England [who] experienced radioactive fall-out from the 1986 Chernobyl accident which contaminated their sheep flocks and upland pastures (Wynne 1996:19).

Like Dr Stockmann's fellow citizens in *An Enemy of the People*, the farmers were advised by scientists of whom they were suspicious. After first being told "that there would be no effects at all from the Chernobyl ... fall-out," a ban on sheep sales was announced due to radioactivity levels; scientists then advised farmers to "hang on because ... the contamination would fall soon," but "once again the advice was badly over-optimistic" (Wynne 1996:24–5).

> Only later did it emerge that these predictions were based on a false scientific model of the behavior of caesium [in alkaline clay soils, but the uplands] have acid peaty soil ... in which caesium remains chemically mobile [rather than] locked up by chemical absorption ... This mistake only became apparent over the next two years, as contamination remained stubbornly high ... What was not lost on the farmers ... was that the scientists had made unqualified reassuring assertions then been proven mistaken, and had not even admitted making a serious mistake (Wynne 1996:25–6).

Scientific credibility on other issues was therefore undermined by this "exaggerated sense of certainty and arrogance" (Wynne 1996:26). Moreover, scientists ignored the "farmers' own knowledge of their local environments, hill-sheep characteristics, and hill-farming management realities," which knowledge was sometimes superior to alleged scientific knowledge:

> A graphic example of the scientists' denial of the specialist knowledge of the farmers was the scientists' decision to perform experiments ... [in which] bentonite was spread at different concentrations on the ground in different plots; the sheep from each plot were then tested at intervals, and compared with controls on zero-bentonite land. However, in order to do this the sheep were fenced in. The farmers pointed out that the sheep were used to roaming over open tracts ..., and that if they were fenced in they would waste (lose condition), thus ruining the experiment. Their criticisms were ignored, but were vindicated later when the experiments were quietly abandoned for the reasons that the farmers had identified (Wynne 1996:26).

Finally, through direct contacts with the conduct of experiments on their land, the farmers became "aware of the sheer number and variety of less controlled assumptions, judgments, and negotiations that underpin scientific facts"—by "accident, as it were, the farmers entered the 'black-boxes'[4] of constructed" science (Wynne 1996:32–3). Wynne concludes that "reflexive recognition of its own conditionality is a pre-requisite for science's greater public legitimation and uptake" (1996:39).

It should be noted that Collins and Evans issued a warning concerning the proper interpretation of Wynne's influential study:

> [What the] study shows is not what it has often been taken to show—that scientific expertise is to be found among the public—but that, in this particular case, there were not one but two sets of specialists, each with something to contribute. The sheep farmers [possessed] a body of knowledge as esoteric as that of any group of qualified scientists. The sheep farmers were not 'lay' anything—... they were experts who were not certified as such (Collins and Evans 2002:261).

In Collins and Evans' typology of the three levels of expertise—no expertise, interactional expertise (enough expertise to interact interestingly with scientists), and contributory expertise (enough expertise to contribute to the science)—the sheep farmers were not simply a "public" with no expertise, but like the scientists, the farmers had contributory expertise (the problem was that the sheep farmers, like the scientists, seemed to lack sufficient interactional expertise to absorb the expertise of the other experts) (Collins and Evans 2002:254–6). This argument

---

4 In social studies of science, the term "black box" refers to the hidden or unacknowledged aspects of the scientific enterprise, such as its social, institutional, and rhetorical features. For example, when a scientific report does not include information about funding, negotiations to reach consensus in the laboratory, or ethical concerns of the scientist, that information is said to be "black-boxed." *See generally* Caudill 2002a.

is part of Collins and Evans' effort to initiate a "third wave" of science studies focused on expertise and experience, which would acknowledge the importance of non-credentialed experience-based expertise, while challenging the notions of "lay expertise" (an oxymoron for Collins and Evans) and wholesale public participation in scientific decision-making (that is, even when the public does not possess expertise) (Collins and Evans 2002:238). In response to those who would see all of science as politicized (and therefore "indistinguishable from politics"), Collins and Evans argue that it is

> important to retain a notion, even [if] it is an idealized one, of a core-set community in which expertise is used to adjudicate between competing knowledge-claims and to determine the content of knowledge. The wider society still has a role to play in forming a view about the socially acceptable use of knowledge and what to do while such knowledge remains contested, but this contribution lies in the political sphere. Lay people as lay people, however, have nothing to contribute to the scientific and technical content of debate (Collins and Evans 2002:280–81).

This resurrection of "the old distinction between the political sphere and the sphere of expertise" is not meant *always* to decrease public participation in science, but rather to shift the "old" boundary (in idealized conceptions of expertise) from a boundary "between the class of professional accredited experts and the rest" to one "between groups of specialists [even experienced-based experts] and the rest" (Collins and Evans 2002:263, 270).

As discussed in Chapter 2, this "third wave" framework is controversial and the dust has not yet settled as to whether Collins and Evans "sidestep the very issues that are relevant to the epistemological status" of the outcomes of particular institutional processes such as courts of law, namely how certain core-set "sciences emerge in the first place, and how protected spaces for such sciences are maintained" (Rip 2003:420–21). For my purposes in this present chapter, the knowledge of judges as outsiders or "public" with respect to scientific expertise in the courtroom is relatively sophisticated. Indeed, the judiciary may well constitute a "pocket of expertise" in Collins and Evans' framework, that is, a narrow group of experience-based experts educated by the certified experts testifying on behalf of opposing parties (Collins and Evans 2002:250). Nevertheless, the fact that judges adjudicate between contradictory scientific opinions, by virtue of a legal institution, gives judges what Collins and Evans identify as a political role as a representative of the citizenry. Indeed, even as Collins and Evans acknowledge that "non-scientists can lend credibility to decisions concerning science" in the courtroom, they thereby seem to suggest that the scientific decision is actually made by the expert who is recognized by the judge as credible (Collins and Evans 2002:276-277). My own analytical framework in the following section is less deferential toward "certified" expertise, and more critical of the deficit-model of the public understanding of science that Collins and Evans impliedly defend.

Judges as Public Actors

> [S]cience, and its practitioners, are not the only, and perhaps not the principal, actors involved in the social construction of scientific authority. It is not a one-way process. The whole of society participates in identifying 'science' and 'expertise,' as it does in the identification of any important symbolic boundary (McKechnie 1996:130).

The analogy between a suspicious public and trial judges is not self-evident, particularly in light of law's precommitment to science as a stabilizing force in legal controversies, but judges are used to seeing two scientists in conflict, both speaking with as much certainty as their client's attorney can encourage. Judges know that some experts act more like advocates than disinterested scientists (Saks 1987: 42, 49).

> An expert can be found to testify to the truth of almost any factual theory, no matter how frivolous, thus validating the case sufficiently to avoid summary judgment and force the matter to trial. At the trial itself an expert's testimony can be used to obfuscate what would otherwise be a simple case (Weinstein 1986:482).

Indeed, a judge's prior experiences with experts might render her suspicious of courtroom science, even though she would have more confidence in neutral or independent scientific views. In that respect, judges are very much like the "public" in a recent study of two urban, industrial areas within Greater Manchester (in the north west of England) where housing was constructed close to chemical plants (Irwin et al. 1996:47–64). Public concern in these localities over pollution and other environmental hazards was documented through questionnaires and interviews that focused on the community's knowledge and understanding of science (Irwin et al. 1996:50). Not surprisingly, in light of Wynne's observation that "trust and credibility are major contextual factors influencing the uptake and understanding of scientific messages" (Wynne 1996:20), the source of scientific information (e.g., a chemical company) affected its persuasiveness in Greater Manchester:

> Despite the regular assumption by those in scientific institutions that 'science' is a straightforward and unitary category (so that the problem of 'public understanding of science' is seen as one of getting *more* science to the public ...), the picture here is of local citizens discriminating between different 'knowledges' according to ... the perceived social credibility of that source (Irwin et al. 1996:53–4).

Because information about pollution "does not exist in a social vacuum, but is weighed in terms of previous experience and cultural evaluations," any "perceived disparity between reassurances offered and subsequent (or previous) pollution incidents will be seized upon by the community as a measure of untrustworthiness" (Irwin et al. 1996:55). Citizens' suspicion concerning industry's self-interested and "very partial account of environmental hazards," and therefore skepticism "regarding local industry as a source of information" (Irwin et al. 1996:56), parallels judicial skepticism, sometimes unjustified, regarding "courtroom" or "litigation" science prepared by one "side" for trial.[5] Similarly, citizens' desire for independent or neutral advice, "seen as potentially valuable in offering an alternative to industry-based information," parallels the frequent call (by judges and others) for neutral or court-appointed "science panels" to adjudicate legal controversies (Weinstein 1986:483–6; Thornburgh 1998:468).

The parallel with Ibsen's *An Enemy of the People* is not so obvious in this context, because the figure of science, Dr Stockmann, is not aligned with corporate interests (the owners of the polluted spa), while the "public"—the citizens who distrust him—are! On reflection, however, Dr Stockmann is "no exception to the rule of self-interest," and "his motives are not pure" (Hornby 1981:152, 156). He, too, is *interested*, personally if not financially and politically, in defeating his successful brother the mayor, who is chairman of the board of the spa (Hornby 1981:155–7).

> The conflict between the [successful and unsuccessful] brothers is most obvious ... when Dr Stockmann ... parades about, saying, "Some respect, if you will, [mayor]. I'm the authority in this town now." Obviously, what is going on here is more than political; Dr Stockmann's glee is the result of his supposing that he has at last defeated his hated older brother (Hornby 1981:157).

The "public," that is, considers the source of the scientific message—Dr Stockmann's "[s]piteful, rambling, overwrought speeches ... are hardly those of a high-minded scientist in search of the truth." Recall as well Wynne's observation that the "exaggerated sense of certainty and arrogance" on the part of scientists, together with their naïve overconfidence, undermined their credibility in the eyes of the Lake District sheep farmers (1996:26, 31). Dr Stockmann, likewise, was "self-righteous," exhibited a "boundless egotism," and had "a rather grand and exaggerated way of seeing himself in relation to a small town political squabble" (Hornby 1981:150). Ibsen's fictional representation of what happens to a "scientific fact" in "society" highlights, perhaps unwittingly, the social aspects

5 "Litigation" or "courtroom" science is often contrasted with scientific experiments or reports completed before, and not in the context of, litigation; the latter are typically considered more reliable. *See, e.g.*, *Lauzon* 2001:693 (district court, which found expert's research was not sufficiently independent of litigation, reversed because expert's involvement with past litigation did not infect his research); *Metabolife* 2001:843 ("rather than disqualify the study ... because it was commissioned by Metabolife, the district court [on remand] should examine the soundness of the methodology employed").

of science itself. Rather than conceiving of "science" as the fact (say, pollution), and "society" as the "public" which receives that fact (and wisely accepts it or foolishly rejects it), Ibsen reminds us (i) that on the side of science there is a set of social aspects or features—a scientist, arrogance, self-interest, motives—and (ii) that these features affect the public reception of science.

Indeed, studies of public understanding of science reveal that PUS involves two "societies"—scientists and the public—interacting. In the study of Lake District sheep farmers, for example, Wynne defines science not as "cognitive content" but as a social and institutional practice based on assumptions that often conflict with public understandings (1996:19). That is, Wynne

> identified [among scientists] certain commitments which were institutionalized and taken for granted ... These assumptions *shaped* scientific knowledge, they were not *extra* to it ... These were elements of cultural prescription posing ... as objective knowledge. They included the assumptions ... that uncertainties in scientific knowledge could be contained within the private discourse of the scientists and would be misunderstood if disclosed in public; [and] that local lay knowledge was effectively worthless (1996:19–20).

The discord between such assumptions and the local knowledge of *consumers* of expertise obviously affects the credibility of scientists and therefore the "uptake" of science by the public. Again, the oversimplified picture of scientific "expertise" delivered to a public with a knowledge deficit is replaced by a complex description of *two* cultures in conflict, each with its own knowledges, each "just as socially grounded, conditional and value-laden as the other" (Wynne 1996:38). The Greater Manchester study, concerning public understanding of pollution and chemical industry hazards, clarified this reformulation:

> Rather than assuming [that the central issue is the public failure to understand science, we] portray the provision of technical information as part of an *interaction* with other forms of knowledge, understanding, and communication ... [W]e highlight those context-specific (or 'local') knowledges [that potentially] match with, contradict, or simply ignore the 'official' technical statements emerging from industrial sources (Irwin et al. 1996:48).

Reminiscent of the citizens in *An Enemy of the People* who ignored Dr Stockmann's warning, the subject communities in Greater Manchester viewed environmental hazards as

> just one part of everyday life ... [F]rom the perspective of local people, science has no necessarily special or privileged status alongside such routine concerns as unemployment [or] rent increases (Irwin et al. 1996:52).

Moreover, in light of (i) the mistaken advice given to the Lake District sheep farmers and (ii) the "partial" account of hazards offered by chemical plant scientists to the communities in Greater Manchester, we should not assume

> that local understandings are inadequate or deficient in comparison to formal, scientific understanding. On the contrary, they may well represent a more robust and well-tested body of advice, information, and practical assistance than any new or externally generated piece of technical evidence (Irwin et al. 1996:55).

Knowledge from the scientific community therefore competes with understandings in the local community.

Mike Michael's study of some British communities' reactions to the dangers of ionizing radiation likewise challenges the "deficit model" of the public understanding of science (wherein "people are treated as essentially repositories of information" (1996:109)). In his interviews, Michael found

> that people do not simply possess knowledge about scientific 'facts' and scientific procedures and processes [;] they can also reflect upon the epistemological status of their knowledge ... [T]his active reflection can directly affect their responses to science and scientific experts (1996:107).

For example, a lay person's sense of ignorance concerning science may manifest itself as a desire to know more, but it can also manifest itself as (i) "a bracketing of science knowledge" as to which one cannot aspire ("they are saying that they are constitutionally not naturally equipped to fathom the mysteries of science") or (ii) a deliberate choice to ignore or avoid scientific knowledge because it obscures "the real issue" ("extra knowledge is redundant, or a distraction from the central issue—that radiation is dangerous") (Michael 1996:115–17, 120). In the latter case, ignorance is "mobilized to challenge or attack the relevance of a given body of expert knowledge" (Michael 1996:119–20).

> The texture of science, the minutiae, the arcane—all these only obscure the real (political) issues. Here, to assimilate specific scientific knowledge (for example, about ionizing radiation) would be to assimilate a particular (inferred) set of social interests and values which are anathema (as opposed to merely beyond one's capacity) (Michael 1996:121).

Self-ascriptions of ignorance are therefore part of a complex relationship with science in which

> the causes or reasons behind [lay people's ignorance of science] reflect their social identity and their relations of dependence, co-operation, or challenge—that is [,] relations of power *vis-à-vis* science (Michael 1996:112).

In *An Enemy of the People*, these power relations are dramatized by the community's rejection of Dr Stockmann. People feel threatened by his discovery, which may result not only in higher taxes (to fix the problem), but also in an economic disaster (by losing tourism). Some of Stockmann's fellow citizens even consider him a revolutionist: "What're you trying to do, make a revolution here?"; "You're just trying to blow up everything!" (A. Miller 1950:91, 94). The appropriate model for public understanding of science is therefore not to contrast the "scientific" with the "social," because the scientific side of things is already too social—alongside "cognitive content" we find institutionalized commitments, social values, scientists with particular identities (and perhaps questionable interests and motives), and assumptions about scientific authority and public ignorance, all of which come into play when the public interacts with science.

Again, it is my contention that judges who evaluate expertise, and decide to admit or disallow an expert's testimony, can be usefully identified with the public (in their reception of science) in both Ibsen's play and in the PUS studies discussed above. That is, instead of viewing the judge's gatekeeping role as an extension of science's own institutional gatekeeping—e.g., requiring methodological rigor, ensuring peer-review, etc.—the judge can be seen as the public's gatekeeper, as an outsider (with respect to the scientific community) who is critical rather than deferential toward scientific knowledge.

Less Deference, More Criticism

> [T]he last thing in the world I ever expected was to be ignored. That wasn't even represented in my calculus of possible outcomes. I thought that it was only the objective merits of the work itself that mattered, especially in science. If not in science, then where else? I thought that everyone would just evaluate what a man had done on the basis of ... how closely it approximated [to] the truth. I didn't know how things really work in this world (Goldstein 2001:69).

It bears reiterating that the PUS fieldwork I have been discussing—Lake District sheep farmers, Greater Manchester communities close to chemical plants, and lay understanding of ionizing radiation—all belong to the critical or qualitative perspective toward the public understanding of science. Traditional or quantitative PUS is viewed by critical scholars as "neglect[ing] the reflexive and social character of understanding" (Michael 1996:109). More specifically, traditional PUS measures deficits in scientific literacy as established by accredited scientific knowledge; for critical PUS, by contrast, PUS "is not about the cognition of facts but about interpretation of social relations, about culturally informed judgments on the trustworthiness of the sources of knowledge" (Michael 2002:361–2).

> For traditional PUS, ... people [are] assimilators of knowledge, that is, cognitive repositories [for] information ... In contrast, ... critical PUS rests on a model of the member of the public as a socialized, culturalized human ...

> For critical PUS, what is important in the uptake ... of scientific knowledge are issues of trust, credibility, and understanding of social relations (Michael 2002:365, 364).

For traditional PUS, expertise in the form of universal knowledge is transmitted into a local, social site "beyond" science; on the other hand, in

> critical PUS, both the publics and science are local. Science ... is a local site where knowledge is produced in local contexts, contingent on local parameters ... So we have two locals, one of which (science) is in a privileged position (Michael 2002:369).

Moreover, when a traditional PUS survey concludes that we need more science education, science is thereby conceived as "the active disseminator [while] the public are merely the passive receivers"—this remedy "reinvoke[s] the power-relation of a dominant science and a subservient public" (Michael 1996:109).

The recent survey of state trial court judges to determine their level of scientific literacy (Gatowski et al. 2001), it turns out, falls squarely within the deficit model of traditional PUS. Judges were "judged" as not having the required scientific literacy or understanding of science (as represented by *Daubert* principles such as "testability" and "low error-rate") (Gatowski et al. 2001:433). The survey concluded that more scientific training is needed to remedy this deficit (Gatowski et al. 2001:454–5). By appropriating the analytical framework of critical PUS, however, the judicial survey can be shown to oversimplify the "uptake" of expertise by judges in a *Daubert* hearing on admissibility. Deficit models, as exemplified in the aforementioned survey, tend to idealize science, ignore its local (e.g., social, institutional, and rhetorical) character, and defer to or privilege scientific knowledge. Many federal judges, however, seem to have developed a more sophisticated and pragmatic conception of science as an enterprise with local and practical goals and limitations, and they tend not to defer to abstract scientific authority. For example, recent post-*Daubert* jurisprudence in the federal courts reveals that:

1. Some appellate judges "seem to be adopting a pragmatist view of the scientific enterprise itself: naturalistic but representational, useful but model-based, rigorous but approximate, social but empirical, evidence-based but probabilistic" (Caudill and LaRue 2006:18). For example, trial judges have been reversed for failing to understand that:
    a. Medical diagnosis often relies on patient reports, not objective measurement techniques;
    b. Science involves uncertainly, teamwork, and alternative explanatory models;
    c. Science is probabilistic, not certain;
    d. Not all scientific knowledge is peer-reviewed and published; and

e. The limitations of social science do not make it unscientific (Caudill and LaRue 2006:19–23).

Federal district court (i.e., trial) judges are not only reversed for failing to understand and properly apply the *Daubert* guidelines, as implied by the aforementioned survey, but also for failing to understand the social, institutional, and rhetorical aspects of the scientific enterprise.[6]

2. Some appellate judges do not defer to science, but insist on understanding an expert's "logic, which implies education by the expert, and not simply credentials and a claim of general acceptance, as a prerequisite to admissibility" (Caudill and LaRue 2006:34–6). Federal district court judges are not only reversed for failing to be rigorous in their *Daubert* inquiries, but also for failing to understand the social authority, the "cloak" and "mantle" of expertise that can exist apart from methodological reliability and can therefore illegitimately persuade trial judges and juries (Caudill and LaRue 2006:36–41).

Viewing these developments in light of contemporary studies of the public understanding of science, the parallel between judges and the "public" is further justified. Recall that in Wynne's fieldwork among the Lake District sheep farmers, whose knowledge was deemed effectively worthless by the scientists, the farmers noticed the inconsistencies and uncertainties of science and, on the basis of "different presuppositions and inferences," actually constructed an alternative "science" based on their own evidence and unsatisfactory experiences with experts (Wynne 1996:32–3). In the study of public understanding of pollution risk in some Greater Manchester communities, the authors noticed "the critical climate within which technical information is received and, in particular, a local awareness of the importance of the information's *source*" (Irwin et al. 1996:58). In Michael's interviews concerning public understanding of ionizing radiation, the "participants construct[ed] a more or less critical relation with science and the institutions of science" (1996:111). Far from being ignorant recipients of expertise, the "public" in these studies is more accurately described as "critical (if not downright hostile)" (Irwin and Wynne 1996:219) toward a scientific enterprise that itself was either suppressing its "cultural limits and precommitments" or surprisingly ignorant of its own "socially grounded, conditional, and value-laden" knowledge (Wynne 1996:38–40). Indeed, it is the "public" whose views are aligned more closely with

6 *See* Caudill and LaRue 2006:23–8, discussing cases where judges failed to understand science as a social practice, not just an abstract ideal. Indeed, even methodological ideals are local and dependant on the relevant [scientific] community's standards. Science, that is, should be understood as frequently inconclusive, based on reasonable belief, evolving, and subject to (i) internal disagreements, (ii) limitations of resources, and (iii) techniques of persuasion.

historians, philosophers, and sociologists of science who have reflected on the epistemological limitations of mainstream science.

> Lay attitudes toward science, technology and other esoteric forms of expertise, in the age of high modernity, tend to express the same mixed attitudes of reverence and reserve, approval and disquiet, enthusiasm and antipathy, which philosophers and social analysts (themselves experts of sorts) express in their writings (Giddens 1991:7).

Although viewing judges in their post-*Daubert* gatekeeping role as "public" recipients of scientific expertise may seem counter-intuitive, they remain on the public and not the scientific side of legal controversies. Moreover, some tend not to defer to science, but to see science as a pragmatic problem-solving enterprise not unlike law in its social, institutional, and rhetorical dimensions.

Conclusion

> Western science derives from an earlier art of rhetoric, chronologically (i.e., with regard to the sequence of developments in our tradition), as well as systematically (regarding the nature of scientific activity). Paul Feyerabend goes as far as declaring that propaganda belongs to the essence of science, a view also held, but less outrageously formulated, by T.S. Kuhn in his theory of scientific paradigms. Far from dismissing science as mere rhetoric—a hopeless attempt in view of its practical and technological triumphs—this position states the obvious fact that all sciences ... are social endeavors which must be carried out through the channels and means, and according to the rules, of communication available to a community of practitioners and to the wider society of which they are a part (Fabian 1983:109).

When environmentalists read *An Enemy of the People* as a story about risk, safety, and an ignorant and *interested* public (or press, corporation, and local government), they reduce the play to a "deficit model" of the public understanding of science. While situations do recur in which a genuine, serious environmental risk is ignored because the public does not understand science, Ibsen's play is more complex. *An Enemy of the People* reveals the social and rhetorical features of science itself; that is, the scientific enterprise is not simply a producer of abstract "knowledge" but is instead another community distinguishable from the "public." Dr Stockmann's own limitations and his own ignorance explain the failure of his warning as much as the interests and ignorance of the citizenry do.

In the contemporary debates over "junk science" in the courtroom, a deficit model is also apparent when the argument is made that judges are to blame for not understanding genuine science. A more accurate description of the judiciary is available in contemporary studies of the public understanding of science, as judges seem to be behaving like all non-scientists do when faced with scientific expertise—they notice conflicting claims, elitist assumptions, unjustified certainty, and a lack of reflexivity or self-awareness on the part of experts. In the courtroom, where an expert is aligned with a party, these problems are only exacerbated, so we would expect to see, and we do, not only deferential judges who consider themselves ignorant, but also some judges who de-mystify expertise. Science is seen by the latter judges as an enterprise with local and practical goals and limitations, such that deference must be earned.

In the next chapter, I explore the distinction between competing visions of images of science in law. Just as some judges have an idealized image of science, while others have a more pragmatic image of the scientific enterprise (as not only social, but seemingly unreflective concerning its social dimensions), these two images of science are evident in cinematic representations of science in the courtroom.

Chapter 5
Idealized Images of Science in Film: The Expert Witness in Trial Movies

Apologia: Law and Film

> It is too early to say whether the law-and-cinema discourse will … succeed in creating modes of analysis that are capable of withstanding conceptual, empirical, and ethical critique. Ornamenting our jurisprudential analysis with a reference to such or such a film or attaching an analysis of a film to a legal or moral statement of one type or another are liable to ultimately be but a transient fashion. Yet the conclusion that the discourse of law and cinema is doomed to be just a fad is equally hasty (Reichman 1977:45).

Scholarly reflection on the portrayal of lawyers and legal processes in film is a growing practice. As to its status as a sub-discipline of law, it may be identified as Law and Film Studies ("there has been an explosion of study linking law and film from the late 1980s") (Greenfield et al. 2001:11)), and as part of the law and literature movement (as in "filmic literature"):

> Much like in [the] law-and-literature domain, we … can talk about … the manner in which law is portrayed in various films. Conversely, we can discuss cinema in law, namely the manner in which cinema is integrated in legal texts and practices. We can also think about law as cinema, by referring to legal practices as a specific type of cinematic-dramatic practices …. Lastly, we can place law alongside cinema, thereby using the practices as arenas from which insights can be gained regarding human culture, or the human condition.
>
> Yet [this] should not lend to the erroneous conclusion that cinema is but a type of text … Cinema has its own unique features … (Reichman 1997:6–7).

Law-and-film is also a primary focus of Law and Popular Culture Studies, and exists (as do all of the foregoing) under the umbrella of Law, Culture, and the Humanities (as that sub-discipline is represented by the Association for the Study of Law, Culture, and the Humanities) (Sherwin 2006), although the field and its focus are not clearly defined (Greenfield et al. 2001:10, Reichman 1997:16, 45). The purposes of such reflection are varied (Reichman 1997), and include a sense that those in the discipline of law should pay attention to popular culture (Friedman 1989:1606). There is general agreement that the images of law and lawyers in popular fiction and cinema reflect how people view and understand legal processes, although there is less agreement that such images create new views and understandings (Posner 1989:1660, Asimow and Mader 2004:7). In any event, lawyers arguably should know how the general public feels about law, because its members are (i) potential clients or jurors with whom they will need to communicate, or (ii) potential law students (and *potential* lawyers) who need to have a realistic vision of the profession (both when deciding whether to study law, or after they enter law school).

It is also evident that films about law and lawyers can sometimes be used as effective teaching tools in law schools, whether to illustrate (good or bad) trial advocacy skills, to serve as hypotheticals for legal education ethics training, or to reflect on justice and fairness in contemporary or past society (including issues of gender, race, and power) (Reichman 1997:30, 33, 34).

> The idea is to show that the provisions of a certain statute or a decision of a certain court do not realize their purpose and/or lead to injustice because they do not take into account certain elements of the reality of human life—elements about which one can learn through watching films (Reichman 1997:32).

Thus it has been suggested that feature films and documentaries could be used in first-year law school courses to "humanize" law students, for example, by showing the social consequences of legal controversies (Day and Murphy 2009). However, some argue that "to confine the use of film within teaching to the merely pedagogic would be a tragic waste of its full potential" (Greenfield et al. 2001:6). We should also be interested in how the portrayal of "internal legal culture ... affects the external legal culture" (Greenfield et al. 2001:5) including the "Perry Mason effect" (jurors expect confessions of guilt during a criminal trial), the "People's Court" phenomenon (jurors find witnesses credible if judges do not shout skepticism), and the "CSI effect" (jurors expect highly conclusive science in every criminal case) (Sherwin 2006:4). That is, we should be interested in the capacity of film to *construct* law, insofar as the audience of a law film may eventually recognize and understand (legitimate or illegitimate) legal categories by visual identification and experience (Bond 2010).

Films also may offer insights as to "how law operates in the larger culture" (Denvir 1996:xii). Even when lawyers sometimes find the representations of law and lawyers in film unrealistic, they "tend to be taken as credible representations of ... reality" by the public and therefore create a context with limitations and possibilities for law in society (Sherwin 2006:7). Finally, popular cinema can be seen as a jurisprudential activity, offering insights into contemporary legal philosophy and revealing a "jurisprudence of popular culture" (MacNeil 2007).

On the other hand, some doubt that popular fiction, which clearly could include popular cinema in the age of electronic mass media, is useful for "the permanent and fundamental issues of law that we call jurisprudence" (Posner 1989:1661). Judge Posner concedes that "we may be able to learn something about the popular understanding of law from popular fiction about law," but he only looks to classic works of literature (e.g., Kafka, Shakespeare, Melville, Dickens)—"the body of writings that are somehow able to speak to people living under other skies, in other times, from those of the author and his original audience"—for insights about "law at the jurisprudential level" (1989:1654–5, 1660–61). And even as to great works of literature, Posner doubts that most novels about law are interesting in any "way that a lawyer might be able to elucidate":

> If I want to know about the system of chancery in nineteenth-century England I do not go to [Dickens'] *Bleak House* ... There are better places to learn about law ... [In] a culture that has non-literary records, those records generally provide more, and more accurate, information about the legal system than does literature (1986:1356).

Posner's critique also suggests that great literature has little to offer legal historians, other than "insight into how law was perceived by non-lawyers" (Little 2006:2, citing Posner 1989:1356–7). However, Professor Little argues that literature can elucidate the atmosphere of a period, better than non-fictional sources can, and therefore offer a supplementary "way of contextualizing legal history and engaging with particular legal issues" (2006:3–8, discussing Holdsworth 1929, Meron 1993, and Treitel 1984). Moreover, the effect of great literature about law on the public is likely greater than the effects of legal texts, such that "canonical literature ... is of crucial significance in terms of shaping the development of the popular imagination of law, and that of lawyers themselves" (Little 2006:8–9, discussing Ward 1998). Finally, when literary depictions are combined "with a range of non-fictional sources [such as diaries, autobiographies, and private papers, they] can be used to build understanding of [general] socio-cultural attitudes and perceptions, which can then inform the analysis of specific aspects of social and legal history" (Little 2006:11, discussing Finn 2003).

The debate over the utility of literature for legal historians illuminates several important aspects of this chapter on images of expertise in trial movies. First, I will use trial movies as an indicator of popular beliefs about expert witnesses. While numerous "empirical studies show that expert evidence influences jury decisions"—especially when (i) the link between the research relied upon (by the expert) and the facts of the case is clear, and (ii) the expertise is presented early in the trial—studies also indicate that jurors likely have trouble discriminating between good and bad science.[1] This suggests that other factors are in play when jurors decide which expert to believe, and just as an "immensely popular

1 See Green et al. 2002:232–3. Research "demonstrated that expert testimony describing studies containing a confound, missing a control group, or having the potential for experimenter cueing effects is just as influential as valid research" (Green et al. 2002:233). Long before such studies confirmed juror confusion about scientific issues, there were "calls ... for the elimination of the jury. Charles H. Dana argued as early as 1853 that 'in a process that had become highly professionalized, it was incongruous to entrust

contemporary novel about law may … afford a better glimpse of how lay people regard law than a public opinion poll would do" (Posner 1989:1655), popular trial movies that reflect public sentiments may help supplement empirical studies of how juries evaluate expertise. Second, to the extent that popular culture, including cinema, shapes the popular imagination concerning science in law, the representation of experts in trial movies becomes important for understanding new developments in legal contexts and for framing a response. Finally, the interdisciplinary methodology of legal historians (who seek a broader understanding of culture to illuminate legal culture) is implicated in this chapter, which considers popular views of science and scientists in its analysis of trial movies. That is, popular conceptions of lawyers and legal processes combine with presuppositions about science in public responses to cinematic representations of expertise.

In the next part of this chapter, I acknowledge the existing discourse concerning the reputations of lawyers (in movies about law) and scientists (in science fiction movies), and introduce the thesis that the representation of science and scientists in trial movies is consistent with the idealized image of science that persists in law. Next, I identify the study of the images of science in lawyer movies as a point of intersection between literature-and-science studies (or science and popular culture studies), which includes the analysis of images of science and scientists in science fiction *films*, and the law-and-literature movement (or law and popular culture studies), which includes the study of images of law and lawyers in *cinema*. (Another point of intersection, not relevant to the present chapter, is the study of images of law in science fiction—for example, the essays on law in *Star Trek* that appear in *Star Trek Visions of Law and Justice* (Chaires and Chilton 2003).) The parallel between law-and-film studies and science-in-cinema studies confirms that a hybrid enterprise—namely the study of scientists in lawyer movies—is relatively easy to construct on the basis of existing theoretical frameworks and research. Then I turn to examples from recent trial movies to show that the image of the biased, bought-and-paid-for expert, as well as the image of the expert as bringing closure to the contradictory arguments in a trial, both reflect the idealization of science in law. Lawyer movies, that is, often deliver a message that when science is appropriately disinterested and untainted by advocacy and rhetoric, it will solve the legal controversies concerning science that are brought on by advocacy and rhetoric in the courtroom. There are exceptions, however, to these images, such that a third category of lawyer films can be identified in which science is represented more modestly. I conclude not only that most cinematic representations reflect the idealization of science in law generally, but that there are adverse consequences of those representations for litigation involving experts.

---

the evaluation of the experts' arguments on technical points to uninformed laymen …'" (*See* Johnson-McGrath 1998:188, quoting Nelson 1964:181).

Moreover, the "legal and medical journals of the first half of the [twentieth] century are filled with lamentations of juries' refusal to acknowledge scientific circumstantial evidence" (Johnson-McGrath 1998:191–2).

Reputational Contours in Trial Movies

> Within the last two decades, lawyers have gone over the cliff as far as public esteem for the profession is concerned. Legal popular culture reflects this dismal phenomenon quite accurately, presenting most lawyers in a strongly negative manner (Asimow 2000:582).

> U.S. adults who consume popular culture frequently (habitual viewers) are more likely than infrequent viewers to hold negative opinions about science, to believe that science is dangerous, [and] to consider scientists odd and peculiar people ... (Kirby 2000:12).

Given that lawyers have such a bad reputation in popular culture, and that scientists are contemporaneously viewed as strange if not dangerous, it would seem that the combination of these two professions in a trial movie (e.g., a lawyer presenting the testimony of a scientific expert) would be a public relations disaster for both law and science. Of course, the negative image of lawyers could hardly get worse, and their teaming up with scientists is not likely to help their public reputation for trying to win at any cost, for manipulating the system and the truth, and for corruption[2]—it is more likely that lawyers' procurement and use of expert witnesses would be viewed as just another questionable tactic. As to scientists, as portrayed in science fiction movies, their traditional popular culture images as arrogant, Godless, inhuman, mad, dangerous, impersonal, and amoral (Haynes 1994) would seem likely to accompany them when slumming in the cinematic courtroom—but again, how much worse could their reputation become? Oddly, however, science and scientists do not seem to suffer reputational losses in trial movies. This phenomenon can best be explained by the twin, oscillating images of scientific experts in law: (i) when the expert is negatively portrayed, it is often because lawyers and the legal process have tainted science; and (ii) when the expert is positively portrayed, it is often because science is represented as better than law a curative to law's rhetorical and institutional instabilities. Both images reflect the shift in popular culture toward more positives images of science, which corresponds to the growing cultural authority of science. Both images, however, also reflect the actual idealization of science in law, and both images immunize the scientist from reputational harm. In short, cinematic lawyers continue to look bad, but scientists fare quite well when they team up with lawyers in trial movies.

2 "The American public says that lawyers are greedy; lawyers are manipulative; lawyers are corrupt; and that the legal profession does a poor job of policing itself" (Shapiro and Associates 2002:7). Seventy-four percent of survey participants agree that lawyers are more interested in winning than justice, lawyers "are believed to manipulate both the system and the truth", and some say lawyers' tactics "border on the unethical, and even illegal" (Shapiro and Associates 2002:7–9).

By the term "idealization," of science in law, I refer to the expectation that science is a stable body of relatively objective knowledge on which the law can draw to settle legal controversies. Historically, this can be explained in part by advances in forensic science:

> Throughout the twentieth century, politicians, prosecutors, and forensic scientists sought to ensure juries' appreciation of and belief in scientific evidence through a widespread public relations campaign … The campaign was carried out through magazine articles, World's Fair exhibits, short stories, books, and Hollywood movies: the propaganda had supporters ranging from Harvard University and Erle Stanley Gardner to local police departments eager to convince taxpayers of the need to fund a municipal or state forensics lab. The message was simple: disinterested, "objective" science was the best weapon against crime (Johnson-McGrath 1998:192).

In the "construction of science's cultural authority as pure, unbiased, and objective," the forensic scientist's testimony is therefore expected to be "unaffected by his or her own background, beliefs, and social and intellectual biases …" (Johnson-McGrath 1998:193). That expectation may seem benign, except that it often corresponds to a romantic notion of the scientific enterprise and thereby eclipses not only the instabilities and controversies within science itself, but also the social and rhetorical aspects of even the best science. We see the idealization of science in law whenever there is a presumption that if two scientific experts disagree, one of them must be a "junk scientist," which presumption ignores the limitations of data and theoretical presuppositions that lead to genuine scientific disputes. We also see the idealization of science in law whenever we associate "bias, interest, and motivation" with unreliable expertise, which association misses the practical advances made by scientists who have strong theoretical biases, institutional interests, and financial motivations. Finally, we see the idealization of science in law whenever a legislator, administrator, or judge demands certainty from science, not recognizing its probabilistic nature and dynamic history. It is neither an exaggeration, nor a critique of scientific progress, to acknowledge scientific debates, the variations of scientific methodologies, the importance of networking and "social capital" with respect to publications and grants, and the persuasive elements in scientific discourse. To think that these features are somehow markers of bad science is to idealize science.

In my recent study (with L.H. LaRue) of post-*Daubert* admissibility opinions, two different conceptions of the scientific enterprise were identified among the federal judiciary (2006). The first, a romantic view, was associated with those trial judges who expect more from science than it can reasonably deliver. Such judges tend to make two types of errors: (i) sometimes these judges were too strict, and disallowed good science because the expert witness did not live up to their idealistic image of science (Caudill and LaRue 2006:15–30); and (ii) sometimes these judges were (paradoxically) too lenient, and allowed bad science on the basis of its social authority alone (Caudill and LaRue 2006:31–47). Examples of the first error include cases where the testimony of a scientist was not admitted because it was based on less-than-perfect or incomplete information, or because it involved alternative explanations or a probabilistic conclusion. Examples of the second error include cases where testimony of a scientist was admitted solely because the expert had impressive credentials, notwithstanding an unreliable opinion. In both cases, judicial failure to understand the practical goals and limitations of science resulted in admissibility decisions that were out of sync with the realities of scientific practice and explanation. On the other hand, a modest, non-idealized vision of science was also identified among some members of the federal judiciary. Such judges tend to recognize that science is a cultural enterprise, with its own controversies, that relies not only on logic and methodology but also on social conventions, rhetorical moves, and institutional credentializing. And such judges are not surprised by experts who disagree with each other, by credentialed experts with weak methodologies, or by qualified scientists who are not willing to testify with absolute certainty (Caudill and LaRue 2006:xv–xvi). Moreover, judges who hold a more modest view of science tend to make better admissibility decisions.

The present chapter is not concerned with the judiciary, but with the public and potential jurors in our adversary system. Nevertheless, judges, as I argued in Chapter 4, seem to be on the side of the general public and to share in the public understandings of science in our culture. To the extent that cinema about law reflects public understandings, (i) the idealization of science in popular culture, as well as (ii) more modest views of science in popular culture, represent the same perspectives that can be identified in judicial opinions involving expert admissibility decisions. While the focus of this chapter is on trial movies as the producer of images of scientists in their interactions with legal institutions, an idealized image of science in popular culture can have effects on both judges and juries who are called upon to evaluate scientific expertise in the courtroom. Moreover, the lawyers who present expert testimony, and their clients, will have to deal with the effects of popular culture images of science and scientists. The significance, therefore, of trial movies far exceeds their entertainment value.

Parallel Enterprises Redux

As suggested in Chapter 2, those who study the images of law and lawyers in popular culture have a lot in common with those who study cultural images of science and scientists. Both enterprises are worrisome, since the images they identify over the last several decades are overwhelmingly negative. At least lawyers enjoyed a golden age in cinema in the decades prior to 1970, wherein the "prototypical ... lawyer was skillful, devoted to his clients, and ethical" (Asimow 2000:575). "But negative lawyer portraits began to appear in the 1970s ... During the [80s and 90s], a great many attorneys on the big screen have been ... rude, crass, selfish, ... greedy [,] unethical, disloyal, or incompetent" (Asimow

2000:576–7). Scientists, on the other hand, have most often been portrayed throughout cinematic history as frightening, from the "Nazi-like scientists creating 'supermen' through scientific manipulation" in *Man Made Monster* (Universal Pictures: 1941) and *The Boogie Man Will Get You* (Columbia Pictures: 1942), to the science-bashing 1997 film *Gattaca* (Columbia Pictures), which warns of a discriminatory "world dominated by genes" (Kirby 2000:2, 5, 13). Kirby notes that the geneticist in *Gattaca* who can engineer "the qualities that society finds desirable" is different from the earlier Doctor "Moreau stereotype, since here the figure of the scientist, rather than tyrannically enforcing his vision, merely plays upon existing popular beliefs and attitudes" (2000:7).

Because lawyers and scientists were both the subject of negative portrayals in film, both professions could worry about the impact of public misconceptions. Indeed, Michael Asimow "speculates that negative [movie] images can lead public opinion as well as follow it," therefore "such portrayals are [not only] an important social datum" reflecting the public's low esteem of lawyers, but "they have real world consequences" (2000:535). In a similar fashion, Theodore Roszak urges scientists to "face up to the warning" in the persistent folklore of "Dr Faustus, Dr Frankenstein, Dr Moreau, Dr Jekyll, Dr Cyclops, Dr Caligari, Dr Strangelove" (Roszak 1974:31).

Both professions likewise worry about the career effects of negative popular culture images. Michael Asimow points out that the public demonization of the legal profession "lowers self-esteem" of law students, "causes lawyers to devalue the work they do," leads to "career dissatisfaction and stress," and contributes to distrust of lawyers on the part of clients and jurors (2000:541–2). Scientists are similarly concerned that negative film depictions have made viewers "feel that a career in science is undesirable," and even that "decreasing federal funding of the sciences is due in some part to negative portrayals in popular-culture sources" (Kirby 2000:12). Moreover, it does not seem to matter, with respect to the cultural power of negative images, that those images are unrealistic. Even if

> law professors, lawyers, law students, film theorists, or filmmakers ... are apt to discount the strongly negative portrayals of lawyers ... because [such images] contradict ... their own experience [or because] the films [are] poorly written, implausible, or just absurd ..., the relevant introspective community is ... people who have only fragmentary, mostly erroneous, knowledge of what ... lawyers are like and what they do... These are people who are prepared to accept radically negative statements about law and lawyers ... (Asimow 2000:553).

Likewise, because "much of the public's exposure to science is through fictional representations" (Kirby 2000:12), movie

> audiences make judgments about what is "plausible" within the film's diegesis, not necessarily [about] what is "real"... In the end, ... "a picture is not only worth

> a thousand words; however inaccurate, it may be worth a wealth of documented evidence to the contrary" (Kirby 2003, quoting Padian 1987).

Just as those who have limited contact with law and lawyers are taught, through fictional films or television, "what lawyers do, what kind of people they are, ... and how the legal system actually functions" (Asimow 2000:552), science fiction can go beyond "a genre of fiction per se, and become instead a mode of awareness about the world" (Banash 2003:2, quoting Kraus and Ayer 2000:5).

This is not to say that the problem with lawyer movies and science fiction films, respectively for the legal profession or for scientists, is that they are not accurate in their legal-procedural of scientific theoretical aspects. James R. Elkins, for example, bristles at the notion that lawyer movies should be viewed as "failed documentaries," or that we should demand that they "be legally realistic about law and lawyers before they can be taken seriously" (Elkins n.d.). Likewise, John Denvir sees public and pedagogical value in lawyer movies—their "very quantity ... demonstrates ... the human appetite for justice"—notwithstanding their lack of "verisimilitude," the artistic license taken, and oversimplification of "messy reality in their pursuit of a clear battle between good ... and evil ..." (Denvir 2003). While a focus on procedural inaccuracies in a lawyer movie may have some limited use in a law school evidence classroom, that exercise does not begin to exhaust the significance of lawyer movies for the public relations problem of the legal profession. And the same is true of movies about science and scientists, which are frequently followed by "The Real Science of ..." books and articles "in which a scientist critiques the 'scientific accuracy' of a fictional film" (Kirby 2003:7). For example, Mark Glassy's *The Biology of Science Fiction Cinema* (2001) summarizes 75 films and "systematically provides an overview of the plot, of what science worked and what did not, and of what science in the film could actually happen" (Kirby 2003b:11). David Kirby thereafter observed that science fiction

> scholars will question whether such intense scrutiny of scientific accuracy is a worthwhile exercise. Obviously, the science in ... *The Ape Man* (1943) will be out of date when compared to the current state of scientific knowledge ... Such extensive analysis of scientific verisimilitude does not add anything to our comprehension of ... the cultural significance of their films ... or American attitudes toward science ... In the end, the only audience well-served by this book is biology teachers who use science fiction films ... as a teaching aid (2003b:8).

On the other hand, "the role that fictional films can play in the formation of consensus and closure in scientific disputes" is worthy of attention: "Film not only has the ability to act as virtual witnessing technology, but also forces consensus on the public by presenting a single vision of nature in a perceptually realistic structure" (Kirby 2003:8, 11). Thus it is not the fact that film directors exercise license, or cut corners to develop a plot line, that worries scientists, but rather that the public is persuaded to accept contested representations as settled. Likewise, lawyers are worried that even though most lawyers are "decent, socially responsible people who work hard for their clients, successfully check government overreaching, ... are pretty ethical most of the time, and do not earn inordinate amounts of money" (Asimow 2000:54), lawyer movie audiences experience negative portrayals of the legal profession as real.

Amidst all this worry, there are some positive signs and activist efforts with respect to the public perception of lawyers and scientists. In response to its consumer research on negative public perceptions of lawyers generally, the A.B.A. Section on Litigation has proposed that bar associations (i) do more to educate consumers about law and lawyers, (ii) do more to educate lawyers about maintaining good client relationships, and (iii) become more active in disciplining lawyers and in encouraging *pro bono* work (2002:37–8). Michael Asimow observes that television (as opposed to film) creates more favorable opinions of law and lawyers, and concludes that it "seems likely that the negative impact of film on the public perception of lawyers is more than cancelled out by the positive portrayals of lawyers on television" (2000:558). And there are, of course, numerous examples of lawyer movies that represent the legal profession in a positive light—somewhere over one-third of lawyer movies in the last several decades are categorized as "positive" in Asimow's survey (2000:568–9).

On the scientific side of cinema, there is even more optimism and activism concerning positive portrayals of scientists. In the past, Hollywood chewed "scientists up and spit them out" as arrogant, aloof, creators of monsters:

> Then along comes Jodie Foster in *Contact*, playing an impassioned ... astronomer trying to get in touch with her inner extraterrestrial. Or Sean Connery, in *Medicine Man*, playing a crusading botanist trying to cure cancer and save tropical forests. [And] Russell Crowe [in *A Beautiful Mind*] as John Nash, a cranky and crazed, but curiously empathetic, mathematician ...—each movie showed the scientist in a positive light—as an impassioned seeker of truth ... (Toburen 2002).

Spielberg's *War of the Worlds* (Paramount Pictures, 2005) and *Minority Report* (Cruise/Wagner Productions, 2002) similarly "portray science in a positive light—they portray science as the answer to ... disaster problems" (Kirby 2005). The use of science advisors, notwithstanding the risk that an advisor might promote his or her own view in the case of disputed science, makes contemporary science fiction films more realistic—"science advisors can utilize fictional films to ... disseminate their concepts among the general public" (Kirby 2003b:3). And "popularization is akin to promotion, especially with regard to obtaining funding or other support for scientific research" (Kirby 2003b:5).

> The more realistically things are portrayed, the better it is for everyone—producers and public alike ... The fact that the movie [*Deep Impact*, Dreamworks SKG: 1998] made an effort to portray [the threat of comet impacts] realistically

> helps convey [the message that the threat can be mitigated] and raise awareness of a real issue (Kirby 2003b:6).

The so-called "*War Games* effect," named after the 1983 MGM film, refers to the capacity of a realistic fictional film to raise public awareness and increase research funding (Kirby 2003b:5). All things considered, there seems to have been a shift in popular culture toward a much more positive view of science and scientists.

The parallel to the "*War Games* effect" in television programs about law—the so-called "CSI effect" — is not as encouraging (Willing 2004). Jurors, having watched forensic scientists (in the various CSI episodes) flawlessly solve crimes in highly sophisticated laboratories, come to expect that level of evidentiary proof in criminal trials (Rincon 2005).[3] Strangely, the popularization and lofty expectations of forensic science comes at a time when the reliability of most of the forensic sciences is being questioned by legal scholars (Moriarty and Saks 2005). Nevertheless, it seems that science is held in high esteem, and that lawyers and their real experts will tend to disappoint the public by not living up to an idealized view of science.

In the next section, I discuss how lawyer movies involving scientific experts tend to support an idealistic view of science, whether by representing science as the extra-legal solution to contested courtroom disputes, or by representing attorneys as manipulators of weak or greedy experts in order to win lawsuits. I concede that some trial movies concerning experts, which I identify and discuss, do not seem to fall into those two categories—a more modest image of science is sometimes evident. My analysis confirms, nevertheless, the notion that scientists seem to be overcoming the public relations problems created in decades of negative portrayals in science fiction cinema, while lawyers continue to look bad.

Experts in the Movies

> Despite their ubiquity, experts continue to generate concerns for the judicial system. Doubts have been voiced about overly biased experts, inaccurate conclusions, misleading testimony, jury incomprehension, and the fear that scientific expert testimony may possess an "aura of infallibility" (Moriarty and Saks 2005:22–3).

3 This phenomenon is not new; *see*, *e.g*., Leitch 2005, in which Leitch argues that the popularity of the "Perry Mason" television series tended to make potential jurors expect a confession, and to be critical of prosecutors who could not produce one.

Tainted Science: The Expert as Advocate

In two relatively recent movies, *A Time to Kill* (Warner Bros., 1996) and *A Few Good Men* (Columbia Pictures, 1992), trial experts are characterized as biased advocates, bought and paid for by lawyers and their clients. Both of the opposing experts in *A Time to Kill* are called upon to opine as to the temporary sanity of the defendant, Carl Lee Hailey, who is charged with murdering (on the steps inside the courthouse) two accused rapists of Hailey's young daughter. The prosecutor and the defense attorney each present a psychologist, and each lawyer tries to discredit the other's expert. The science in the case is presented to the viewers as debatable—this is not a movie about the clarity or credibility of psychological evaluations of sanity. That is, there is no direct idealization of science as a producer of truth to stabilize a controversy, because science is not an element of the plot. Rather, the idealization of science is indirect, insofar as the clear message is that junk expertise in the courtroom can be purchased from experienced witnesses. The implication is that such witnesses will not be concerned about *real* science, which could actually help in the search for truth, but only with saying what they are paid to say. The prosecution's expert, Dr Rodeheaver, holds a university chair in psychiatry and directs a facility for the criminally insane. He looks distinguished, with a polished and confident demeanor, but in his many years as a courtroom expert he has never found a defendant insane (including one housed in his own care for over ten years). The expert for the defense, Dr Bass, impliedly also highly-credentialed, is an overweight, sloppily-dressed alcoholic, but otherwise seems pleasant, professional, and trustworthy. Bass testifies that even the insane can premeditate a crime, which is the opinion for which he was hired. Instead of attacking his testimony as unreliable, the prosecutor discredits the witness by revealing Dr Bass's conviction at the age of 23 for statutory rape (of a 17 year old he eventually married). Neither expert ends up looking good (although Dr Bass is not as bad as Dr Rodenheaver), but it is their role as advocates, and not their background in science, that brings them down. Indeed, they have impliedly abandoned their credible profession as a condition for their utility in the courtroom.

A Time to Kill highlights the process of acquisition of scientific knowledge for litigation—each side hires an expert to help that side's lawyer advocate a legal position in a controversy. That problem, of filtering science through the needs of a client, is likewise illustrated in *A Few Good Men*, where a single expert helps to cover up the scandalous death of a soldier (with an undiagnosed heart condition) following a hazing ritual. Dr Stone, an experienced physician and Chief of Internal Medicine at a hospital, is portrayed as an obedient colleague of the military officers involved in the cover-up. Dr Stone's credentials, appearance, and bearing are stellar, but his testimony is easily discredited because he knows that his opinion—that the murdered soldier died of poisoning—is untrue. He abandons medical science, which is never an object of scorn in the film, to become a liar.

While the lawyer's role in finding an expert willing to support that lawyer's arguments is quite conventional, it is arguably a "negative" aspect in terms of public perception. Viewers of the films just discussed are likely not versed in the professional ethics of lawyers, and may not know that lawyers are ethically permitted to present doubtful or shaky expertise (as long as it is not *known* to be false).[4] Significantly, however, these films are not an indictment of science or scientists generally. *Some* disreputable scientists, the audience learns, are willing to become biased advocates, but science as a discipline abhors fraud; so it is these scientists' association with law and lawyers that taints their scientific profession.

Another example of expert as a biased advocate appeared over 50 years ago in *Anatomy of a Murder* (Columbia Classics, 1959). Dr Raschid, the medical examiner testifying for the prosecution, appears to have only made examinations that would help the prosecutor, to the exclusion of others that might help the defendant. The contemporary fascination with forensic science, represented by the popularity of the various CSI television programs, mirrors the public trust in forensic science in the mid-twentieth century:

> An exhibit on the scientific virtues of the medical examiner system … at the 1933 Century of Progress Fair in Chicago [explained that a medical examiner was] "a non-political official, expert in medicolegal pathology, who conducts a scientific investigation into the cause of death, whose work is purely medical [and whose findings are] impartial" (Johnson-McGrath 1998:22).

Notwithstanding such idealizations, some medical examiners may give in to the influence of unethical prosecutors, as in *Anatomy of a Murder*.

Likewise, the figure of Dr Towler in *The Verdict* (20th Century Fox, 1982) confirms the image of the expert as advocate. Prior to his testimony for the defense in a medical malpractice suit, Dr Towler is coached by a roomful of lawyers from the large law firm representing the defendant hospital. While this is a conventional practice, viewers would likely get the impression that the witness is being taught how to respond to cross-examination to avoid telling the truth. Indeed, the doctor is portrayed as both naïve and honest until he is trained by defense counsel.

In all of these films, science is not an object of disdain – it is fraudulent science, in the service of advocates, that is the target. These films are complimented by another type of film that glamorizes science as a perennial producer of stable knowledge to bring closure to legal conflicts.

Idealized Science: The Expert as Saviour

> Science is mechanical, technical, value-free, and nonhumanistic. Science pronounces the law as supplied by nature. Law seeks justice [and] is dialectical, idealistic, non-technical, value-laden and humanistic (Markey 1984:527).

---

4 *See ABA Rules* 2002: 3.3(a)(3). Lawyers do not vouch for their experts; lawyers are permitted to do the best they can to serve their clients in the circumstances.

If scientists can avoid the temptation to become advocates—thereby avoiding accusations of bias, interest, and motivation—they can maintain an image of objectivity even in the contested world of lawyers. Some lawyer movies promote this image of expertise, including *Erin Brockovich*, *Primal Fear*, *Presumed Innocent*, and even the comedy *My Cousin Vinny*.

In the true story of *Erin Brockovich* (Jersey Films, 2000), the heroic file clerk (played by Julia Roberts) working for a plaintiff's lawyer discovers a cover-up of industrial poisoning of a city's water supply. In the midst of a moving drama portraying the stress upon working single mothers, the devastating damage caused by the poisoning, the arrogance of defense counsel, and the oblivious plaintiff's attorney for whom Erin works, the image of expertise can be easily missed. However, Erin meets with a professor who offers the scientific information confirming the cover-up; the professor even calls her later with more information, and she is able to help win the largest settlement ever paid in a direct-action lawsuit. As an image of science in law, this one is pristine—the professor is not even *dealing* with a lawyer, and he does not appear in court or even get paid; he's completely untainted. He is neither slick nor polished, but rather a modestly dressed professor who holds the determinative scientific knowledge to bring justice in the wake of a tragedy.

Primal Fear (Paramount Pictures, 1996) is the story of a teenager, charged with the murder of a Chicago archbishop, who is represented by an unlikable defense attorney (played by Richard Gere). Dr Weil, a medical examiner, is able to establish that a left-handed person, like the defendant, inflicted the wounds on the victim. Weil's clear and simple explanation leads the audience to the truth. Even though judicial reservations have been expressed concerning the reliability of "science for litigation"—i.e., testimony based on research done after a lawsuit has been filed—resulting in a preference for untainted pre-trial research as the basis for courtroom expertise, forensic scientists have traditionally escaped this condemnation (Edmond 2007). When *Daubert* was remanded to the U.S. Court of Appeals for the Ninth Circuit, Judge Kozinski supplemented the U.S. Supreme Court's "factors" (to consider in admissibility decisions) with the statement:

> One very significant fact to be considered is whether the experts are proposing to testify about matters growing naturally and directly out of research they have conducted independent of the litigation, or whether they have developed their opinions expressly for purposes of testifying … [W]e may not ignore the fact that a scientist's normal workplace is the lab or the field, not the courtroom or the lawyer's office (*Daubert* 1995:1317).

As this standard would cast doubt on forensic scientists, including medical examiners, Judge Kozinsky immediately drops a footnote;

> There are, of course, exceptions. Fingerprint analysis, voice recognition, DNA fingerprinting, and a variety of other scientific endeavors closely tied

> to law enforcement may indeed have the courtroom as a principal theatre of operations … As to such disciplines, the fact that the expert has developed an expertise principally for purposes of litigation will obviously not be a substantial consideration (*Daubert* 1995:1317 n.5).

The exception for forensic science is likely, however, unjustified:

> Many of the forensic techniques used in courtroom proceedings, such as hair analysis, fingerprinting, the polygraph, and ballistics, rest on a foundation of very weak science, and virtually no rigorous research to strengthen this foundation is being done (Risinger and Saks 2003).

Thus, the infallibility that is often attributed to forensic science in popular culture is illusory and best explained by the public's idealization of science in law.

Presumed Innocent (Mirage, 1990) is also a murder mystery involving a prosecutor who is accused of killing his lover, also a prosecutor. A fingerprint specialist is able to establish a match between the defendant's print and a print on a bar glass found at the crime scene. Even though there is some doubt because the glass cannot be produced at trial, the fingerprint evidence is presented as conclusive. Evidence scholars, it bears noting, have become increasingly critical of latent fingerprint identification—it does not have a tradition "of disinterested self-testing," the "verification process [conducted by law enforcement officials] is 'vulnerable to unconscious bias or deliberate malfeasance' by examiners," and appropriate "measures of error rates for fingerprint examiners do not exist" (*Note* 2002). Indeed, fingerprint analysts provide the clearest example of the strategy in forensic science ("a growing body of unreliable research funded by law enforcement agencies with a strong interest in promoting the validity of" their techniques) of placing its claims beyond the realm of empirical research:

> [Fingerprint examiners claim] that their technique has a "methodological error rate" of zero and that any errors that occur are therefore lapses on the part of individual examiners. Because the technique can never be performed except through the subjective judgment of human fingerprint examined, it is impossible to test the claimed division of responsibility for error empirically. The claim is thereby rendered unfalsifiable (Risinger and Saks 2003).

Yet courts and the public often continue to view fingerprint analysis as conclusive, due in part to the history and progress of forensic science in the early twentieth century:

> Forensic scientists … [presented] their opinion as to the truth the evidence tells. By invoking science's cultural authority and alleged objectivity, scientists sought to transubstantiate opinion into fact. To do so, they had to ignore or deny

> that this truth was inevitably filtered and shaped by professional experience, interests and personal biases (Johnson-McGrath 1998:193).

Even though forensic science "differs significantly from what most of us consider science to be," there "has been a carefully fostered public perception of near-infallibility" (Risinger and Saks 2003). While research can undermine that perception, cinema can strengthen it.

Finally, *My Cousin Vinny* (20th Century Fox, 1992) highlights the decisive role of technical knowledge in establishing the innocence of co-defendants in a murder trial. The story involves the legal victory of an inexperienced lawyer over the experienced prosecutor,[5] which parallels the scientific victory (over the prosecutor's tire mark expert) of the defense attorney's fiancée, Mona Lisa Vito, an unemployed hairdresser who used to work as a mechanic in her father's automobile repair shop. She is unfazed by trick questions on the witness stand, and thereby rises above the world of advocacy into the realm of scientific certainty. The stabilizing force of technical knowledge thereby settles the rhetorical instability of the trial.

These films reflect an idealized image of science in the courtroom, which is consistent not only with public perceptions of expertise but also with the identifiable idealization of science by many judges. Indeed, all of the films discussed above, whether representing experts tainted by law or experts who rise above law to provide determinable knowledge, rely upon an idealized view of science as significantly different from and better than law. Another category of films, however, reflects a more modest view of science as a human and cultural enterprise.

A Measured Assessment: The Expert as Human

Some lawyer movies offer relatively positive images of trial experts, while at the same time acknowledging the pragmatic limitations of the scientific enterprise. For example, in *Suspect* (TriStar, 1987), a homeless individual is (falsely) accused of murder, and the prosecutor calls two witnesses. The first, a forensic pathologist, is represented as professional and competent, but is a bit uncomfortable when challenged. On cross examination, it becomes clear that his testimony concerning whether the murder weapon (a knife) belonged to the defendant was inconclusive, and he overlooked the fact that the defendant was left-handed (he had testified that the knife wound indicated a right-handed killer). The second expert, a police

5 This motif, with roots in jokes about the wisdom of rural individuals over the arrogant city-slicker, is also evident in *Legally Blonde* (MGM: 2001), where a law student prevails over experienced opposing counsel, and in *Erin Brockovich*, where a file clerk prevails over a large law firm. *See* Harris 1987:102, explaining that the "classic" elements of courtroom drama include "the humble country lawyer versus the city slicker, with the former defeating the latter by virtue of his essential honesty".

detective, testified on the basis of his experience that homicides are usually committed by the most obvious suspect. The detective is also represented as confident and competent, but on cross-examination the defense attorney rebuts his testimony by revealing past discoveries of falsely accused individuals on death row. Viewers of the film are, perhaps unwittingly, introduced to the persistent problem of "over-claiming" by experts (and "over-valuing" by jurors) in the presentations of expertise. Because evidence of guilt (or liability in civil cases) is often inconclusive, some experts exaggerate and express "a confidence not warranted by the evidence" (Gross and Mnookin 2003:143).

Although the experts in *Suspect* are ultimately shown to have exaggerated, such that their testimony is not represented as decisive truth, they are not portrayed negatively as brought-and-paid-for advocates. Rather, the experts in *Suspect* are characterized as doing the best they can with inconclusive data, limited resources, and human frailties. The difference between these experts and biased witnesses who will say anything to serve a client is subtle, but in *Suspect* it is the reasonable limitations of science, rather than the dishonesty of experts, that are represented as problematic.

That distinction is clearer in the comedy *My Cousin Vinny*, where the forensic expert for the prosecution is portrayed as almost neutral—with 18 years of FBI experience, he appears to be a professional doing his job, not a recruited advocate. His confident delivery, based on carefully-collected crime scene samples and technically-advanced analysis, is compelling. He is, however, wrong, which the outsider-expert—Mona Lisa Vito—is able to demonstrate with her superior street-knowledge. There is an analogy here with recent research into public understanding of science discussed in Chapter 4. We should not assume

> that local understandings [of non-scientists] are inadequate or deficient in comparison to formal, scientific understandings. On the contrary, they may well represent a more robust and well-tested body of advice, information, and practical assistance than any new or externally generated piece of technical evidence (Irwin et al. 1996:55).

Two other films, *I am Sam* (New Line Cinema, 2001) and *Agnes of God* (Columbia Pictures, 1985), highlight the human side of science. In *I am Sam*, the court-appointed psychologist is represented as biased against Sam, a mentally-challenged father trying to get custody of his young daughter. The science is almost beside the point, as the psychologist's confident testimony is obviously weakened by her preconception of Sam as an unfit parent. When the psychologist is confronted with her own history—her son died from an overdose—she bursts into tears. Interestingly, any message in the film about the unreliability of expertise is eclipsed by a message about the sources of unjustified prejudice in our society. The expert's bias is not due to intentional scientific fraud or unethical lawyering, both of which might support an idealized image of science *when it is* methodologically sound and untainted by lawyers. Rather, occasional bias is represented as unconscious, unfortunate, and unavoidable in science because it is a human enterprise.

Agnes of God also similarly involves an expert with preconceived notions about a novice nun accused of manslaughter in the death of her baby. The expert is determined to see the accused put in prison, but her anti-Catholicism is due to her sister's death in a convent. Throughout the film, she softens and changes her mind about the culpability of the accused. Like *I am Sam*, *Agnes of God* illustrates the instability of expertise, although in both films the expert begins with a personal bias that is overcome. (In neither film, however, does the expertise improve—it just goes away.) My categorization of *I am Sam* and *Agnes of God* as representing a modest view of expertise is based on the manner in which these films neither glamorize nor critique science. Even if "science in the long run gets most things right," the

> sources of error … are numerous: the small size of many studies, for instance, often leads to mistakes, as does the fact that emerging disciplines, which lately abound, may employ standards and methods that are still evolving. Finally, there is bias, which [can be considered] ubiquitous. Bias can take the form of a broadly held but dubious assumption, a partisan position in a long-standing debate … or … a belief in a hypothesis that can blind a scientist to evidence contradicting it (Babbs 2006).

The latter type of error—blinding belief in a hypothesis—is illustrated by the experts in *I am Sam* and *Agnes of God.* While the experts are clearly portrayed negatively, the indictment is personal to them, thereby tempering any idealization of science but not rejecting their *fields* of expertise.

Another example of a modest view of expertise is in the film *Music Box* (Caralco Pictures, 1989), the story of a Hungarian immigrant represented by his daughter when he is arrested for Nazi wartime atrocities. The expert for the prosecution, a senior forensic document examiner, uses scientific techniques to authenticate a photograph. He is challenged, however, for his potential bias as a Jew, but his testimony turns out to be accurate despite his desire to see the defendant convicted. The implication is that all experts have biases, but such biases do not necessarily signal bad science. *Music Box* thereby illustrates that a modest view of the scientific enterprise is neither a critique nor a skeptical view of science.

Finally, in the film *Primal Fear*, a psychologist for the defendant attempts to demonstrate that the accused is mentally ill. The defendant, however, lies and puts on a show to help the psychologist, which results in a faulty evaluation. While there is nothing wrong with the science or the scientist, the "outside" influence of the defendant renders the expertise useless. The representation of science in *Primal Fear* therefore rounds out the modest view of expertise in the courtroom. Science is not, by virtue of its methodological conventions and cultural authority, flawless. Sometimes there is external interference, sometimes a scientist has an unconscious bias, and sometimes there is fraud; but even at its best, science is a cultural activity with limited data, measurement technologies, and resources, such that genuine debates and uncertainties are inevitable.

Such films can be contrasted with the films discussed in the first two categories—bought-and-paid-for experts and those who deliver extra-legal truth—because science is not idealized. The modest or nonromantic view of expertise nevertheless represents a positive and realistic assessment of the scientific enterprise. If the only problem with courtroom expertise was that some experts are frauds, and otherwise experts uniformly rise above the rhetorical fray to produce determinable knowledge, then the idealization of science would be justified. But the field of possibilities for science in law are not thereby exhausted—realistically, even the best science is often as contested, rhetorical, and unstable as the legal context into which it is delivered.

Conclusion

The representations of law and lawyers, and science and scientists, in lawyer movies are complex and diverse. Even when legal scholars say that lawyers are generally portrayed negatively in film, there are numerous positive images, such that one can only speak of "the majority of lawyer movies." Similarly, while the images of experts in lawyer movies are predominantly positive, there are numerous negative portrayals. Even so, the negative portrayals, as well as the representations of science as a modest, human enterprise, in cinema about law do not seem to condemn science and scientists as dangerous, arrogant, or amoral—as did early science fiction cinema. Just as the popular perception of scientists represented in cinema about science is nowadays quite positive, the portrayal of science and scientists in lawyer movies is correspondingly positive. At the intersection of law-and-literature studies and literature-and-science studies, the stock of science and scientists is rising, even as law and lawyers remain in trouble. While this phenomenon is likely to benefit the scientific enterprise, in terms of attracting funding and promoting science careers, the idealization of science in popular culture has even more adverse consequences in the legal context (i.e., beyond the comparative loss of reputations on the part of law and lawyers). Judges and jurors who do not recognize the limitations on the cultural authority of science may alternatively accept the unreliable testimony of experts who claim certainty, and reject the reliable testimony of experts who concede their uncertainties.

In the next chapter, I re-visit Capote's *In Cold Blood*, and highlight a marginal theme concerning the inability of the legal system, at times, to keep up with scientific progress. While Capote attempted to write a non-fiction account, albeit stylized, of a multiple murder and the trial of the two defendants, his efforts ended up challenging any clear distinction between fact and fiction in stories about science in law.

Chapter 6
"Faction": Truman Capote, Legal Ethics and *In Cold Blood*

Introduction

> [As "Capote"] screenwriter Dan Futterman has admitted, reading *In Cold Blood* left him with a sense of an absence, an awareness "that Capote, who was the most interesting character in the book by far, wasn't there" (Kermode 2006).

As filmgoers in 2006 know, Truman Capote's *In Cold Blood: A True Account of a Multiple Murder and Its Consequences* (1965) involves two stories. The first, including the subject matter of the book and two earlier films (the 1967 movie directed by Richard Brooks, and the 1996 television miniseries directed by Jonathan Kaplan), not only details the brutal murder of a Kansas farm family but comprehensively critiques a murder trial. Even as he claimed to refrain from judgment, Capote's indictments of the prosecutors, the defense attorneys, the judge, the jury, and an outdated doctrine of insanity strongly suggest a miscarriage of justice. This alone is reason enough to include *In Cold Blood* in the canon of conventional law and literature studies, insofar as the book can be read as a critique of capital punishment[1], but Capote's narrative also provides vignettes of seemingly unethical conduct, possible community bias infecting a trial, and a particularly bad law regarding the requirements for psychiatric evaluation.

The other story is about the author himself while he was writing *In Cold Blood* (including his personal life, his research practices, and his aesthetic goals) and is the subject of the recent films *Capote* (directed by Bennett Miller and based on Gerald Clarke's *Capote: A Biography* (1988)) and *Infamous* (directed by Doug McGrath and based on George Plimpton's *Truman Capote: In which*

---

1 *See* Gemmette 1998, which does not claim to represent the "canon" of law in literature, but which includes an annotation by Teree E. Foster on *In Cold Blood:*

> Truman Capote's dark non-fiction novel ... chronicles the [Clutter murders] and its effects upon all persons touched by it ... However, the essence of the novel is its depiction of capital punishment ... Capote compels us to ask ... whether execution of even sociopaths like Hickock and Smith is any less random and brutal than the crimes for which they were executed (Genette 1998:35).

Capote believed that capital crimes should be prosecuted by federal courts and that "those convicted should be imprisoned in a special Federal prison where, conceivably a life sentence could mean, as it does not in State courts, just that." (Plimpton 1966:42–3).

various Friends, Enemies, Acquaintances and Detractors Recall his Turbulent Career (1997)). Each film raises ethical questions of immediate interest to "new" journalists and "creative" reporters who share in Capote's heritage or write in the "true crime" genre.[2] Klein mentions Judith Miller's inaccurate *New York Times* stories about Iraq's weapons capabilities, and discredited journalists Jayson Blair and Stephen Glass, as recent examples of journalistic ambition—the film *Capote* represents "the beginning of the end, the top of that slippery slope down which the profession of journalism has slid" (2006). Even if Capote's account of the Clutter murders would have been accurate, his techniques were disturbing:

> Capote lied to his interview subjects, defiled the corpses of the murder victims, arranged for legal representation for two cold-blooded killers, and may have even fallen in love with one of them. For Capote, the end justified his unscrupulous means, and he surely sent a message to some aspiring journalists over the years.[3]

The more illusory ethical conflict in the films, however, concerns the writing of Capote's "true account." As biographer Kenneth Reed explains, creative reportage involves setting "down a continuum of factual information in such a way that it carries a fictive quality"; artistic order, structure, and coherence are imposed on "a body of information" (Reed 1981:84). However, just as Capote seemed to value the completion of his book more than the lives of its subjects—the film "Capote" portrays the author as alternatively arranging for delay of the defendants' hanging in order to get his story, and later hoping that the execution happens quickly to provide a needed, spectacular ending to his book—he seems to have valued artistic structure over journalistic accuracy. As John Richardson (biographer of Picasso) charged in his interview with George Plimpton,

> Truman had absolutely no respect for the truth ... He felt that as a fiction writer he had license to say whatever came into his head as long as it had a surprising point or shape to it, or an unexpected twist to its tail (Plimpton 1997:308).

Capote had "wanted to write ... a nonfiction novel—a book that would read exactly like a novel except that every word of it would be true" (Grobel 1985:112). Though

2 *In Cold Blood* thereby paved "the way for a string of artfully constructed works which attempted to capture the human components of those 'monsters' who habitually fascinate the public and media" (Kermode 2006). Kermode lists, as owing "a debt to *In Cold Blood*", Joe McGinnis's *Fatal Vision* (1983) (the story of convicted murderer Jeffrey MacDonald), Emlyn Williams's *Beyond Belief* (1968) (regarding the Moors murders), Gordon Burn's *Somebody's Husband, Somebody's Son* (1985) (about the Yorkshire Ripper case), and Brian Masters' *Killing for Company* (1995) (about Dennis Nilson).

3 *See* Klein 2006, who notes that Capote "was apparently able to throw the weight of his name around and get just what he wanted," though it is "hard to imagine that the *New Yorker* sanctioned this obvious breach of journalistic conduct."

he claimed to have succeeded, many of his interviewees, including a KBI agent and the chief prosecutor, said he did not (Plimpton 1997:175, 207, 222).

The risks of nonfiction storytelling—of imposing aesthetic structure on information—present challenges not only to new journalists, but also to lawyers and judges. *In Cold Blood* therefore becomes relevant for another aspect of law and literature studies (in addition to its conventional law-*in*-literature aspect), namely law *as* literature. Every law student learns early in law school that facts, in lawyers' arguments and judicial opinions, can be selected and manipulated—that facts are as interpretable and unstable as legal doctrine. This phenomenon raises the question of the ethical limitations on legal storytelling.

The purpose of this chapter is to introduce Capote's *In Cold Blood* as a point of reflection on the ethical obligations of lawyers and judges with respect to expert testimony. In the next section, I focus on Capote's accounts of the prosecution's use of expert witnesses, and his suggestion that defense counsel were (i) unable or unwilling to deal with personal conflicts of interest, and (ii) incompetent, the latter of which became the subject of disciplinary investigations and federal court review. In terms of the duties of an advocate, Capote sees the prosecution as going too far, and the defense as failing to go far enough. In the next two sections, I acknowledge the problematic status of Capote's account of the trial, and I explain how the relevant scientific issues were eclipsed in the novel and in the Kansas Supreme Court's opinion that followed after the defendants appealed their verdicts. I conclude that Capote's nonfiction novel, and the circumstances surrounding its writing, provide valuable ethical insights concerning the goals and limits of trial advocacy and judicial story-telling.

In Cold Blood and its Lawyers

Capote did not claim, as I do, that *In Cold Blood* is a critique of law. Indeed,

> Capote himself did not apparently think of *In Cold Blood* as espousing a thesis or message. He told Perry Smith that [he had no] "moral reasons worthy of calling them such—it was just that I had a strictly aesthetic theory about creating a book that would result in a work of art" (Reed 1981:115).

Capote conceded that he felt "moved" by the circumstances in Kansas, but he also felt "detached" in his narration (Reed 1981:116). "For the nonfiction novel to be entirely successful," Capote explained, "the author should not appear in the work" (Plimpton 1966:38). Kenneth Reed thought it "significant that Capote at no time renders a judgment about the criminals," such that a reader might make his or her own judgment without interference by the author (1981:107). One might ask, however, whether such detachment was achieved (or is even possible), given Capote's characterization of the accused defendants, Hickock and Smith, as "moral perversions of decent men brought about by the poverty, violence, and ill luck that reached back for at least one generation" (Reed 1981:107). Capote showed it is "possible to view the Clutter murders as the logical outcome of sociological and psychological forces that had gained momentum over the years" (Reed 1981:107). Nevertheless, Capote claimed that one reason a nonfiction novel is harder to write than a conventional novel is that he "had to get away from [his] own particular vision of the world" (Weingarten 2006:3).

Even if Capote managed in some degree to reserve judgment on the Clutter murder defendants, his disdain for the legal system is not hidden. Capote once remarked:

> The only person at this moment on the [U.S.] Supreme Court whose grave I wouldn't spit on is Brennan. The rest of them, I would spit on their graves. Except the lady [O'Connor]. She hasn't been there long enough ... (Grobel 1985:119).

In his account of the Clutter murder trial, Capote was unimpressed with the trial judge (who did not allow psychiatric evaluations of the defendants), the jurors, (one "sat with drugged eyes and jaws ... utterly ajar"), and the insanity defense in Kansas (which did not take account of the rapid maturation of the field of psychiatry) (Capote 1965:266–8, 302–303). Moreover, Capote suggests that the prosecutors were too zealous, and defense counsel not zealous enough, the result of which was that the truth about the Clutter murders would not come to light within the formal legal processes and resulting legal-textual accounts.

Prosecutors and Experts

> A prosecutor has the responsibility of a minister of justice and not simply that of an advocate. This responsibility carries with it specific obligation to see that the defendant is accorded procedural justice and that guilt is decided on the basis of sufficient evidence. Precisely how far the prosecutor is required to go in this direction is a matter of debate ... (*ABA Rules* 2002:3.8 comment 1).

After the arrest of defendants Perry Smith and Richard Hickock, who could not afford to hire counsel, Judge Roland H. Tate appointed Harrison Smith to represent Hickock and Arthur Fleming to represent Smith (Capote 1965:257). Soon after the defendant's arraignment in Garden City, Kansas, defense counsel moved to urge the court to send the defendants to the state mental institution in Larned, Kansas, for a comprehensive psychiatric assessment of their sanity and their capacity "to comprehend their position and aid in their defense" (Capote 1965:266). Harrison Smith had visited the facility and conferred with some of its staff, and he argued that there were "no qualified psychiatrists in our own community ... Larned [has] doctors trained to make serious psychiatric evaluations ...; and ... being a state institution it won't cost the county a nickel" (Capote 1965:267).

Logan Green, appointed as special assistant to prosecutor Duane West, opposed the motion because he was

> certain that "temporary insanity" was the defense his antagonists would attempt to sustain [and he was afraid] that the ultimate outcome of the proposal would be, as he predicted in private conversations, the appearance on the witness stand of a "pack of head healers" sympathetic to the defendants ("Those fellows, they're always crying over the killers. Never a thought for the victims") (Capote 1965:267).

Green pointed out that under the M'Naghten rule in Kansas, "if the accused knew the nature of his act, and that it was wrong, then he is mentally competent";[4] moreover, he argued that

> there was nothing in the Kansas Statute indicating that the physicians chosen to determine a defendant's mental condition must be of any particular qualification: "Just plain doctors. Medical doctors in general practice. That's all the law requires ... It's no great job to find whether a man is insane or an idiot or an imbecile ... It is entirely unnecessary, a waste of time to send the defendants to Larned" (Capote 1965:267).

Defense counsel Smith, in rebuttal, argued that psychiatry had "matured rapidly in the past twenty years," that "federal courts are beginning to keep in tune with this science", and that "we have a golden opportunity to face up to new concepts in the field" (Capote 1965:268). Judge Tate, in response, merely appointed

> a commission of three Garden City doctors and direct[ed] them to pronounce a verdict upon the mental capacities of the prisoners. (In due course the medical trio met the accused and, after an hour or so of conversational prying, announced that neither man suffered from any mental disorder) (Capote 1965:268).

Harrison Smith, in defeat, arranged for Dr W. Mitchell Jones, an "exceptionally competent" and "sophisticated specialist in criminal psychology" (from Larned State Hospital), to meet with the defendants and testify if needed (Capote 1965:268).

At the defendants' trial, Dr Jones was called as an expert, and Harrison Smith (following the M'Naghten Rule) asked if he had an opinion as to whether Hickock knew right from wrong at the time of the crime:

---

4 For a discussion of the M'Naghten Rule in Kansas at the time of the Clutter murders, *see State v. Boan* 1984 (discussing two aspects of the M'Naghten Rule: a defendant is not criminally responsible if the defendant did not know (i) the nature and quality of the act, *or* (ii) did not know right from wrong with respect to the act). Kansas abolished the insanity defense in 1996, *see* K.S.A. 22-3220, but evidence of mental disorder can still be introduced to disprove criminal intent. *See generally* Borum and Fulero 1999:127.

> "I think that within the usual definitions, Mr. Hickock did know right from wrong."
> Confined as he was by the M'Naghten Rule ("the usual definitions"), a formula quite color-blind to any gradations ..., Dr Jones was impotent to answer otherwise ... Hickock's attorney hopelessly asked, "Can you qualify that answer?"
> It was hopeless because ... the prosecution was entitled to object—and did, citing the fact that Kansas law allowed nothing more than a yes or no reply ... (Capote 1965:293–4).

Dr Jones would have testified, Capote reports, that Hickock may have had organic brain-damage (from a serious head injury), and that tests should be done to determine whether such damage "might have substantially influenced his behavior ... at the time of the crime" (Capote 1965:294–5). Later in the trial, when Arthur Fleming called Dr Jones to testify with respect to Perry Smith, Jones stated he had no opinion. Fleming then said, "You may state to the jury why you have no opinion," but Green objected: "The man has no opinion, at that's it" (Capote 1985:296). Again, Capote argued that Dr Jones would have explained that while more extensive evaluation would be necessary, Perry Smith seemed to be a paranoid schizophrenic (1965:298). Moreover, Dr Joseph Satten, a "widely respected veteran in the field of forensic psychiatry" on the staff of the Menniger Clinic in Topeka, consulted with Jones "and endorsed his evaluations of Hickock and Smith" (Capote 1965:298).

In terms of legal ethics, any flaws in Kansas doctrine of insanity cannot be blamed on Logan Green. The only ethical question implied in Capote's account is whether the prosecutor's handling of the insanity defense was somehow inappropriate, but the special responsibilities of a prosecutor do not appear to have been neglected: the charge was supported by probable cause, the defendants had counsel (and their initial waiver of counsel and a preliminary hearing was not sought by the prosecutor), and no mitigating evidence was withheld from the defense.[5] These matters were addressed in federal habeas corpus proceedings, following conviction of the defendants; on appeal from the district court's denying the petitions, the appellate court ruled:

---

5 *See*, e.g., *ABA Rules* 2002: 3.8:
The prosecutor in a criminal case shall:

> (a) refrain from prosecuting a charge that the prosecutor knows is not supported by probable cause;
> (b) make reasonable efforts to assure that the accused ... has been given reasonable opportunity to obtain counsel;
> (c) not seek to obtain from an unrepresented accused a waiver of important pretrial rights, such as right to a preliminary hearing;
> (d) make timely disclosure to the defense of all evidence ... known to the prosecutor that tends to negate the guilt of the accused or mitigates the offense ...

> [After their arrest,] each petitioner was fully advised of his rights, including the right to representation by counsel ... [Their] confessions were ... voluntary ... They were advised by the judge that they were entitled to a preliminary hearing and ... such hearing was waived (*Hickock v. Crouse* 1964:97).

As to the prosecutor's opposition to the request that the defendants undergo psychiatric examinations at Larned, the court noted that the defendants were examined "by a panel of three doctors as provided for by Kansas Statute. Kan.Gen. Stat. § 62-1531" (*Hickock v. Crouse* 1964:99 n. 7). Finally, the court observed:

> There was not substantial evidence then, and none has been produced since the trial, to substantiate a defense of insanity. The attempt to establish insanity as a defense because of serious injuries in accidents years before, and headaches and occasional fainting spells of Hickock was like grasping at the proverbial straw (*Hickock v. Crouse* 1964:99).

Capote, in his account of the trial, includes evidence of insanity (Hickock's severe character disorder; Perry's dissociative trances) that did not make it into the trial record because of the limitations of the M'Naghten Rule, but his implication of injustice does not seem to implicate the prosecutor's special ethical responsibilities (Capote 1965:267–8, 294–306).

Capote also implies, however, that because Logan Green "feared" the prospect of defense experts and "predicted" their sympathetic testimony, Green knew that the three local physicians who pronounced the defendant's sanity were wrong. *ABA Model Rule* 3.3(a)(3) provides that a lawyer cannot knowingly "offer evidence the lawyer knows to be false" (*ABA Rules* 2002:3.3). However, this is a notoriously low standard for policing bad evidence, because a "lawyer's reasonable belief that the evidence is false does not preclude its presentation to the trier of fact" (*ABA Rules* 2002:3.3 comment 8). Nevertheless, a "lawyer's knowledge that evidence is false ... can be inferred from the circumstances," and a "lawyer cannot ignore an obvious falsehood" (*ABA Rules* 2002:3.3 comment 8). Moreover, prosecutors are held to a higher standard than are other lawyers, and are expected to "voluntarily refrain from using potentially unreliable evidence" (Moriarty 2007:24). There is also a special duty not to mislead the tribunal, and the "mere offer of known inadmissible [i.e., not reliable under the standards of admissibility] evidence" is improper (*ABA Standards* 1993:3-5.6, Gershman 2008–2009: §10.37). But if Green genuinely believed that "[i]t's no great job to find whether a man is insane," and that it would have been a "waste of time" to engage in comprehensive psychiatric examinations of the defendants (Capote 1965:267), then he would neither have *known* that the defendants were insane, nor believed that the evidence he did submit was inadmissible. We simply do not require attorneys to know, in a battle of medical experts, which physician or psychiatrist is telling the truth (Caudill 2003:343–8). Even scientists disagree about the validity of many hypotheses. Thus it hardly makes sense to require that lawyers make evaluations of complex scientific validity, or to assume that lawyers know when a complex hypothesis is "true." Moreover, the dismissive language in the habeas corpus appeal (to the U.S. Court of Appeals for the 10th Circuit), with respect to the insanity plea, did not suggest any prosecutorial misconduct:

> The defendants did not testify and their defense was limited to a report of a psychiatrist who had examined them, and who stated that Hickock knew right from wrong, but he had no opinion as to Smith (*Hickock v. Crouse* 1964:99).

Defense Counsel and Fair Trials

> Everett Steerman, Chairman of the Legal Aid Committee of the Kansas State Bar Association, was disturbed by ... allegations ... that [the defendants] had not had a fair trial ... [The defendants complained that their] two defense attorneys, Arthur Fleming and Harrison Smith, whose "incompetence and inadequacy" were the chief cause of their [convictions, had offered] no real defense ..., and that this lack of effort ... had been deliberate—an act of collusion between the defense and the prosecution (Capote 1965:326).

The Kansas Supreme Court, on July 8, 1961, affirmed the judgments rendered and death sentences imposed on the defendants (*Smith v. Kansas* 1961). Fleming was Perry Smith's attorney on the joint appeal from the verdicts of guilt, while Hickock was appointed new counsel because Harrison Smith became Finney County Attorney in January, 1961 (*Hickock v. Hand* 1962). Claims of error included the refusal to appoint a psychiatrist to the commission examining the defendants, and failure to recognize the claims of temporary insanity (as well as setting the trial date just after the Clutter estate auction, and failure to grant a change of venue—which had not been requested) (*Smith v. Kansas* 1963). After the convictions were affirmed, motions for rehearing were filed, but the Kansas Supreme Court

> immediately began to receive letters from the petitioners complaining about the court-appointed counsel. Soon the court was informed that counsel had been discharged. In a short time petitioners were writing to various legal aid groups in Kansas seeking counsel (*Hickock v. Hand* 1962).

The Wichita Bar Association legal aid committee asked attorney Russell Shultz to investigate the situation, and Shultz asked for a delay in the motion for rehearing, which the Court granted while requesting a copy of his report when completed (*Hickock v. Hand* 1962). The report disturbed the Court, and after Schultz was appointed to bring habeas proceedings, retired Justice Thiele was appointed as a commissioner to take evidence and produce another report (*Hickock v. Hand* 1962). The latter report was adopted by the Kansas Supreme Court in its opinion denying the writ (*Hickock v. Hand* 1962). Shultz was recognized for giving his time to represent the petitioners, but his charges that appointed counsel were incompetent and their representation inadequate (for failing to meet enough with the defendants, to seek a change of venue, to seek separate trials, to object to certain jurors, and to introduce evidence) were rejected (*Hickock v. Hand* 1962).

Just before the hearing on the writ of habeas corpus in the Kansas Supreme Court, Perry Smith criticized Shultz and moved to have new counsel (namely a penitentiary inmate, who was rejected for not being a member of the bar) (*Hickock v. Hand* 1962). Capote was also, though somewhat guardedly, critical of Shultz.

> It would appear that Shultz's investigation was rather one-sided, since it consisted of little more than an interview with Smith and Hickock, from which the lawyer emerged with crusading phrases for the press: "The question is this—do poor, plainly guilty defendants have a right to a complete defense? I do not believe that the State of Kansas would be either greatly or for long harmed by the death of these appellants. But I do not believe it could ever recover from the death of due process" (Capote 1965:326–7).

In the commission hearing before retired Justice Thiele, Shultz emphasized the failure to request a change of venue (although Fleming defended his decision on the basis that local ministers opposing the death penalty could make the local jury lenient), and suggested that "because of community pressure, Fleming and Smith had deliberately neglected their duties" by failing to meet sufficiently with their clients, by waiving a preliminary hearing (the attorneys, however, had not yet been appointed), by making damaging statements to the press concerning the defendant's guilt (Harrison Smith denied the newspaper quotes), and by "failing to prepare a proper defense" (Capote 1965:328–9).

After the state denial of the defendant's writ of habeas corpus, Hickock's new counsel Joseph Jenkins brought a petition for writ of certiorari to the U.S. Supreme Court (denied in February, 1963), and also (together with Perry Smith's new counsel, Robert Bingham) habeas proceedings in the U.S. District Court for Kansas (*Hickock v. Crouse* 1963). The habeas petitions were denied, and on appeal to the Tenth Circuit, those denials were affirmed:

> [Jenkins and Bingham] have prosecuted [their] petitions with commendable vigor. It is quite obvious [that] ... the present attorneys are convinced that due to local prejudice and pressure the appointed attorneys ... during the trial did little or nothing to protect [the defendants'] rights .... We think, however, that these attorneys ... have lost sight of the problems which confronted attorneys Smith and Fleming[:] each petitioner had made a full [and voluntary] confession ... Under these circumstances, they would have been justified in advising that petitioners enter pleas of guilty and throw themselves on the mercy of the court (*Hickock v. Crouse* 1964).

Good faith representation, the court continued, "does not contemplate that miracles will be performed," and the decisions not to request a change of venue, not to object during a trial, and not to "resist the introduction of the confession in evidence do not necessarily suggest incompetence" (*Hickock v. Crouse* 1964). On appeal from the 10th Circuit, the defendants' petitions for writs of certiorari and for rehearing were denied (*Hickock v. Crouse* 1965).

The requirement that lawyers provide competent representation (*ABA Rules* 2002: 1.1) is ambiguous enough to support the various courts' and the commission's conclusions that Harrison Smith and Arthur Fleming provided an adequate defense. Harrison Smith had 24 years' experience, and Fleming about 40, in their Kansas law practices (*Hickock v. Crouse* 1964). Capote points out, however, that Shultz's "principal objective," in asking these attorneys why they did not request a change of venue, was "to discredit them and prove that they had not supplied their clients with the minimum protection ..." (1965:328). But they "withstood the onslaught in good style, particularly Fleming," who explained why he had not done so because of "some aversion to capital punishment in the community" (Capote 1965:328). Even the failure to demand separate trials was explainable (whoever was tried first might become a witness against the other), and the failure to demand a record of *voir dire* was not prejudicial because "all of the jurors who served at the trial" were called as witnesses at the commission hearing (*Hickock v. Hand* 1962). Seeming incompetence was never translated into actual incompetence despite a great deal of scrutiny.

Although the term was never used in Capote's account or in the various proceedings that considered the fairness of the murder trial, there was also a charge of conflict of interest brought against Fleming and Smith. Rule 1.7 of the *ABA Model Rules* provides that a lawyer shall not represent a client if "there is a significant risk that the representation … will be materially limited … by a personal interest of the lawyer." There is an exception if "the lawyer reasonably believes that the lawyer will be able to provide competent and diligent representation to [the] affected client," *and* "the affected client gives informed consent, confirmed in writing" (*ABA Rules* 2002:1.7(b)). Capote writes that underlying all of Shultz's charges, including the failure to consult with the defendants sufficiently, making damaging remarks to "newsmen," and "failing to prepare a proper defense," was "the implication that because of community pressure, Fleming and Smith had deliberately neglected their duties" (1965:328–9). And Jenkins and Bingham, in their federal habeas proceedings, were

> convinced that due to local prejudice and pressure the appointed attorneys representing the petitioners prior to and during the trial did little or nothing to protect their rights. As a result, they contend the petitioners did not have a constitutionally fair trial, and that the defense offered [by appointed counsel] was a reflection upon the integrity of the Kansas bar … (*Hickock v. Crouse* 1964:99).

Both Fleming and Harrison Smith had resisted their appointments, and Harrison Smith even said he doubted that doing his best would "make me too popular around here," but both felt obligated to serve (Capote 1965:257). Whether they bowed to community pressure is left for the reader of *In Cold Blood*, and for the adjudicators of the various hearings on the fairness of the trial, to decide. While Hickock experienced a "hostile atmosphere" in Garden City, Judge Tate testified after the trial:

> It is my opinion that the attitude toward [the defendants] was that of anyone else charged with a criminal offense—that they should be tried as the law provides; that if they were guilty they should be convicted; that they should be given the same treatment as any other person. There was no prejudice against them because they were accused of crime (Capote 1965:328).

That seemingly pollyannaish assessment undoubtedly helped the "imperiled" careers—"because of the apparent credit the Bar Association bestowed upon" the allegations of the defendants—of Judge Tate as well as Arthur Fleming and Harrison Smith (Capote 1965:327).

Finally, Capote's account of the challenges faced by Fleming and Smith includes Shultz's question to Harrison Smith concerning statements to the press:

> Are you aware that a reporter, Ron Kull of the Topeka *Daily Capital*, quoted you, on the second day of the trial, as saying there was no doubt of Mr. Hickock's guilt, but that you were concerned only with obtaining life imprisonment rather than the death penalty? (1965:329).

Rule 3.6 of the *ABA Model Rules* prohibits any "extrajudicial statement that the lawyer knows or reasonably should know will be disseminated ... and will have a substantial likelihood of materially prejudicing" a trial in the matter. Any "opinion as to the guilt or innocence of a defendant ... in a criminal case" is identified in the comments (to Rule 3.6) as "more likely than not to have a material prejudicial effect," so there is little doubt as to the impropriety of such a statement. Harrison Smith, however, denied making the statement: "If I was quoted as saying that it was incorrect" (Capote 1965:329).

While Capote does not focus on the rules of professional conduct in his account, *In Cold Blood* easily functions as a point of reflection on the ethics of lawyering. Its vignettes of attorneys in action are especially relevant because of their recency and actuality in Capote's "true account." However, it is the status of Capote's account as "truthful" that suggests another reason to include *In Cold Blood* in the canon of law and literature studies. As persuasive storytellers bound by the obligation to tell the truth in a trial (*ABA Rules* 2002:3.3), lawyers risk making the same errors of which Capote is accused.

Lawyers and Judges as Storytellers

Fact, Fiction, Faction

> The decision [to write *In Cold Blood*] was based on a theory I've harbored since I first began to write professionally ... It seemed to me that journalism, reportage, could be forced to yield a serious new art form: the "nonfiction novel," as I thought of it. Several admirable reporters—Rebecca West for one, Joseph Mitchell and Lillian Ross—have shown the possibilities of narrative reportage ... (Plimpton 1997:197).

The substantial literature concerning Capote's role in creating, sustaining, or even giving a bad name to the various movements termed narrative reportage, new journalism, and creative or literary journalism is beyond the scope of this chapter. However, some brief background and a few comparisons help illuminate the ethical controversies that followed the alleged invention of the "nonfiction novel." Capote mentions Rebecca West, who admired *In Cold Blood* as a "grave and reverend book" (West 1966:114), and whose own work included crime and trials reportage (West 1947, 1955). The similarities of *In Cold Blood* with, for example, West's report of a brutal "torso murder" in England (entitled "Mr Setty and Mr Hume"), are apparent (West 1955). While West's fiction has been criticized ("only one [of her nine novels is] worth reading today"), her journalistic art is considered superb—her abundant strength as a novelist "to tell an absorbing story and to portray the intricacies of human character ... flowered in her journalism ..., not in her novels ..." (Bell 1985:33). Perhaps her

> art needed the steel scaffolding of facts on which to build the unique structure of narrative and ideas she fills with human beings who convince us in every word and look that this was how they were, and not otherwise (Bell 1985:33).

Thus her "ruthlessly observant" account of a murder case in "Mr Setty and Mr Hume" is "packed with unforgettable sketches of the people she encountered in her slow retracing of what actually happened" (Bell 1985:35). Even West, however, as Capote would later be, was accused of lacking "the kind of truth which is fully supplied only by simple warmth and compassion—the wall of her superior powers would seem to rise between Miss West and these suffering human beings" (Trilling 1955:3). Capote was accused of "winning the friendship" of Smith and Hickock, "and then failing to help them" (Goldstein 1985). Notwithstanding the similarities between Capote and West, and her admiration of *In Cold Blood*, Capote dismissed West — "always a good reporter"— as never really using

> the form of creative reportage because the form, by necessity, demands that the writer be completely in control of fictional techniques—which means that, to

> be a good creative reporter, you have to be a very good fiction writer (Plimpton 1966:2).

Those "fiction" skills, however, would haunt Capote when he was later accused of blending fact and fiction—which criticism is discussed in detail below.

Another helpful comparison is the new journalism of Tom Wolfe, who included Capote in his anthology in *The New Journalism* (1973). Combining "the skills and stamina of an ace reporter with the techniques of fiction" (Sheppard 1987:101), Tom Wolfe and his fellow New Journalists wrote "journalism that would ... read like a novel" (Wolfe 1973:9). Significantly, when asked about New Journalism, Capote distanced himself from "Tom Wolfe, and that crowd," and claimed that

> they have nothing to do with creative journalism—in the sense that I use the term—because neither [James Breslin nor Tom Wolfe], nor any of that school of reporting, have the proper fictional technical equipment. It's useless for a writer whose talent is essentially journalistic to attempt creative reportage, because it simply won't work (Plimpton 1966:2).

Wolfe, on the other hand, closely aligns with New Journalism the literary devices of scene-by scene construction (avoiding sheer historical narrative), dialogue in full, third-person point of view, and recording minute details, all in the realist tradition of Dickens, Balzac, Fielding, Trollope, and Smollett (Wolfe 1973:31–3). Whether this is new is therefore often debated (Hough 1975:16–23, Weingarten 2006:8), but the concern of many journalist critics is that despite the careful and extensive research of writers like Wolfe and Capote, they add too much to the story. For example:

> The mid-1960s brought New Journalism, or at least a new label and new found popularity to an old technique: intermingling fact with fiction ... *Harper's Magazine* tried defining New Journalism metaphorically as "somewhere west of journalism and this side of history," the "place where reporting becomes literature." In this uncharted territory, writers embellished quotes, burrowed into characters' interior thoughts, created scenes that may have happened but did not, and made up characters who were collages of real people. Among the leading practitioners were Tom Wolfe, Gay Talese, Norman Mailer and Truman Capote (Goldstein 1985:211).

Wolfe remarks that his own initial reaction to Gay Talese's *Esquire* article on Joe Louis, which read like a short story, was similar:

> *What the hell is going on?* ... My instinctive, defensive reaction was that the man had ... made up the dialogue ... [M]aybe he made up whole scenes ... [T]hat was precisely the reaction that countless journalists and literary intellectuals would

> have over the next nine years as the New Journalism picked up momentum (1973:11).

Wolfe, on the other hand, considered that modern journalism bored readers "to tears without understanding why ... To avoid this I would try anything" (1973:17–18).

When Wolfe wrote his first novel, *Bonfire of the Vanities* (1987), it was not so much a break with New Journalism as "an experiment in radically journalistic fiction" that was true to the movement—it implied "a claim that all this has been observed rather than created" (Vigilante 1987:48). His portrayal of New York Society is so accurate and devastating (Vigilante 1987:48) that to

> call *The Bonfire of the Vanities* Wolfe's first novel is to make a distinction without too much difference. The ingeniously rigged plot is clearly fictional, but the details of New York City life, high and low, leap from the legman's notebook ... [Making] the leading character a Wall Street broker ... meant that Wolfe had to study the breed in its habitat, to examine its plumage, to listen to the roar of "well-educated young white men baying for money" (Sheppard 1987:101).

To those who might claim Wolfe exaggerated, he replied, "If you don't think this is a correct picture of New York today, then do your own reporting. I say you'll come back with what I did" (DeVries 1990:243). Moreover, Wolfe explained, those "things that strike people as mockery or hyperbole were, to me, instances of barely being able to keep abreast of what was occurring." Even so, Wolfe did not claim, as Capote did with respect to *In Cold Blood.*, that he intended to write "a book that would read exactly like a novel except that every word of it would be true" (Grobel 1985:112).

Capote and Journalism

> [*In Cold Blood*] helped show journalists the possibility of using creative writing techniques while holding to the guidelines of journalism; something now commonly seen [because] many view the style as crucial to keeping readers (Jensen 2005).

In Cold Blood was the subject of great praise, a "chilling masterpiece," and Capote has been considered a near-genius for his "severe control ... without morose moralizing," for choosing "precisely the right vocabulary," for managing the horror "without collapsing into bathos," and for "pioneering ... a new style of novel writing" (Michener 1985:9–10). He was also considered "a creative, but still objective reporter" who brought the imaginative "techniques of a fiction writer to his reporting" (Reed 1981:119–20). From an ethical perspective, however, two concerns persist with respect to *In Cold Blood.*

First, and only peripheral to the focus of this chapter, is the convergence of amoralism, questionable journalistic techniques, and personal ambition or careerism within Capote as he researched and wrote *In Cold Blood*—this convergence is the subject of the films *Capote* and *Infamous*:

> [T]he most scathing examination of U.S. culture in *Infamous*, settles on issues of ethics versus personal ambition and careerism. As Capote feigns sympathy and a supportive emotional bonding with Smith in the bid of the accused man for a life sentence, he harbors at the same time a secret desire that Smith be executed as quickly as possible ... in order to provide a potent finale to his book in an impatient bid for a bestseller (P. Miller n.d.).

> Capote's relationship with murderer Perry Smith is depicted in all of its self-serving strangeness, with the writer first falling in love with his subject ..., then later abandoning him and longing for his execution in order that he may finish his wretched book.
>
> In one key scene, Capote is seen lying to Smith about the title of his magnum opus, claiming that *In Cold Blood* is just a publisher's puff (Kermode 2006).

The "cunning tricks Truman Capote used to obtain the information he needed" has been called the second crime in *In Cold Blood* (Burdeau 2006:32–3), and Capote's alleged remark, that he could "hardly wait" until "they're executed" so that the book could be published, is unforgettable (Plimpton 1997:265). For some journalists, such behavior exemplifies the failure of journalistic ethics:

> If there is a scandal in the making of the best-selling non-fiction book of 1966, it's not about the facts contained in the 368 pages of Truman Capote's *In Cold Blood*. Virtually every detail about the brutal murder of the Clutter family has stood up to forty years of scrutiny. When it comes to Capote, the devil is not in the details, it's in how he got to those details in the first place (Klein 2006).

Others, however, are less comfortable with the accuracy of Capote's "details," and for them the scandal of Capote's unscrupulousness should not eclipse the second ethical controversy, namely the scandal of the fictional aspects of *In Cold Blood*.

Before turning to the problem of accuracy in Capote's storytelling techniques and its parallel in trial advocacy, it bears mention first that the notion of unethically betraying an informant's trust, in journalism, has a parallel in the professional regulation of conflicts of interests for lawyers. Consider that Capote is virtually blamed for the duplicity of contemporary "true crime" authors—for example, convicted murderer Jeffrey MacDonald claimed that Joe McGinnis (in *Fatal Vision* (1983)) "inveigled his way into [MacDonald's] confidence, gaining unique access to his personal life under the guise of writing a sympathetic account of his innocence, while, in fact, penning a damning indictment of his guilt" (Kermode 2006). The ethical dilemma of author-lawyers who become "true crime" reporters of their client's experiences in court arises from the same risk of duplicity. Rule 1.8 of the *ABA Model Rules* prohibits negotiation, prior to the conclusion of representation, "of an agreement giving the lawyer literary or media rights to a portrayal of account based in substantial part on information relating to the representation." The comments to that rule confirm the "conflict between the interests of the client and the personal interests of the lawyer," and that those actions "suitable in the representation of the client may detract from the publication value of an account of the representation." While unethical journalists have to work to gain a subject's trust before obtaining access to materials that they could use with which to betray their subject, attorneys have ready-made access due to the trust that characterizes attorney-client relations. The idea that an attorney may refrain from taking actions that would benefit a client, in order to make the lawyer's forthcoming book more exciting, is actually illustrated by the accusation that the wealthy Capote had the resources to help Smith and Hickock, by providing them better counsel—"$50,000 might have saved them ... only the poor must hang"—but he did not in order to speed both their executions and completion of the book (Plimpton 1997:215). That said, the more striking parallel between Capote's construction of *In Cold Blood* and the ethical obligations of lawyers lies in the nature of nonfiction storytelling techniques.

As depicted in the film "Capote," Truman Capote was famous [or infamous] for his claim that he could

> transcribe conversation without using a tape recorder ... I could get within 95% of absolute accuracy, which is as close as you need (Plimpton 1997:202).

When challenged concerning the accuracy of the details in *In Cold Blood*, Capote replied:

> One doesn't spend almost six years on a book, the point of which is factual accuracy, and then give way to minor distortions. People are so suspicious ... All of [*In Cold Blood*] is reconstructed from the evidence of witnesses (Plimpton 1997:207).

Even biographer and apologist Kenneth Reed was not disturbed by the charges that Capote blended fact and fiction:

> Capote had managed to orchestrate the story of the Clutter murders, not through the distortion of fact, but by the reordering and proportioning of it ... [W]hile the reader can depend upon the high degree of accuracy in Capote's documentation, it should be borne in mind that the selectivity of detail and the particular points singled out for emphasis are elements left to the discretion of the artist himself (Reed 1981:112).

But that is not the end of the story. Contemporary assessments typically concede that Capote

> blurred the line between truth and untruth, despite his claims of impeccable accuracy. His embellishments—which vary from allegedly misquoting people to making composite characters to ending the book with a scene that never happened—have bred ill will from some in the book who felt falsely portrayed and distrust from readers who, upon learning of Capote's changes, are left to wonder where reality ends and fiction begins (Jensen 2005).

It was Phillip K. Tompkins' 1966 *Esquire* article, entitled "In Cold Fact," that catalogued Capote's inaccuracies and caused some readers, who "would have had no problems ... if Capote had not claimed that he never strayed from the truth," to "wonder whether any of the inconsistencies are important" (Spurrill [no date]). And Bill Brown, the former editor of the *Garden City Telegram* who was "enlisted to track down interview sources" for Capote, thought that Capote's portrayal of the Clutter family was so off the mark as to be virtually unrecognizable (Weingarten 2006:31, 34).

Numerous individuals portrayed in *In Cold Blood* have questioned Capote's recollections of their meetings with the author (Tompkins 1966). The lead prosecutor who tried the Clutter case, Duane West, later complained that he had been "portrayed unjustly and grievously underrepresented" in *In Cold Blood* (Smith 2005). Logan Green is presented as responsible for the convictions, and West appears to be playing second fiddle (Smith 2005). West said,

> I've heard various people say that Truman didn't quote them directly ... I know he mistakenly described my part in the book ... I handled all the investigation, worked with the investigators, prepared the trial brief, handled all the evidence ... Mr. Green was hired to assist me [, but] I made the opening statement to the jury. Truman took part of what I said and attributed it to Mr. Green ... This business of a new art form—"nonfiction novel"—is a bunch of *garbage* (Plimpton 1997:221–2).

Similar complaints were made by K.B.I. Agent Harold Nye, to whom Capote sent some galleys from *In Cold Blood*; Nye called the work "a fiction thing," and refused to approve the galleys because Capote "didn't tell the truth":

> What he did was take this lady who ran the little apartment house ... where Perry Smith had been, and fictionalize her way out of character. Accuracy was not his point ... I was under the impression that the book was going to be factual, and it ... was a fiction book (Plimpton 1997:175).

Even as Capote was being accused of taking "the latitude of the fiction writer," a technique he associated with the "documentary novel—a popular and interesting but impure genre," he insisted that his "nonfiction novel" had the distinction of combining "the persuasiveness of fact" with "the poetic attitude fiction is capable of reaching" (Plimpton 1966:3).

Trial lawyers, in their opening and closing statements, are storytellers who likewise hope to combine persuasive facts with compelling narrative techniques. Moreover, as advocates, they need not pretend to complete objectivity, which suggests a parallel with New Journalists and even Capote (whose claims to objectivity are belied by his seeming, perhaps unconscious, advocacy for the murderers).

> While the New Journalists are not the first to recognize the difficulty of being "objective," they do articulate the problem more zealously than their predecessors. They question what constitutes objectivity and whether it is even desirable. Their criticism focuses on ... time-honored assumptions underlying traditional journalism (Kallan 1975:9).

For example, New Journalists view "neutrality as an impotent response to social problems," and believe that the attempt to be "detached and impersonal ... leads to sterile, meaningless, and often misleading journalism;" in short, the "canons of objectivity ... function to insulate the truth" (Kallan 1975:9). Indeed, even Capote said that the reporter, "above all, ... must be able to empathize with personalities outside his usual imaginative range ..." (Plimpton 1966:2).

The contrast of truth with objectivity is evocative of the role of legal advocates, where objectivity is excused but where truth becomes the ethical limit on advocacy. As to judges, however, objectivity returns to the fore as essential to their role in trials.

"Somewhere West of Journalism and This Side of History": The Eclipse of the Scientific Issue

> [Federal] courts are beginning to keep in tune with this [new psychiatric] science as related to people charged with criminal offenses (Capote 1965:268, quoting defense counsel Harrison Smith's argument on behalf of Hickock).

The narrow issue of whether the state court in Garden City, Kansas, failed to acknowledge advances in psychiatric science, is easily lost in the clutter of Capote's account. Notwithstanding the numerous challenges to the accuracy of Capote's novel, his identification of the court's reliance upon local physicians for evidence of sanity is confirmed in court records and in the Kansas Supreme Court's opinion on appeal from the trial. Those opinions, however, can themselves be characterized as creative journalism.

On appeal from their verdicts, the defendants "claimed the trial court erred in refusing to appoint a psychiatrist to the commission that examined them" for sanity (*State v. Hickock and Smith* 1961). The court replied:

> Without laboring this point it may be said it has been determined by this court adversely to defendants' position in well considered decisions to which we adhere. See *State v. Lammers*, … "the statute does not require that any other than doctors of ordinary medicine be on the commission …" (*State v. Hickock & Smith* 1961).

As to the defendants' claim of temporary insanity,

> the utmost that can be said of [such] contentions … is that a psychiatrist … stated that … Hickock knew right from wrong at the time of the commission of the crime and that he had no opinion on the subject as far as Smith was concerned. In any event, the very most that can be said for defendants' position on this point is that the question of their sanity … was determined by the jury upon the evidence introduced … (*State v. Hickock and Smith* 1961).

Finally, as to the three local doctors, who "after an hour or so of conversational prying," found no "mental disorder" (Capote 1965:268), the Kansas Supreme Court *could* have ignored the issue of the lack of psychiatric qualifications of the doctors, and stopped writing their opinion—since it was the very most, the utmost, that could be said—by relying on the statute (requiring only doctors of ordinary medicine), the M'Naghten rule (requiring only that a defendant knows right from wrong), and the jury's determination of guilt. But the court offers a background account, stating that the defendants simply requested a "commission to examine the defendants" and got one (*State v. Hickock and Smith* 1961); however, according to Capote's account, defense counsel asked for a comprehensive psychiatric examination at the state mental institution (Capote 1965:266). Without mentioning the availability of expert psychiatrists who examined the defendants and found evidence of mental disorders, the court stated that the local doctors were "conceded to be reputable, qualified, experienced and respected practicing physicians" (*State v. Hickock and Smith*, 1961). Capote's narrative suggests that these ordinary physicians were neither experienced nor qualified in psychiatry, but his is an alternative account, offered to the reader to compare to the official legal account. In that latter narrative, for perhaps obvious reasons, the justices took a "poetic attitude" and engaged in "creative reportage" (Plimpton 1966:2–3), to construct a scene not witnessed by Capote.

The significance for this book of these competing narratives is that, according to the unofficial, marginalized literary account, modern science was seemingly eclipsed by legal processes. The defendants Hickock and Smith are hardly sympathetic figures in this true-crime drama, but Capote succeeds in raising questions about the pretense, at times, of law's reliance on science.

Conclusion

> [Capote:] What I think is that reporting can be made *as* interesting as fiction, and done *as* artistically ...
>
> [Plimpton:] ... I suppose the temptation to fictionalize events, or a line of dialogue, must be overwhelming. With "In Cold Blood" was there any invention of this sort to speak of—I was thinking specifically of the dog you described trotting along the road ... and Dick [Hickock, when on the run with Perry Smith,] swerving to hit the dog. Was there actually a dog at that exact point in the narrative or were you using ... a fiction device ...?
>
> [Capote:] No. There was a dog, and it was precisely as described (Plimpton 1966:41).

Capote claimed no moral or message for *In Cold Blood*, except that he vowed to tell the truth. To the extent that lawyers are storytellers, *In Cold Blood* is perhaps a warning about the limits of drama, emplotment, and identification with one's client. Moreover, whether fact or fiction, the representation of lawyers in *In Cold Blood* provides points of reflection on the role of prosecutors and defense counsel in criminal trials. The way in which the prosecution dealt with the insanity defense, and the questions about the competence of, and conflicts of interest affecting, the defense attorneys provide heuristic images of ethical misconduct for law students and lawyers. Thus the year of Capote (2006) was a good one, for law and literature studies and for the legal profession's perennial need to reaffirm the ethical aspects of advocacy and judging.

But Capote's account of outdated science also provides an exemplary literature-and-science and law-and-science text for a hybrid analysis. Moreover, beyond the description of legal processes operating without the benefit of the best science, Capote's true-crime novel betrayed rhetorical contours, an inevitable point of view, and unwitting advocacy. Those might be expected in an artistic text, but the next chapter considers the rhetorical aspects of a medical publication, where objectivity is presumably the norm.

Chapter 7
Historical Narratives: Mad Alchemists, Experts Attacking Experts, and the Crisis in Forensic Science

> At this point it is hard to make a mistake; filter the solution, acidify it, take the Kipp, let hydrogen sulfide bubble through. And here is the yellow precipitate of sulfide, it is arsenious anhydride—in short, arsenic ... the arsenic of Mithridates and Madame Bovary (Levi 1984:17).

A True Story

In the late winter of 1828, in Northumberland, Pennsylvania, 160 miles northwest of Philadelphia, Mrs William Logan was accused of poisoning her late husband with arsenic; in the "public mouth," her "virtue began to be suspected, and it was reported that she had been intimate with a neighboring gentleman" (Jackson 1829:238). She was arrested and sent to prison on the basis of a report by four physicians who conducted a "variety of chemical examinations" (of the deceased's stomach and its contents) that "clearly indicat[ed] the presence of" arsenic (Jackson 1829:239). Thanks to the efforts of Dr Samuel Jackson,[1] William Logan's own physician who later catalogued the numerous errors and weaknesses in the board of physicians' "ominous" report, "this woman was acquitted ... by the *grand jury*, twenty-three to one" (Jackson 1829:248).

> Science had triumphed over gossip; an innocent life had been saved. Lest the lesson be lost, [Jackson] published the story in the *American Journal of the Medical Sciences*, being careful to list by name the four practitioners whose lack

1 In his account of the Logan case, Mohr mistakenly, I believe, identifies Dr Samuel Jackson as a "former president of the Philadelphia Board of Health and a leading medical educator" (1993:68). Mohr is referring to Dr Samuel Jackson (1787–1872), Professor of the Institutes at the University of Pennsylvania. The Dr Samuel Jackson (1788–1869) involved in the Logan case graduated from the University of Pennsylvania medical department in 1812, and one year later moved to Northumberland to practice there; indeed, he is often referred to as "Dr Samuel Jackson of Northumberland" to distinguish him from Professor Jackson. Dr Jackson of Northumberland, nevertheless, was prolific and well known as a skilled practitioner; he returned to Philadelphia in 1837, became a member of the College of Physicians and Surgeons, and was president (1852–1853) of the Philadelphia County Medical Society. *See* Salvador 1900:116–17, Scharf and Westcott 1901:1616, Ripley and Dana 1874:495).

> of medical jurisprudence skills might in an earlier era or in a less sophisticated region have sent the wife to the gallows (Mohr 1993:68).

The lesson, alas, *was* lost, for in January of 2007, a jury in San Diego convicted Cynthia Sommer of murdering her husband with arsenic (*California v. Sommer*); it was reported that she contacted an internet dating service before her husband's death, and that soon afterwards she "hosted boisterous parties," used life insurance proceeds for breast augmentation surgery, and took "up with another man" (*Associated Press* 2005). On the basis of "laboratory testing and expert opinion evidence that [Marine Sergeant] Todd Sommer died of arsenic poisoning," Cynthia Sommer spent over two years in the Las Colinas jail (*People's Motion to Dismiss* 2008:1). Thanks to "the fresh insight of neutral experts" ("who had no connection with the previous litigation") from the Quebec Toxicology Center ("considered the 'gold standard' for metal testing worldwide"), the murder charge was dropped; the experts tested previously untested tissue samples from the deceased, and not only found no arsenic, but declared that the earlier reported tissue distributions of arsenic were "physiologically improbable" (*People's Motion to Dismiss* 2008:2). Again, "Science had triumphed over gossip; an innocent life had been saved" (Mohr 1993:68).

In contemporary accounts of the images of science and scientists (often negative) in popular culture, the portrayal of a "mad scientist" in science fiction film and literature figures heavily as reflecting or causing the persistent, though hardly universal, fear and distrust of science in our culture (Tudor 1989:133–57, Haynes 1999). More specifically, the identifiable fear of chemicals and distrust of chemistry likely is rooted in older fictional images of the "mad *alchemist*," whose greed, secrecy, fraud, and arrogance together provide an exemplar for the dangerous, amoral, godless image of the "mad scientist" generally:

> Western culture relies on and reveres science .; yet, paradoxically, the master narrative of scientific knowledge in both literature and film focuses on an evil and dangerous maniac, obsessive, secretive, ruthless, and arrogant, drawing on many of the qualities popularly associated with medieval alchemy (Haynes 2006:5).

Concerns about scientific hubris and amorality are, however, not limited to the untrained public, but are evident in numerous episodes in the history of scientific expertise in the courtroom. The advancements in toxicology in the first half of the nineteenth century, particularly with respect to detection of arsenic, left in their wake (in the "arsenic wars") numerous accusations of arrogant over-confidence, and not merely understandable analytic errors, within the scientific community. Because of the seriousness of a criminal investigation, scientific hubris was viewed by some scientists as particularly dangerous and morally reprehensible.

> The identifying … of arsenical colours [when testing for arsenic] … has deceived some experienced chemists, and it is not to be expected that the laborious village practitioner can have such knowledge of chemistry as may enable him to pronounce on this tremendous business of life and death—a business which the most experienced ought to approach with fear and trembling, with terror and dismay (Jackson 1829:248).

The link between hubris and amorality, grounded in fictional images, was thereby established in scientific discourse.

Drawing upon the substantial literature concerning the history of scientific experts in British and American trials in the nineteenth century, this chapter focuses on several scientific controversies outside of, but related to, the early nineteenth-century courtroom. Much has been written about the origins of scientific expertise in trials, the difficulties faced by nineteenth-century judges and juries due to disagreements among scientific experts, and the corresponding loss of public confidence in science in its interactions with the legal system (Golan 2004, Landsman 1995 and 1998, Hamlin 1986, Mnookin 2007). My own analysis is centered on several debates (before, during, and long after the "arsenic wars" that began in late 1830s Paris) that illustrate the manner in which scientists reflected upon and responded to the relation between legal proceedings and advancements in science. That law often needs scientific knowledge is obvious, as is the fact that science progresses over the years in its capacity to provide accurate information; one would expect, therefore, to find scientists criticizing their forebears, and revising their views, on empirical grounds. More surprising, however, is to find scientists employing the terminology of popular culture discourse concerning dangerous, arrogant, and amoral "mad" scientists when discussing the advancement of "medical jurisprudence" in arsenic poisoning cases.

To explore such discursive contours, this chapter draws upon the distinction, influential in science studies (including science and technology studies, or the sociology of scientific knowledge) between empirical and contingent "interpretive repertoires" in the discourse of scientific controversies. Briefly, the distinction implies that scientists typically employ two different narrative styles, rhetorics, and/or vocabularies when communicating among themselves: (i) a formal, empirical repertoire to describe their own work, and (ii) an informal, contingent repertoire to describe critically the work of those scientists with whom they disagree. The former is exemplified in scientific papers, explaining in agentless prose the results of rigorous research; the latter is exemplified in accusations that a rival was less than rigorous, perhaps influenced by funding, or that a rival's work reflects insufficient training, arrogant over-confidence, or a lack of integrity. Examples of these repertoires are evident in Dr Jackson's report on the Logan case, in the "arsenic wars" in mid-nineteenth century France and England, and in the recent Cynthia Sommer trial in San Diego.

This chapter then highlights the parallels between (i) scientific discourse just before and during the arsenic wars, and (ii) contemporary debates over expertise in the courtroom. Specifically, I note that claims of over-confidence and ethical failures play a role in the current criticism of forensic identification experts—the so-called crisis in forensic science (Pyrek 2007, Fisher 2008)—which criticism reflects the same contingent discourse that earlier scientists employed in condemning the work of some chemical experts in criminal trials involving accusations of arsenic poisoning. Beyond the manifest historical lesson that the crisis in forensic science is not new, I argue that the crisis is not limited to forensic identification techniques, but sometimes extends even to those techniques, such as forensic toxicology, that are grounded in basic science. The post-trial criticism of the experts who confirmed the presence of arsenic in the Sommer case, by other experts, not only involved a contingent discourse implying hubris and ethical failure, but also served to break down any strong distinction between discredited "police science" and credible forensic techniques grounded in "basic science."

I conclude that the ever-present "contingent" aspects of science, including ambition, advocacy, and confidence, are not always flaws to be corrected, though they may be in some cases. Moreover, uncertainty is part of the scientific enterprise, and also is not always a correctible flaw. Most importantly, the dynamic advances in arsenic detection techniques in the first half of the nineteenth century are not unlike the rapid changes in forensic science in the last several decades; the modesty and moral circumspection of some chemists just before and during the arsenic wars provide a model for the appropriate attitude toward forensic science in contemporary courts.

Mad Alchemists: Hubris and Amorality

> The belief that science is dangerous is … central to the horror movie … In just over [250] films …, science is posited as a primary source of disorder, and in 169 of them that impulse is given flesh in the person of a "mad scientist"(Tudor 1989:133).

In his cultural history of the horror movie, Andrew Tudor identifies the prominence of mad-scientist movies in the "classic period" (1931–1936), many "rooted in the Frankenstein story," which pattern continues in the "war years" (1941–1946) and into the late 1950s (1989:29, 34, 40–42).

> In the *Frankenstein* tradition of mad-scientists' movies, the key protagonists are directed to the pursuit of knowledge at the expense of humane values. … These men (they all are) are not simply mad, bad and dangerous. …
>
> … Dazzled and corrupted by the prospect of progress, scientists ignore the proper limitations, the everyday values ... (Tudor 1989:137, 141).

While numerous other themes and perceived threats are identified within the horror movie genre, it is the image of the hubristic and amoral "mad scientist" that reappears in the debates between chemists leading up to and in the "arsenic wars."

As Peter Weingart explains at the outset of his study of chemists in fiction films, chemistry "is the iconic discipline of the 'mad scientist,' reflecting the alchemical imagery that was prevalent until recently … in the depiction of science in films" (2006:31). Alchemy, "a metaphor for the pursuit of material goods and immortality," was criticized in eighteenth-century romantic literature as "the amoral pursuit of mere knowledge about nature" (Weingart 2006:34).

> One of the most common stereotypes about science is that scientists generate dangerous knowledge, ... which is associated with hubris. … The ambivalence and potentially threatening nature of scientific knowledge and the technical inventions that accrue from it is expressed in a conflict between scientific knowledge and ethical values (Weingart 2006:32).

The link between chemistry and the twin dangers of hubris and amorality is highlighted in Joachim Schummer's study of "mad" chemists in nineteenth-century literature (2006).

> Taking chemistry as the embodiment of the enlightenment ideas of science, writers related chemistry to atheism, materialism, nihilism, and hubris, and eventually reinforced the negative view by transforming the "mad alchemist" into the mad scientist (2006:101).

Indeed, Mary Shelley's Dr Frankenstein—"of course, a chemist of the late eighteenth-century"—through his ambitious involvement "in the chemical investigation of nature, i.e., the secrets of divine creation," was necessarily "driven to commit the sin of hubris with disastrous results" (Schummer 2006:119, 121). And while moral perversion is implied in Frankenstein's hubris, Nathaniel Hawthorne's story *Rappaccini's Daughter* (1844) combines "the hubris theme with moral criticism of the obsessed and unscrupulous scientist who knowingly runs the risk of doing harm to other people" (Schummer 2006:123).

Finally, Roslynn Haynes, an English literature scholar with a background in chemistry, explains the endurance of the alchemist stereotype as due in part to the parallels between early science and alchemy in terms of their associations with arrogance, power, ambition, maintenance of secret knowledge, and desire to overcome or transcend conventional human limitations (2006:14–24). However, modern science is also subject to the same ethical suspicions and negative literary representations that confronted early scientists, from (i) Dickens's depiction (Boz 1837) of the members of the British Association for the Advancement of Science "as having lost all humanitarian sympathies and values, as socially irresponsible and emotionally and morally deficient" to (ii) Balzac's "romantic belief that preoccupation with science atrophies the normal emotions that sustain … social responsibilities" in *The Quest of the Absolute*, and (iii) Wells' view in *The Island of Doctor Moreau* (1967) of scientists as "ruthless in their idealism, prepared to sacrifice people or animals in the cause of their experiments" (Haynes 2006:18–19). Modern scientists themselves, Haynes concludes, "have continued to provide writers and film-makers with ongoing instances of the alchemist stereotype" with their mystery and obfuscation, ruthless determination, and failure "to show concern about the social and moral impact of their research" (2006:22–3).

All of the foregoing observations are intended to provide insights into the popular or public understanding of science as a potentially dangerous enterprise. Chemists, by contrast, who "see themselves as ... benefactors of humankind," would find their "stereotypical public image as the sorcerer's apprentices who befoul the environment" as "way off target ... a caricature" (Laszlo 2006:99). One would therefore not expect to find chemists discussing their colleagues' work in terms of hubris or amorality. However, the notion persists that scientists employ two different repertoires in their discourse, one of which preserves the terminology of the public's fear of science and scientists.

Contingent Repertoires

> She worked listlessly in the lab…, negligently washing the precipitates, weighing the nickel dimethylglyoxime, and I had hard work convincing her that it was not quite the thing to pad the results of the analysis: something she tended to do, in fact she confessed to having done often, since, she said, it didn't cost anybody anything and pleased the director ... (Levi 1984:72).

In their influential study of scientists' discourse, Gilbert and Mulkay contrasted the "empirical" repertoire by which scientists frequently present their own work, with the "contingent" repertoire often used in discussing the work of other scientists (1984). The empirical repertoire "portrays scientists' actions and beliefs as following unproblematically and inescapably from the empirical characteristics of an impersonal natural world," while the contingent repertoire depicts the "activities and judgments of specific individuals acting on the basis of their personal inclinations and particular social positions" (Gilbert and Mulkay 1984:56–7).

> This suggests that scientists have available and make recurring usage of two contrasting formulas to represent science: one employs an impersonal, abstracted, agent-absent discourse, which makes claims of *universal* applicability, regardless of human action or belief; a second employs a personalized, localized, agent-centered discourse, which makes claims *arte*factual, *particular* to specific human actions and beliefs (Locke 2001:13).

When one scientist makes a "universally formulated" knowledge claim, for example, "this person died from arsenic poisoning," another scientist can create a controversy with a counter-claim of "particularity"—i.e., that the first claim was the "outcome of experimental error, personal bias, or ideological interest" (Locke 2001:13). This is not to say that technical discourse among scientists is "*mere* rhetoric, but as *a* rhetoric, [it is] part of the resources that scientists have available to construct accounts of their work" (Locke 2001:12).

In a recent study of crop geneticists working in conditions of controversy, Kevin Burchell confirmed the alternative use of empirical and contingent repertoires—the former when describing themselves, the latter when describing others with whom they disagreed—among the scientists interviewed (2007). Burchell also enhances Gilbert and Mulkay's notion of empirical and contingent repertoires by extending it "to include methodological and ethical considerations" (2007:146). Thus

> the empiricist repertoire describes the view that beliefs and actions flow unproblematically from ... a method that is distinctive for its objectivity and rigor, and from an ethical framework. By contrast, the continent repertoire describes the view that beliefs and actions flow from ... prejudices and interests, from methodological shortcomings, and are perhaps unethical (Burchell 2007:147).

Among the criticisms made by the scientists (in Burchell's study) against other scientists, Burchell identifies the claims that some "others" do not take the time to replicate experiments due to the pressure to publish (rigorous checks and balances rely "upon the integrity of the individual"), in particular journals (which are a "badge" and potentially "not even about the science"), where peer review breaks down ("There isn't enough time to do it properly or there are personal things overriding a fair assessment"), raising even the possibility of fraud "where there are large amounts of stress to publish, and you're in a highly competitive field" (2007:150, 154–5). Such claims, referring not to impersonal "natural" phenomena but to the "personal inclinations and particular social positions" of individuals, exemplify the contingent repertoire of scientists.

In another recent study of an (anonymous) internationally renowned environmental scientist, the authors focused on how the Canadian scientist constructed his identity in their interview with him (Lee and Roth 2004). Referring to the distinction between empirical and contingent repertoires as "useful in showing how scientists manage their identities through talk," the authors noted that their "participant came out of the interview as a full-fledged member of the scientific community with traits typically ascribed to scientists such as expertise, objectivity, passion, and disinterestedness" (2004:6, 8). The interviewee "was not just telling a story about his life ...; he was *making* himself ... [He] came out to be a scientist with a particular identity" (Lee and Roth 2004:8–9). In his self-presentation, the scientist claimed that he "saw what even scientifically competent people were unable to see"—namely, that

> most of the processes drinking water utilities use [are] … treatment and disinfection while quality of water is actually a function of the source water you start with. And … I started thinking …, "If we could actually develop some models and understanding of how ecosystems function at the source water, [we] would be able to help the water utilities better manage the quality of water at the tap and improve human health" (Lee and Roth 2004:9).

While others were mired in a "mindset" focused on treatment and disinfection, he "was the prime mover in the eventual change of mindsets"—the new one still a "mindset," but now one firmly grounded in basic science ("unbiased, disinterested and objective from [his] point of view"):

> He came, he saw (with his trained eye), and he converted. With similarity to the empiricist repertoire of scientists, [he] presented a view that science ultimately triumphs, that the truth would prevail no matter what.
>
> ... [He explained that he] "started talking to utilities, … and the first response … was, 'why do we care about source water?' … It took me about a year and a half … to convince the government and industries that this is something worthwhile ... [N]ow it is a very very well recognized, well respected program ... " (Lee and Roth 2004:10–11).

Although the field of drinking water quality is "closely tied with provincial and federal politics," his integrity required that he ignore outside pressures and offer his "views regardless of whether my funding depends on government, … on industries or not" (Lee and Roth 2004:11). The self-described independent scientist, impliedly unlike some other scientists, "spoke for objectivity and truth which all (rational) others had to listen to" (Lee and Roth 2004:14–15). Framing one's identity as a scientist in terms of ethical independence and fidelity to rigorous methodology exemplifies the empiricist discourse.

Notwithstanding the seeming arrogance, at times, of the renowned scientist discussed above, the empiricist repertoire is not hubristic; accusations of hubris, like accusations of amorality (including ethical failures or lack of integrity, which suggest recklessness or carelessness), are part of the contingent repertoire of scientists. Indeed, the water quality scientist was quite modest with respect to his discovery of the importance of source water—he was surprised that there were "places [in Canada, the "pristine North"] where water quality is so poor, it's amazing that it is still allowed to be used as a source water" (Lee and Roth 2004:9). Although he "did not remain in the dark for long," he was "astonished initially about the extent of environmental problems" ("Even a scientist can be fooled …") (Lee and Roth 2004:10). But he was an "unassuming servant of science," committed to "doing and applying basic science" without regard to job security or an attractive salary (Lee and Roth 2004:10–11). Moreover, his unique success with source water programs was due to his "team," including economists, environmental psychologists, public health officials, and "terrestrial people who do … remote sensing type of modeling so that we can quantify land use on a watershed from an image and then link it to the water quality at the source" (Lee and Roth 2004:12). Although at times he seems to "blow his own horn," he moderates his claims to acknowledge the support of "an interdisciplinary team of professionals," thereby walking a fine line between hubris and belittling his own accomplishments in the service of science (Lee and Roth 2004:12–13).

With that framework in mind, I re-visit (in the next section) the medical article, regarding the death of William Logan, published in 1829 by Dr Samuel Jackson of Northumberland, Pennsylvania.

Dr Jackson's "Humble" Diatribe

> This publication, it is hoped, will have its use by exciting the reflections of those who are better qualified than the author; with these humble views, therefore, and no other, he offers it to the profession "with the spirit of a man that has endeavored well"—of one whose position and feelings are fortunately such, that he has neither interest to serve nor malice to gratify (Jackson 1829:246).

So ends Dr Jackson's article on the case of the supposed poisoning of William Logan with arsenic. No hubris, no interest or malice—simply the self-described "position and feelings" of an alert observer of nature. Indeed, the first two pages of Jackson's report explain Logan's death by natural causes: "inflammation of his vein from bleeding" (1829:237). Jackson was initially called to the Logan household because William, who had gone out on a very cold day and returned home drunk, came down with a fever, was suffering pain in his head, neck, and limbs, and developed a cold and cough as well as inflammation of a vein in his arm; Jackson treated him by bleeding, providing firewood to keep Logan's house warmer, and administering small doses of emetic tartar (to induce vomiting), but Logan became faint and delirious, and died ten days after his illness began (Jackson 1829:237). Dr Jackson joined a colleague, Dr Rodrigue, to examine the corpse, and while the former comforted the widow, the latter "dissect[ed] out the inflamed vein" to reveal "the most perfect specimen of intense inflammation we had ever seen" (Jackson 1829:238). Dr Jackson had seen similar cases (including Logan's brother), and

> did conceive that poison could have no part in the matter, for during the whole course of his disease there was no puking, no purging which was not the effect of medicine, no pain nor sensation of heat in the stomach or bowels, no nausea which was not apparently the effect of febrifuge doses of tart. emet. [,] no spitting nor hiccough, no cold sweats, the teeth were never on edge that I heard

> of, no inordinate thirst, no cramps, numbness, or paralysis of the extremities, stools not unnatural, countenance not changed, the blood was not dissolved, the lungs were said to be sound (1829:238).

It would be "incomprehensible and without a parallel" for the "erosion which was afterwards supposed to be seen in the stomach" to have been caused by arsenic "without exciting some corresponding symptom. … To reconcile the phenomenon of the disease with the known effects of arsenic, we conceived to be impossible" (Jackson 1829:238).

But a few days later, Jackson continues, "popular clamour" intervened—suspicions arose because Logan's "wife had procured arsenic from an apothecary," seemingly to keep rats and mice from her butter; the coroner therefore "took various depositions" in the community which, in Jackson's opinion, reflected hasty assumptions as well as "trifling or irrelevant" testimony that "when properly understood went rather to clear than to convict the woman" (1829:238–9). Nevertheless, the body was disinterred and delivered to a board of four physicians for examination; after only two days, they issued an "ominous" report that Logan died of arsenic poisoning, "in consequence of which the woman was committed to prison" (Jackson 1829:239).

Before analyzing the shortcomings of the board's report, Jackson surveys the "circumstances favorable to the accused," including William Logan's good relationship with his wife and her faithful care of him, Logan's complaints about rats and desire to poison them, as well as the lack of motive "for so hideous a crime "— "there was no hope … of her being bettered by his death" (1829:240). Jackson also highlights the fact that he "was most carefully excluded" from "the whole business of the examination," despite his age, experience and doctor-patient relationship with Logan (1829:240).

Reviewing the minutes of the board's proceedings, Jackson first points out the contradictions among the physicians' respective descriptions of Logan's stomach—"as to the supposed inflammation, it appears to be a mere matter of opinion whether any existed" (1829:241). The "whole phenomenon" was explainable in terms of Logan's "intemperance," his enjoyment of country whiskey, which "appears more reasonable than to suppose an acute inflammation by arsenic, without puking or any mode of distress" (Jackson 1829:241–2). Moreover, Jackson warns:

> Even the most *expert* have mistaken vascularity and congestion for inflammation, and a coagulum of blood for an ulcer in the stomach from arsenic. To our present purpose, Dr Shaw,[2] *Anatomy*, p. 51, [states:] "… I have come to the conviction

2 John Shaw (1792–1827) was a British surgeon whose influential MANUAL OF ANATOMY (1822) was republished in the U.S.; it bears mention that Jackson's article also referenced numerous other sources, including the TRACTS ON MEDICAL JURISPRUDENCE (1819) compiled by Dr Thomas Cooper (1759–1839), an article in the MEDICO-CHIRURGICAL REVIEW by M. Louis (the author of MEMOIRES ET RECHERCHES ANATOMICO-PATHOLOGIQUES (1826)),

> that the appearance of the stomach … alone, in a question of poison, is not to be depended on" (1829:242).

Adding an ethical component to his critique, Jackson quotes Shaw's hope that "this degree of uncertainty will prevent the anatomist from being called on to decide a question which may involve the life of a fellow creature" (1829:242).

Jackson "readily" excuses the board of physicians for their "hasty assumption" that arsenic was present, even "before any chemical experiment," blaming instead their lack of "knowledge of morbid anatomy"—they saw a black spot, which appeared "imposing … to the minds of the unphysiological" (1829:242). Jackson also forgives the four physicians for their chemical experiments, which "were as fallacious as the appearance of the stomach," blaming instead the author of the pharmacological treatise on which they relied,[3] Dr John Ayrton Paris (1785–1856), a well-known Edinburgh physician (1829:243–6). Jackson details the ambiguous results of the various liquid tests performed by the board of physicians, noting that comparing "colours is extremely difficult" and "even experienced eyes may be deceived;" that the "sulphus cupri" test detects arsenic *but also* "other matters which are sometimes found in the stomach;" that "the copper and silver tests were used in the most objectionable forms;" that the sulphuretted hydrogen test allows tartar emetic to be mistaken for arsenic; and that the physicians failed in their attempts "to obtain the alliaceous odor" and "to metalize the supposed arsenic" (Jackson 1829:246). The latter

> negatives conspire with other facts to prove that none of the metal existed in the stomach. They leave us destitute of all *positive* proof, and greatly debilitate the *circumstantial*; therefore, since such strong suspicions arose in their minds, it is greatly to be regretted that they did not proceed further with the enquiry (Jackson 1829:246).

The failure to "metalize the supposed arsenic" was not, however, considered disproof, since one physician "accounted for [it] by the presence of moisture, a second by their having too little heat and a third by their using too much—all of which circumstances were surely within the power of the chemist to obviate" (Jackson 1829:243). Moreover, some "important [and easily performed] leading tests were omitted," no microscope was used ("a very powerful one was within their reach"), and no drawings of the (destroyed) stomach were made, even though

---

and works by the Italian chemist Dr Luigi Valentino Brugnatelli (1761–1818), the British physiologist Dr John Bostock (1773–1846), and the Scottish anatomist Matthew Baillie (1761–1823) (Jackson 1829:239, 242, 245–6).

3 Burchell (2007:154) includes in the contingent repertoire the claim that other scientists fail "to reach the standards of practice that are demanded by the empiricist repertoire;" such failings can be attributed to "personal preferences which might be linked to such poor training."

"some excellent delineators were at hand" (Jackson 1829:246). How can all these misjudgments be explained?

The answer is in the hubris of Dr Paris—"here then is the reason they were so easily satisfied at the presence of arsenic" (Jackson 1829:246). In "an opinion peculiar to himself, and … deeply fraught with error and homicide," Dr Paris advises that the silver and copper tests furnish "striking and infallible indications":

> Dr Paris is so delighted with making these arsenical colours, that, while writing on the subject, he has laid down his pen to "convince himself with how little trouble, and with how much pleasure and profit, such experiments may be conducted." … If this not be mere childish play, it is at least the extravagance of a man transported with novelties. … Does not everyone perceive how much room there is left for the ardent imagination of a man zealous in the pursuit, to play on these colours[?] (Jackson 1829:246).

For Dr Jackson, the colors from liquid tests provide "one degree of evidence only," following which a metal should be extracted from the precipitate (showing that a metal "struck these colours"), and then "this metal [should be proved] to be arsenic by the proper experiments" (1829:246). If the quantity is too small for metallization, then all you have is a presumption, and you cannot "swear the arsenic is there" (Jackson 1829:247).

> Men have been justly or at least truly convicted by presumptive evidence—this is the business of law and not of medicine; we shall therefore conclude with an opinion contrary to that of Dr Paris, … that the copper and silver tests do *not* afford "infallible indications," and that it is grossly negligent if not highly criminal to trust them, when so many others may be so easily and so satisfactorily employed (Jackson 1829:247).

In his hubris and ethical lassitude, Dr Paris left the board of physicians in the Logan case "like mariners in an ocean to them unknown, the rocks and shoals of which were left unnoted in their only chart" (Jackson 1829:247).

In most of Jackson's article, he reserves an empirical repertoire for himself, and a contingent repertoire for the physicians as they are misled by Dr Paris. He carefully considers the symptoms prior to death, finds the cause of death, and is not fooled by appearances; they made hasty assumptions, lacked proper training, failed to make further inquiries when doubts arose, and shared in Dr Paris's childish, zealous imagination. At the end, however, he equivocates by conceding that he has merely pointed "out those omissions which we should most probably have made ourselves." He also mentions "the propriety of sending the stomach with a portion of its contents to Philadelphia," with its chemists and pathologists as would "not be expected on this side of the mountain"—this cautionary procedure "is practiced in Europe" (1829:247). Given the importance of a criminal trial,

> no pains ought to be spared to prevent the cruel catastrophe [on families and children], with the consequent endless and wide-spreading imputation of unmerited infamy. … [And] it is not to be expected that the laborious village practitioner can have such knowledge of chemistry as may enable him to pronounce on this tremendous business of life and death—a business which the most experienced ought to approach with fear and trembling, with terror and dismay (Jackson 1829:248).

Though Jackson includes himself in the group that would be misled by "books of blunders" (1829:248), his modesty appears as mere rhetoric, since he confirms that through his efforts, Logan's wife was acquitted.

A similar controversy, prefiguring the Logan case in certain respects, arose in New York in 1817 (Mohr 1993:66–7). Abraham Kesler was suspected of poisoning his wife with arsenic; her remains were disinterred (two months after her death), and after performing "a superficial series of observations and chemical tests," several local physicians "testified that the woman had ... been murdered with arsenic" (Mohr 1993:66). After Kesler was found guilty and sentenced to death, his attorneys appealed to the governor, whose experts

> concluded forcefully that post-mortem observation of the woman's stomach was meaningless, given ... extensive putrefaction ..., and that the local physicians had not conducted the proper chemical tests for arsenic. The governor thereupon stayed the execution ... (Mohr 1993:67).

However, after "another round of medical opinions on the case," taken by the Courts of Justice committee of the state legislature at the request of the governor, the stay was overridden and Kesler executed—the "legislature's doctors ... decided that they had no quarrel on the whole with the original local procedures" (Mohr 1993:67).

Decades later in Bethlehem, New York, when the chemical tests for arsenic detection were much more sophisticated, a controversy concerning aconite poisoning repeated the pattern of experts attacking other experts for overconfidence and carelessness (Mohr 1993:122–39). In 1853, John Hendrickson was accused of murdering his wife after the coroner and two local physicians, who conducted a post-mortem and suspected poisoning, received confirmation from Dr James H. Salisbury of Albany, to whom they had delivered most of the deceased's intestines, that "Maria Hendrickson had been poisoned (her husband gave her pills he had purchased a week before her death) and the agent of her destruction was aconite, or more precisely aconitine, the alkaloid thought to be the active ingredient of aconite" (Mohr 1993:125). Dr Salisbury, who was highly regarded as an expert medical chemist and who had studied aconite, became the prosecution's star witness against Hendrickson at the ensuing trial (Mohr 1993:126–7). Aconite was, however, "one of the most difficult poisons to detect once it entered the body," and "virtually no one else in the scientific world was prepared to defend

Salisbury's chemical claims" (Mohr 1993:127). Although Hendrickson's defense attorneys accused Salisbury of hubris—"careerist ambitions and perverted professionalism"—as well as carelessness—Salisbury did not save the allegedly isolated aconitine (it was administered to a cat, which "did not die"!)[4]—the jury found Hendrickson guilty and the judge (confident that "science had made another advance [by detecting] a previously undetectable poison") ordered him hanged (Mohr 1993:129–31).

> Hardly had Hendrickson been convicted, however, before his remarkable case began to elicit the attention of professionals outside Albany ... David A. Wells, [who was] deeply immersed in the study of chemistry [,] ... was convinced that Salisbury had erred in his chemical testimony [and] that aconitine could not be detected in the manner Salisbury described ... A formal statement of protest was drafted by Wells's friend, Augustus A. Hayes, [and signed by] an impressive list of American chemists ... (Mohr 1993:132–3).

Wells, like Dr Samuel Jackson, published a detailed critique (of Salisbury's unconventional procedures) in a medical journal (Wells 1854), and although "Hendrickson's case had become a national *cause célèbre* among [medico-legal] professionals" by 1854, garnering criticism from numerous quarters, John Hendrickson was hanged that year (Mohr 1993:134, 136). Nevertheless, Salisbury's career was "crippled" by "those who pegged him from the outset as a skillful but rash young scientist willing to rush forward with grandiose claims on the basis of flimsy evidence" (Mohr 1993:137–8).

---

4 Defense counsel Henry G. Wheaton spectacularly argued:

> Just look at it—the confidence of this Dr Salisbury. He ... says [he] discovered this aconitine ... and yet calls no one in to see his discovery, or to confirm it. He is in too great a hurry; he ... administers it all to a cat. He ... had such a desire to send his name abroad; he could not step a single moment; could not bring a particle of it into court for us to see it ...
>
> Ambition urges him on. If the prisoner is convicted, his name goes forth linked with this case ...
>
> To the cat again: The doctor ... gave it all the substance ... and yet, after about two hours of trifling sickness, it recovered ... [t]he cat did not vomit, retained it all, and in three hours was well. What a cat! What a doctor! What an opinion ... upon such facts!
>
> The cat should have died out of deference to the Dr's opinion ...

Mohr 1993:289, citing David M. Barnes and Winfield S. Hevenor, Trial of John Hendrickson, Jr., for the Murder of his Wife Maria, by Poisoning, at Bethlehem, Albany County, N.Y., March 6th, 1853: Tried in the Court of Oyer and Terminer, at Albany, N.Y., in June and July, 1853 (1853).

The great American pioneer of medical jurisprudence T.R. Beck (1791–1855) warned that

> [m]edical witnesses ... too often get carried away in the competitive atmosphere of the courtroom and overstated their findings. "Pressed by perplexing questions, and probably irritated in their feelings," a doctor "is apt to make declarations more strongly corroborative of opinions that he had formerly advanced, and as his examination advances, he may incur the charge of being *biassed [sic]*, more than facts will warrant" (1828:24).

Interestingly, Beck's remarks were delivered while William Logan lay dying in Northumberland, Pennsylvania, under the care of Dr Samuel Jackson, who was about to confront, and later rebuff, the overconfident and careless physicians who allegedly detected arsenic. Beck's warning, and Jackson's parallel concerns, mirrored a growing controversy over arsenic detection techniques in Europe.

The "Arsenic Wars"

> [The] *British and Foreign Medical Review* … saw the controversies raging in Paris as the result of an overwrought toxicological imagination … Urging British readers of Orfila's experimental reports to "guard against being misled by the enthusiasm of the author," the *Review* devoted two lengthy articles to providing a "cool and deliberate examination" [which] concluded that Orfila had placed too much reliance on his own experimental process, his results representing "the height of transcendental analysis." (Burney 2006:252).

The term "arsenic wars" is, in the first instance, a reference to the debates between Mateu Orfila, a well-known toxicologist and courtroom expert, and his critics in Paris beginning in the late 1830s (Bertomeu-Sánchez 2006:275). Orfila (1787–1853), born in Minorca and educated in Valencia, Barcelona, Madrid, and Paris, was appointed professor at the Faculty of Medicine in Paris in 1819; by 1830 he was dean of the Faculty and a "medical celebrity" (Bertomeu-Sánchez and Nieto-Galan 2006-ix-xiii). His greatest influence as was as a "founding father" of toxicology, and his *Traité des poisons* (1814–1815) was popular and influential in France and abroad (Bertomeu-Sánchez and Nieto-Galan 2006:ix–xiv, xvii). As a frequent forensic expert, he was actively involved in the controversial 1840 trial of Madame Lafarge, who was accused of poisoning her husband with arsenic; Orfila's authoritative detection of arsenic, and criticism of other experts who found no arsenic, put Madame Lafarge in prison and ignited "a fierce debate … in the Paris medical community, soon spreading to other academic contexts and to society as a whole" (Bertomeu-Sánchez 2006:208).

The Lafarge case offers a picture of the numerous tests and practices for arsenic detection, and disagreements over their conclusiveness, prior to the gradual acceptance of the Marsh test (Bertomeu-Sánchez 2006:211). Local physicians relied on autopsies and symptoms, while Orfila encouraged chemical analysis and was critical of "smell" tests (i.e., dangerously attributing a "garlicky" odor to arsenic) (Bertomeu-Sánchez 2006:211). Even the experts in the case who used hydrosulfuric acid to produce a yellow precipitate, a sign of the presence of arsenic, did not seem aware that their results were ambiguous (other substances could produce similar precipitates), and in any event could not finish the test and obtain metallic arsenic (Bertomeu-Sánchez 2006:212). When a second opinion was requested from three pharmacists who employed the new Marsh test (i.e. using the apparatus constructed by James Marsh (1794–1846) to capture arsenic), which was enthusiastically embraced by Orfila[5], they could not obtain any trace of arsenic (Bertomeu-Sánchez 2006:208, 213–14). As doubts remained, Orfila joined yet another team of experts who reapplied the Marsh test to confirm the presence of arsenic and affirm that the detected arsenic did not come from the chemicals used in their analysis, the earth from which the victim's body was exhumed, or from the "normal arsenic" in the human body (Bertomeu-Sánchez 2006:208). Those latter qualifications were important because critics had pointed out that zinc used in the early Marsh test could contain arsenical impurities, that cemetery soils could contain arsenic, and that the evidence for "normal arsenic" was inconclusive (Bertomeu-Sánchez 2006:218, 220–26).

François-Vincent Raspail (1794–1878) was a frequent challenger of Orfila's methods in trials and in scientific publications—Madame Lafarge's lawyer, after Orfila's final report, tried to contact Raspail, but "when Raspail arrived in Tulle, the legal proceedings were over and Madame Lafarge had been indicted for murder and … imprisoned for life" (Bertomeu-Sánchez 2006:208). Raspail, for example, was concerned about (i) arsenic in copper vessels used to boil cadavers, and (ii) the potential effect of transporting cadavers on wood painted with arsenical covering: "There are so many non-criminal circumstances that can bring arsenic or arsenical components into the tissues of buried victims!" (Bertomeu-Sánchez 2006:219). And he supplemented such criticism with "rhetorical remarks about the contrast between [Orfila's] 'purely theoretical experiments' performed in the 'cabinet,' and forensic science, which could decide between the 'life or death' of the accused" (Bertomeu-Sánchez 2006:220). Raspail thereby condemned Orfila's arrogance and suggested he was morally careless. Orfila, however, had the academic and political power to respond, and to "defend his credibility and prestige as a medical expert," in lectures, published papers, reprints of his textbooks, salon discussions, and public experiments, leading Raspail to reflect on how much his "powerful authority"

5 "Credit for using the Marsh test for the first time in a criminal trial is accorded to Orfila in the famous Lafarge case in 1840 in France. Yet [Sir William Brooke O'Shaughnessy (1809–1889)], isolated [in India] from the mainstream of chemistry and law, claimed to be the first to describe results of the test as applied to a legal procedure" (Gorman 1984:59).

> is contrary to the principles of equality in law. How much it is scarcely favorable to the defense's interests, when … an … expert … in advance is showered with praise … An all-powerful expert … who is opposed to simple provincial experts, with no other power than their own good reputation, and with no other authority than their knowledge and probity! Finally, … an expert who decides university appointments and dismissals in Paris … (Bertomeu-Sánchez 2006:223).

Orfila's early role as a skeptic, and as a critic of the over-confidence of the initial experts in the Lafarge trial, was in Raspail's view eclipsed by Orfila's own over-confidence and blindness to the limitations of his own toxicological experimental methods.

The reception of Orfila in Britain, while generally positive, also reflected concern for his hubris. His discovery of "normal arsenic," which had seemingly disastrous implications for chemical proof of an arsenic poisoning charge (acquittals could easily be obtained if normal arsenic was assumed), raised "cautious skepticism" (Burney 2006:251). In "several accounts of the [normal arsenic] controversy Orfila was cast as a brilliant virtuoso who had, in this instance, unhappily over-reached himself" (Burney 2006:252). George Owen Rees (1813–1889), a chemist at Guy's Hospital, thought Orfila to be too enthusiastic about his experimental prowess:

> [Orfila] has excluded some of the most satisfactory and delicate tests … and has somewhat dogmatically insisted upon the infallibility of appearances which, however they may carry conviction to his own mind, will scarcely be considered as sufficient by other chemists (Burney 2006:252).

Orfila's British critics saw him as sacrificing "the higher threshold of interpretive restraint required of an expert operating within the constraints of the criminal courtroom" (Burney 2006:253). Orfila's excesses could also be attributed to the official, authoritative capacity of experts in French courts, which shielded them from the "adversarial testing experienced by British witnesses," but in any event the concerns about Orfila "underscored the need for modesty in the application of chemistry to medico-legal inquiry, and for an acceptance of the contingencies of toxicological fact-making" (Burney 2006:253). Alfred Swaine Taylor's (1806–1880) textbooks referred to Orfila to suggest "the dangers of over-interpretation," and Taylor criticized "Orfila's willingness to confirm the presence of arsenic on the basis of 'ambiguous indicators'" (Burney 2006:254).

Taylor himself, however, was soon accused of over-confidence in his work (with his Guy's Hospital colleague Rees) on the trial of William Palmer[6] in 1856.

6 Palmer was a country physician who was suspected of poisoning his gambling partner Jonh Parsons Cook (as well as his—Palmer's—wife and brother). For lengthy accounts of the Palmer trial, *see* Burney 1999, Ward 2005.

> Taylor had supported the prosecution's charge of [strychnine] poisoning despite the fact that he had failed to detect poison in the body of the alleged victim, relying primarily on clinical evidence for his conclusions. His critics on the defense team [insisted] that if the poison existed even in minute amounts, a skilled analyst should have detected it (Burney 2006:255–6).

Criticism continued in the popular press, and Taylor defended himself in part by recalling Orfila's sins of excess in the Lafarge case, and by drawing an analogy to the experts who opposed him in the Palmer trial—"for Taylor, these dogmatists had simply reversed Orfila's error: instead of declaring the presence of poison on the basis of an insecure infinitesimalism, they testified to its absence on the basis of inflated claims to analytical sensitivity" (Burney 2006:256). Nevertheless, despite Taylor's substantially successful efforts to re-frame the Palmer case in his textbooks, his "public image remained ambiguous until his death," and he was condemned in some quarters "as the harbinger of a new and dangerous set of scientific pretensions" (Burney 2006:255–6). Three years after the Palmer trial, Taylor testified in the arsenic poisoning case of Thomas Smethurst; on the basis of a single result using the Reinsch test, he declared the presence of arsenic and Smethurst was convicted (Coley 1998:145–6, Ward 2005:146–8). However, William Herapath (1796–1868) later showed that Taylor's use of the test was faulty (Taylor used copper gauze containing arsenic (Ward 2005:141, 147)), and Smethurst was pardoned (Coley 1998:145–6).

In the mid-eighteenth century, the tests for arsenic detection were so uncertain that accusations, or even the existence, of hubris among experts are rare. Stephan Landsman notes that in two poison cases in 1752 England, the expertise on poisoning was equivocal (Landsman 1998:463). When Ludgate prisoners Pestell and Johnson were tried for poisoning a fellow inmate, two surgeons testified; the first voiced doubts (about proof of poisoning) and would not charge the defendants "without the clearest physical evidence," the second agreed, and acquittal resulted (Landsman 1998:463). When Mary Carpenter, a servant, was accused of poisoning her employer, a chemist would not swear to the fact that poison was used, an apothecary could not opine to that fact, and a surgeon's autopsy did not support a murder charge—all three witnesses seemed to display "a keen awareness of the high level of proof required" (Landsman 1998:463–4). Ten years later, Landsman reports, "the demand for certainty remained equally vigorous" in the poisoning trial of Jane Sibson (Landsman 1998:464). An apothecary named John Tyrell made a "hasty, overzealous" accusation, but he was attacked at the trial as partisan, dishonest, and lacking medical knowledge; three surgeons and three physicians declared that there was no evidence of poisoning, and upon acquittal of Mrs. Sibson, Tyrell was seized, tried, and convicted for perjury—"as much for his excessive advocacy as his specific misstatements" (Landsman 1998:464, 481–2).

By 1782, however, the hubris of less-than-competent experts was successful in the poison trial of Captain John Donellan, accused of murdering his brother-in-law. The circumstantial evidence was compelling—Donellan's suspicious behavior, potentially sizeable inheritance (which would go to Donellan's wife if her brother died), opposition to an autopsy, and experiments with distilled liquids—and the prosecution provided five doctors to testify, three who attended the autopsy and two "celebrated physicians" (Landsman 1995:141). The "most eminent forensic medical expert in England, John Hunter," testified for the defense on the basis of substantial experience that there was no evidence of poisoning; but he was reluctant "to deliver a fully definitive partisan answer to all the questions put to him," and the jury returned a controversial finding of guilt (Landsman 1995:141–2).

Finally, in an 1826 trial in Sussex, England, Hannah Russel and a lodger were accused of poisoning her husband. Evidence that she had purchased arsenic, together with the testimony of a local surgeon who said he found arsenic in the victim's stomach, resulted in convictions (Watson 2004:164). The lodger was hung, but Hannah's execution was delayed. Dr Gideon Mantell (1790–1852), a Sussex physician and geologist, took an interest in the story (without which "she would certainly have been executed"); Mantell was convinced that the deceased had not been poisoned (he had heart problems); he therefore criticized the surgeon's tests, and sought confirmation of his views from other physicians (Watson 2004:164–5). When Hannah Russel was pardoned, due to Mantell's efforts, the pattern of over-confident and careless experts, later corrected by those with better credentials, was firmly established.

Settling the Controversy?: Modern Arsenic Detection Technologies

> [F]ear of undiscovered crime lay at the heart of the nineteenth-century obsession with poison murder. …
>
> To dispel these fears, what was needed was an effective way to detect and deter poisoning crimes. For centuries, this had been an almost impossible task, but in the nineteenth-century the situation changed. By the 1840s, toxicology had emerged as the first modern forensic science (Essig 2002:181).

In her 2004 study of poison crimes, Katherine Watson identifies four chemical tests[7] for arsenic detection that were considered standard prior to the 1830's: the

---

7 Numerous treatises on poisons (most including descriptions of various tests for detection) were published in Europe in the late eighteenth and early nineteenth century. *See* Niyoki 1980:251 (citing German and French treatises). "In contrast to overall European development of the field of toxicology, nothing had been written in the United States before the beginning of the nineteenth century" (Niyoki 1980:251–2) (noting that American editions of Orfila's works were available by 1817, and that Thomas Cooper, a professor of chemistry at the University of Pennsylvania, described the tests for arsenic in 1818, citing *J.G. Nancrede, A General System of Toxicology* (translation of Orfila's *Traite des Poisons* …, 1817) and Thomas Cooper, "On the Tests of Arsenic", Paper read at American

reduction test and three liquid or precipitate tests (2004:16–17). As early as 1752, Anthony Addington performed a chemical examination in the English trial of Mary Blandy, who was convicted of poisoning her father with white arsenic (Goldsmith 1997:153). Addington found white powder on the bottom of a pan used to serve gruel; when the powder was placed in water, most of it sank to the bottom, while a "gritty and insipid taste was noted, and the odor of garlic was clearly evident upon placing it in a red hot pan"—all of which was identical to the behavior of a sample of white arsenic simultaneously tested (Goldsmith 1997:153–4). Such early tests were described by Joseph Black in 1803, who noted that arsenic could be distinguished by its weight, volatility, ability (when heated) to penetrate metallic copper and give it a whitish color, and qualities when burned (whitish smoke or garlic odor); Thomas Ewell in 1806 observed that arsenical powder thrown on heated coals will produce white flames and a garlic smell; and Benjamin Rush detected arsenic by the smell of garlic, the appearance of a whitish presence on copper plates heating the powder, and the formation of a green precipitate when the whitish powder is treated with alkaline copper sulfate (Goldsmith 1997:154–5). The latter test was a version of the first major precipitate test, known as Green's test, which treated a suspected arsenic solution with ammoniacal copper sulfate to produce a green precipitation of copper arsenic or a greenish-blue precipitation of copper arsenate (Goldsmith 1997:155).

The second precipitation test, described by Joseph Hume in 1809, involved adding a silver nitrate solution in an alkaline environment to produce a bright yellow silver arsenate precipitate (Goldsmith 1997:155). The third test involved "passing a stream of sulfuretted hydrogen … gas into an arsenic solution previously acidified with hydrochloric acid to produce a bright yellow amorphous precipitate of arsenious sulfide" (Goldsmith 1997:156). Each of these tests had limitations and ambiguities resulting in the possibility of misleading results and typically requiring combined tests (Goldsmith 1997:155–6).

The "reduction" test refers to the heating of "white arsenic to decompose it to oxygen and metallic arsenic, which would then form a deposit on glass" that could be dissolved in water and tested with liquid tests (Watson 2006:192). In another formulation, small "amounts of solid arsenic compounds could be reduced

---

Philosophical Society, Sept. 18, 1818)). Cooper's *Tracts On Medical Jurisprudence* were published in 1819, and included (i) the text of his Sept. 18, 1818 paper, at 431–8, as well as (ii) annotated (by Cooper) versions of Samuel Farr, *Elements of Medical Jurisprudence* (1787) and George Edward Male, *An Epitome of Juridical or Forensic Medicine* (1816), both of which describe the available tests for arsenic detection, at 49–54 (Cooper updates Farr's eighteenth century methods) and 154–7 (Male's tests). Most of the tests described are reflected in Dr Jackson's article published after the Logan case. Mohr 1993:56 explains that before "1800 virtually no local practitioners could test a corpse for signs of poisoning; by 1825 there were plenty of physicians around the United States who could." Dr Jackson seems to be one of those who could, and his description of the typical symptoms of an arsenic victim, track closely the descriptions offered by Farr and Male, *see* Cooper, *Tracts…*, at 50 (Farr) and 149 (Male).

by carbonaceous flux, recently ignited charcoal, to the elemental state of arsenic" (Goldsmith 1997:156). James Marsh (1794–1846), from his own account, relied most heavily on the reduction test in his work on the 1833 prosecution of John Bodle for the murder (by arsenic poisoning) of his grandfather, George Bodle (Watson 2006:188–92). John Bodle was acquitted, at least in part, because the tests Marsh "used were simply not delicate enough to detect tiny quantities" of arsenic; that "failure … stimulated Marsh to try to find a better method of detecting arsenic" (Watson 2006:184). Relying on Carl Wilhelm Scheele's demonstration that zinc and arsenic mixed in an acid solution formed a gas (arsine) that when burned produced a metallic arsenic deposit, Marsh devised a simple apparatus[8] in 1836 to capture arsenic (Watson 2006:192–3). Though there were reliability problems in Marsh's early experiments, the method was variously modified and became a standard test in Britain and abroad (Watson 2006:193). (Jöns Jacob Berzelius (1779–1848) modified the apparatus, and though the Marsh-Berzelius test required great skills to avoid errors, it offered a way to discover small quantities of arsenic in the bodies of poison victims) (Watson 2006:193–8). The Marsh test was publicized in the 1840 Lafarge trial by Orfila, and was soon the prominent method of arsenic detection in English trials (Watson 2006:196–9).

Soon thereafter, Hugo Reinsch (1809–1884) "introduced a simple, effective test that could pick up arsenic" at miniscule levels, and it was also used in many poison trials.

> The test consists of placing a copper leaf or copper plate … previously treated with dilute nitric acid into an arsenical solution that had been previously acidified with hydrochloric acid and heated nearly to boiling. Arsenic then reveals itself as a brilliant gray metallic-like coating or a black coat (Goldsmith 1997:159–60).

In the late nineteenth-century, Professor Alfred Naquet's *Legal Chemistry* (English translation, 1884) included a section on detection of arsenic, in which he provided detailed instructions for the best test used prior to Marsh's test, Marsh's test, and Raspail's method ("we have not, however, personally tested its merits"); his translator added the Reinsch test ("the omission in the text … should be supplied") (Nacquet 1884:17–30). In the first half of the twentieth-century, Anton J. Bettendorf's (1839–1902) test (a modification of the Reinsch test), Ernest W.H.

8 For his invention,

> Marsh made a u-shaped glass tube … with one end open, the other terminating in a stopclock. The reagents [including the solution in which boiled organic samples allegedly contained arsenic] were placed at the bottom of the u-shaped tube. … Upon opening the stopclock, the arsenic escaped … and had to be quickly ignited. … When this was done, a glass or porcelain plate was held over the stopclock, and bright metallic arsenic deposited on the plate. If no arsenic was present in the sample tested, the plate remained clear (Watson 2006:193).

Gutzeit's (1845–1888) test (a modification of the Marsh test, still regarded as a valid method), the Hefti tests (using "electrolytic deposition of arsine upon an electrode"), and the Kage modification of the Gutzeit test (using mercuric bromide as the reagent), were used by forensic scientists (Goldsmith 1997:160–61). Nowadays, Curry's modernization of the Gutzeit test by inserting "the framed reagent dried filter paper into a spectrophotometer to take optical readings" can detect arsenic at low concentrations, but the atomic absorption technique and neutron activation analysis are preferred. (Goldsmith 1997:161).

The standard method in arsenic testing since the mid-1980s is the inductively coupled plasma-mass spectrometry used in the Sommer investigation (Middleburg 2008).

> Looking back, a progression can be seen in the tests, beginning with the purely qualitative and intuitive, moving to crude chemical tests, and now arriving at the more sensitive modern tests for arsenic detection. Arsenic may have a reputation as a popular poison, but it now faces a near certainty of being detected (Goldsmith 1997:167).

It is that level of confidence that was expressed by the expert witness for the prosecution in the Cynthia Sommer trial, in late 2006 in San Diego. He was Chief of Biophysical Toxicology in the Department of Environmental and Toxicologic Pathology at the Armed Forces Institute of Pathology ("AFIP") in Washington, DC, held a doctorate in physical chemistry, and was highly published. Sommer was convicted as an arsenic poisoner on January 30, 2007, but in the ensuing post-trial litigation challenging the verdict, sufficient questions were raised concerning the laboratory procedures and results to lead the prosecutor to send newly discovered tissue samples (preserved in paraffin) to the Quebec Toxicology Center, which found no arsenic in any of the samples.

In retrospect, the Sommer trial re-enacted the pattern of over-confident hubris and moral carelessness on the part of a toxicological expert, conviction of the defendant, re-analysis by a better expert, and acquittal of the defendant, that sometimes occurred in the early nineteenth century when arsenic detection technologies were rapidly evolving. The criticism (of the prosecution's experts and evidence) raised by the Technical Director of the Metals Department of NMS Labs (in Willow Grove, Pennsylvania) is not unlike Dr Jackson's diatribe following the conviction and acquittal of Mrs. Logan (*NMS Labs* 2007b). Having testified in the case, the NMS Director received additional information about the procedures at the AFIP, and offered the opinion that (i) the chain of custody for liver and kidney tissues, which allegedly revealed extremely high levels of arsenic, had omissions and unexplained alterations; (ii) the victim's specimens were not properly managed; (iii) AFIP's lab was neither accredited by the American Board of Forensic Toxicology nor did it participate in voluntary performance testing for arsenic (*and* AFIP's standard operating procedures for using Inductively Coupled Plasma Mass Spectrometry ("ICP-MS") were not in place until after the tests were completed); (iv) AFIP did not use Graphite Furnace Atomic Absorption Spectrometry for determination of arsenic in liver and kidney tissues, and therefore did not cross-validate the newly-received ICP-MS technology that was used; (v) this was the analyst's first arsenic test, there were no standard operating procedures, and the analyst did not have the experience that would be required by EPA, for example, to test drinking water; (vi) the possibility of contamination was present (cacodylic acid is used in spectroscopy), but the analyst rejected that possibility on the basis of an unscientific belief that a contaminating source can be monitored; (vii) arsenic speciation in tissues is a questionable procedure, and the method used by AFIP neither followed a peer-reviewed method nor employed appropriate documentation for assessing validity; and (viii) numerous quality control deficiencies corrupted the AFIP tests (*NMS Labs* 2007b). In addition, "the analytical findings of the Sommer case are not in agreement with Sgt. Sommer's activities prior to his death and the autopsy findings": the finding of 100% *dimethylarsenic acid* (DMA) is not consistent with other case studies involving death by inorganic arsenic, and Sgt. Sommer did not display the appropriate symptoms before his death (*NMS Labs* 2007a). While it is not unusual for criminal defendants to challenge the prosecution's forensic scientists, this is a unique case where the evidence against Cindy Sommer was so increasingly doubtful,[9] after her conviction, that the prosecutor dismissed the case:

> District Attorney Bonnie Dumanis said [on April 17, 2007,] "Today justice was done. ... This is how the system is supposed to work. As soon as we had information that pointed to reasonable doubt, we [determined] to get the matter dismissed. ..." Defense lawyer Allen Bloom was unconvinced. "No one should say that this system worked. ... This dismissal wasn't because of the prosecution's efforts; it was done because the defense demanded it" (Littlefield 2008).

Forensic science failures in the "system" have become common enough to lead some to declare a crisis.

The Crisis in Forensic Science

> The increase use of DNA analysis, which has undergone extensive validation, has thrown into relief the less firmly credentialed status of other forensic science

9 At the trial, the author of the letter testified for the defense that, "It is not conceivable that he walked around for 10 days without being ill." "Toxicologist testifies in Poisoned Marine Trial," Jan. 22, 2007, 10NEWS.com, available at http://www.10news.com/print/10817606/detaile.html (quoting Laura Labby). Note that Dr Jackson also, in his evaluation of the four physicians in the Logan case, not only criticized their chemical tests, but also noted that William Logan's symptoms did not indicate arsenic poisoning.

> identification techniques (finger prints, fiber analysis, hair analysis, bite marks, and tool marks). These have not undergone the type of extensive testing and verification that is the hallmark of science elsewhere. … [R]eliable error rates are not known (Kennedy and Merrill 2003).

The primary concern with forensic science is that many identification technologies, unlike DNA profiling, have their origins in law enforcement agencies, and therefore do not share in the usual norms, protocols, and validation techniques that we associate with the best science. The general problem of litigation-driven expertise, associated with civil litigation and the reliance of experts on studies performed after litigation has begun, has been highlighted by those concerned with funding sources, identifiable interests, and partisanship of trial experts (Edmond 2007, Haack 2008). Until recently, however, law enforcement forensic science, which is obviously "litigation-driven" by its association with prosecutors, has not been criticized for its funding sources, prosecutorial interests, and partisanship (Edmond 2007:865). But concerns now arise over

> law enforcement-sponsored research relevant to the reliability of expert evidence in criminal cases, evidence that virtually always is proffered on behalf of the government's cases. Of primary concern is research directly focused on the error rates of various currently accepted forensic identification techniques, which have not been subject to any formal validity testing (Risinger and Saks 2003).

Despite public perceptions of near-infallibility, the research supporting handwriting examination techniques, fingerprint identification, and hair analysis is weak, and independent studies of polygraph tests do not validate their accuracy (Risinger and Saks 2003, Faigman et al. 2003). There is also an "embarrassing lack of empirical research on well-accepted techniques such as … firearms identification, and bite mark comparisons" (Giannelli 2007). Indeed, many of the prisoners recently exonerated by DNA evidence were convicted on the basis of unreliable forensic identification techniques (Giannelli 2007).

Ethical concerns about forensic identification techniques have also been raised:

> The blowing smoke phenomenon [in forensic testimony during criminal trials] is particularly vexing. If there is an answer to the blowing smoke, muddying the waters problem, it will have to come from within the forensic science community in the form of a tighter code of ethics (Fisher 2008:285).

The problem of over-confidence in weak scientific methodologies is compounded by the sense that some of those who testify have little regard for the rights of the accused.

In this critical onslaught, a distinction is typically made between "what we might call 'normal forensic sciences' (e.g., forensic toxicology and forensic chemistry)," on the one hand, and the forensic individualization or identification "sciences" which "have no basic science to under undergird them" (Saks 2000:881–2).

> Normal forensic science does things like determining what substance something is (e.g., what is this white powder?) … [They] borrow and apply principles from normal basic sciences such as … chemistry … The forensic identification sciences … are an enterprise consisting of nearly all application and no science (Saks 2000:881–2).

Without questioning the validity of the critique of forensic identification techniques, one must ask, in light of the history of arsenic detection technologies, whether such a strong distinction is sustainable. Forensic toxicology shares some of the problems identified as weaknesses in forensic identification science. First, even though forensic toxicology has a foundation in the basic sciences, its application in a particular case is "science-for-litigation" and is driven by "a single unambiguous desired result" which will be "presented to a reviewing community (judges and juries) that typically is not scientifically literate" (Risinger and Saks 2003). Second, forensic toxicology is often associated with crime laboratories, some of which are unaccredited, and even the best have been the site of problems.

> [P]erhaps the best example is the Federal Bureau of Investigation (FBI) laboratory, considered to be the country's premier crime lab. A 1997 inspector general's report on the lab found scientifically flawed testimony, inaccurate testimony, testimony beyond the competence of examiners, improper preparation of laboratory reports, insufficient documentation of test results, scientifically flawed reports, [and] inadequate record management and retention … (Giannelli 2007).

Ten years later, the NMS Lab's toxicologists (testifying on a behalf of Cindy Sommer) found the very same flaws in the Department of Environmental and Toxicologic Pathology at AFIP. Finally, the same concerns over partisanship, interest, and sources of funding that worry the critics of forensic identification techniques are just as applicable to assessments of forensic toxicology. Even in the mid-nineteenth century, when there were no law enforcement-sponsored crime laboratories, charges of partisanship among forensic toxicologists can be found. Indeed, from the nineteenth century, when party-driven expertise became the norm in U.S. and English courts, until the present, concerns over partisanship are evident. (Mnookin 2007:769–75). In the famous Palmer case, both Taylor and Herapath, from opposite sides of the case, were accused of partisanship. Defense counsel for Dr Palmer maintained that from

> the very beginning of his association with the case. … Taylor had been the quintessential partisan. Taylor's initial examination had been biased by the stepfather's suspicions that Cook had not died a natural death. His performance

> at the [inquest, where Taylor confidently declared strychnine as the agent of death,] confirmed him as an interested party. Having staked his credentials as an expert witness on a highly speculative theory supported by mere "tearoom gossip," he had publicly backed himself into a corner ... (Burney 1999:81).

Hence Taylor's consistent testimony, even when his chemical tests revealed no strychnine, and his explanation of absorption. But Herapath, testifying for the defense, "was made to confess on cross-examination that he had again and again bragged among friends that he too thought Cook was poisoned by strychnine but that Taylor did not know how to find it" (Golan 2004:99). Taylor therefore later accused Herapath of belonging "to a class of 'traffickers in evidence' who would for a fee align themselves to any cause" (Hamlin 1986:490).

Thus while the recent concerns over the forensic identification sciences focus on its features as science-for-litigation, its association with law enforcement-sponsored crime laboratories, and its potential for partisanship, there is nothing about the scientific foundation of forensic toxicology that removes it from these types of concerns. That is neither to say that forensic toxicology is not more reliable than the commonly-used forensic identification techniques, nor that forensic toxicologists are on the whole partisans who are willing to testify falsely. Rather, it is to say that hubris in the form of over-confidence and overstatement remains a risk in the field of arsenic detection, and that carelessness in the laboratory reflects a moral failure in the criminal justice system.

Conclusion

> In addition to knowledge and experience, complete honesty and objectivity are … required [in my role as an expert witness]. Integrity and reputation are essential in my business (Manuta 2005).

Such aphorisms, I suspect, represent the majority opinion of scientific experts, even though most, in my experience, will concede that they have faced, as opposing experts, scientists who were not so honest or objective and who were willing to testify with much—too much—confidence. That shortcoming is a concern, not a crisis, but the affirmation of experts with integrity and a good reputation illustrates the empirical discourse reserved for self-description and the contingent discourse reserved for others—for example, "I have encountered opposing lawyers who actually try to invent science and have seen some of them unwittingly sound like stand-up comedians" (Manuta 2005). With respect to arsenic detection, the pattern of over-confidence on the part of experts later proven to be unreliable, evident in Dr Jackson's re-analysis of Mrs Logan's conviction (a preview of the "Arsenic Wars" in France and England), repeated itself in the Cindy Sommer "affair" (as they called the Lafarge case) in San Diego in 2007. And the image of the mad scientist, recently kept alive in popular culture by Mr Blue (the character played by Tim Blake Nelson) in the latest *The Incredible Hulk* (2008) film, can be faintly detected in the arrogant over-confidence, the hubris, of the irresponsible treatise writer (Dr John Ayrton Paris) identified by Dr Jackson, and in the careless AFIP toxicologists criticized by NMS Labs toxicologists and impliedly by the experts at the Quebec Toxicology Center. It is not only forensic identification specialists, but all forensic scientists who are tempted, at times, by hubris.

Contingencies will always accompany the empirical aspects of science—funding will come from somewhere, scientists are ambitious, and bias toward a preferred theory is commonplace. Those phenomena do not signal junk science, and in situations of scientific controversy or uncertainty, scientists will disagree, which likewise does not imply that one side is less than scientific. We do, however, expect scientists to have integrity and some degree of modesty, the opposites of amorality and hubris, which might keep them from being persuaded to offer an over-confident opinion in disregard of the consequences for a litigant or criminal defendant.

Chapter 8
Conclusion:
A New Picture of Science in Law

The April 2010 oil spill in the Gulf of Mexico, following the explosion on a BP drilling platform, brought to the fore the complications of the scientific enterprise. The technical questions of precisely what went wrong and what was happening in the Gulf (how much oil and gas were flowing into the Gulf, and what damage was occurring?) involved ethical dimensions, public relations, politics, disagreements among qualified experts, scientific credibility and reputations, limited information and resources, and uncertainty. Any notion that we simply needed to find the objective, disinterested, and fully informed expert (or team of experts) to deliver the truth was revealed as an oversimplification. What, then, should we expect from scientific expertise?

The argument in this book is that we can gain insight into how science works in legal contexts through literary sources; clearly, stories about science in law are not the only source of insights—scientific treatises have their own self-representations of science, and science studies scholarship, including the history, philosophy, and sociology of science and technology, provides critical insights. Political scientists study the place of expertise in regulatory and policy contexts. Journalists report often on scientific discoveries and controversies, and their impact on our lives. Within legal scholarship, fruitful debates persist over how to appropriate the best science in the service of law, whether in the courtroom or in the policy and regulatory settings. Nevertheless, literary and historical sources concerning the appropriation of scientific expertise into law provide another perspective, and a set of popular culture images, about the perils and promise of scientists and scientific knowledge in our legal system.

Methodologically, I introduced in Chapter 2 the analytical frameworks upon which this book is based, namely two movements (law-and-lit, lit-and-science), each of which involves two (parallel) types of inquiry: Law-and-lit either (1) looks to literary works about law and lawyers for legal insights, or (2) looks at legal texts as literary achievements; lit-and-science either (3) looks to literary works about science and scientists for insights about the scientific establishment, or (4) looks at scientific texts as literary achievements. All four enterprises are somewhat objectionable: (1) We should rely on legal history, case law, or doctrinal treatises for legal insights; (2) surely law is not fictional and as interpretable as a poem; (3) we should rely on the history of science and scientific treatises for scientific insights; and (4) surely scientific texts are not fictional and as interpretable as a poem. The first three objections are easier to explain: (1) Stories about law and lawyers encourage ethical reflection; (2) law *is* an interpretive enterprise, involving conflicting narratives and rhetorical instability; and (3) stories about science and scientists reveal popular culture images that affect public attitudes toward science. The fourth objection highlights a deeper controversy over the cultural superiority of science, which is why I included in Chapter 2 an extended discussion of rhetorical studies of science, as well as the place of that enterprise within science studies. In short, the question of how science can be depended upon, while at the same time it evinces paradigm-shifts, cultural components (and not merely influences), interests (social, economic, political, and institutional), and rhetorical strategies, has created a dynamic field of inquiry that can be characterized by turns (semiotic, naturalist, science-as-experiment, science-as-culture, science-as-practice) and waves (first, explaining the success of science; second, deconstructing science; third, prescribing the contours of expertise). Tensions persist within science studies concerning the role of "nature" in cultural constructions of scientific authority, which explains most of the turns and waves, but that has not prevented science studies from becoming popular and influential as a field. The literature associated with science studies has, however, had relatively little impact in legal scholarship and practice; one of the purposes of this book has been to introduce the relevance of science studies for the discourse and controversies concerning scientific expertise in law.

As for the four types of inquiry in law-and-lit and lit-and-science studies, they variously merge and blend in this study of stories about science in law. I therefore will make no attempt to classify each of my analyses, except to say that Chapters 3 and 4 are primarily oriented toward the science-in-literature enterprise, through eliciting images of science, while at the same time attempting to identify their implications for law; Chapters 5 and 6 are primarily oriented toward law-in-literature, although it is the images of *science* in law that are the subject of Chapter 5, while the ethical constraints on lawyers and judges discussed in Chapter 6 involve the use of science in law. Finally, Chapter 7 engages the controversial science-as-literature enterprise, although the medical journal article I discuss involves expertise in the courtroom.

In summary, when a scientist like Ramón y Cajal writes short stories, his representation of science is different from that found in scientific treatises. In his realism, however, Cajal exemplifies early Lab Lit, and each of his "vacation stories" reveals an aspect of science beyond the mere observation of natural phenomena in the laboratory. Cajal highlights not only the ethical limitations on science, but also the social construction of scientific authority (as well as the failure of science when society refuses to grant authority to a scientist). Without challenging the beneficial achievements of science, Cajal demonstrates the necessity of rhetoric and reputation, on the part of scientists, in the public reception and utility of scientific knowledge. And while Cajal's stories are in the canon of literature-and-science studies, he mentions law and lawyers, both as a contrast to science and scientists as well as an analogy—both professions require persuasion to win confidence, and both enterprises are capable of adjusting the facts and finding an argument "to fit the most contradictory theories" (Cajal 2001:183, 232). Both enterprises, moreover, not only form a community in conversation with fellow practitioners, but are oriented to an outside audience in a cultural context that determines their efficacy.

That audience, the public, is the subject of Ibsen's scientific play, *An Enemy of the People*, which emphasizes the importance of public relations for scientific utility. Scientific knowledge is intertwined with political bias and economic interests, not only in the obvious sense that the public reception of science is influenced by citizens' biases and interest, but also in the way that citizens recognize the biases and interests of scientists themselves. Moreover, a community's skepticism about the scientific community, because of science's mistakes and contradictions, is quite similar to judicial skepticism about expertise in the courtroom. While some judges idealize science, others are suspicious of both the experts who come before them *and* the notion that law should defer to scientific experts solely on the basis of credentials; such judges also recognize the limitations of science, its social aspects, and its uncertainty resulting in genuine scientific controversies—disagreement between experts does not signal "junk science" on the part of one of them. On the basis of their experience with experts, such judges develop an ability to discern expertise on the basis of a modest view of science that is distinct from an idealized view of science held by other judges.

Both views of science, idealized and modest, are represented in movies about trials involving expert witnesses. And both views are likely reflected among filmgoers, some of whom might come to understand that law should defer to authoritative science. That is, some trial movies present an image of science, which is otherwise an ideal producer of knowledge, as susceptible to manipulation by advocates who hire experts willing to make whatever "scientific" argument the client needs. Others present an image of law as the solution to a legal controversy—a genuine expert rises above the contested world of lawyer's rhetoric and delivers the truth. Both images idealize science, but there are other lawyer films that present the human side of scientific expertise, and support an image of science as a modest enterprise. Whether lawyer movies reflect public sentiment, or create public sentiment through their powerful images, two views of the scientific enterprise and its relation to the courtroom are alternatively represented in cinema.

Moving away from "pure" fiction to Truman Capote's so-called non-fiction "novel" *In Cold Blood*, we see another representation of scientific expertise in the courtroom. While Capote claimed that his true account of the Clutter murders had no message, an implicit critique of the way law [mis-]uses science is evident in the story. Kansas law, as well as its judicial understanding of insanity, is presented as lagging behind the new develops in psychiatry. Moreover, the lawyers, especially the prosecutors, are complicit in the failure of the legal process to recognize the mental disabilities of the defendants. Ethical failures on the part of the lawyers therefore infect the proceedings. Unwittingly, Capote also demonstrates the difficulty in constructing a true account of anything, as non-fiction authors cannot so easily claim objectivity.

The apparent objectivity of scientific discourse is also called into question in the medical journal article by Dr Samuel Jackson, whose story about an alleged arsenic-poisoning case betrays a rhetorical structure of alternating empirical and contingent repertoires. Whereas one would not expect the literary narratives concerning, and the image of, mad scientists to enter into technical, scientific discourse, Jackson draws upon the images of the amoral and dangerous scientist in his condemnation of other "experts" who claimed to detect arsenic in the body of a patient who died from natural causes. In the decades following Jackson's diatribe, arsenic detection improved to an extent that contemporary toxicology is not included in the recently-condemned forensic sciences with no real basis in science. However, the recent case involving Cindy Sommer, falsely accused (on the basis of expert testimony) of poisoning her husband with arsenic, reveals that a modest view of the scientific enterprise is appropriate in legal contexts.

The "modest view of science" is revealed in each of the literary examples in this book, but I do not mean to associate the modest view with some caricature of social constructivism, as discussed in Chapter 2. Even if the "science wars" neatly bi-furcated the two possible attitudes toward science as involving either worshipful trust in the scientific enterprise to deliver truth, or complete skepticism about science as a merely rhetorical accomplishment, we are not actually left with only those two alternatives. The history of science studies, including rhetorical studies of science, reflects a concern with avoiding either extreme, although the entire field might be conceived as a reaction to a perceived idealization of science in the mid-twentieth-century by philosophers of science seemingly committed to describing why scientific knowledge is superior to all other forms of knowledge, by historians of science seemingly committed to describing the linear advancement (from past errors to current, stable knowledge) of science in each of its disciplines, and by early sociologists of science seemingly committed to describing the methodological norms that consistently lead to scientific progress. The so-called "second wave" of science studies not only highlighted the social, institutional, rhetorical, economic, and political aspects of science, but its adherents refused to see those aspects as mere external influences upon the internal operation of the scientific enterprise. That is, the social aspects of science do not represent failures, but rather are the supports on which science relies. This is not to say that there cannot be adverse external influences that produce bad science; a regulated industry might pay a scientist to misrepresent laboratory results, or an expert in court might over-testify to help her client win a lawsuit. Nor is this an argument for the unreliability of science. The point is that even the best science is a cultural production, involving audiences, cultural contexts, shared conventions, interdisciplinary alliances, and language.

A picture of science emerges (from the images in stories about law's appropriation of scientific expertise) that challenges the view that science is completely different from law. Law *is* rhetorical, social, and institutional, involving ethical dimensions, credibility, cultural authority, and unstable interpretations. But so is science, and those features need to be acknowledged and their implications understood in legal contexts.

Bibliography

A Few Good Men (dir. Rob Reiner, 1992).

A Time to Kill (dir. Joel Schumacher, 1996).

ABA Model Rules of Professional Conduct. 2002, as amended, 2009. Chicago, IL: ABA Publications.

ABA Standards for Criminal Justice: Prosecutor Function. 1993. Chicago, IL: ABA Publications.

Agnes of God (dir. Norman Jewison, 1985).

Anatomy of a Murder (dir. Otto Preminger, 1959).

Anderson, C. 1987. Literature and Medicine: Why Should the Physician Read … or Write?, in *Literature and Science: Theory and Practice*, edited by S. Peterfreund. Boston, MA: Northwestern University Press, 35–48.

Aron, R., et al. 1990. *Impeachment of Witnesses: The Cross-Examiner's Art.* Deerfield, IL: Clark Boardman Callaghan.

Asimow, M. 2000. Bad Lawyers in the Movies. *Nova Law Review*, 24, 533–93.

Asimow, M. and Mader, S. 2004. *Law and Popular Culture: A Course Book.* New York, NY: Peter Lang.

Associated Press. 2005. Did Wife Poison Marine? Woman Charged with First-degree Murder for Financial Gain. Available at http://www.msnbc.com/id/10479896/print/1/displaymode/1098.

Atkinson, R. 1999. Liberating Lawyers: Divergent Parallels, in *Intruder in the Dust* and *To Kill a Mockingbird. Duke Law Journal*, 49, 601–748.

Banash, D. 2003. Book Review. *Science Fiction Studies*, 30(1), No. 89. Available at http://www.depauw.edu/sfs/birs/bir89.htm.

Baron, J. 1999. Law, Literature, and the Problems of Interdisciplinarity. *Yale Law Journal*, 108, 1059–86.

Battalio, J. 1998. Introduction, in *Essays in the Study of Scientific Discourse: Methods, Practice, and Pedagogy*, edited by J. Battalio. Stamford, CT: Ablex Publishing Corporation, vii–xix.

Bazerman, C. 1988. *Shaping Written Knowledge: The Genre and Activity of the Experimental Article in Science.* Madison, WI: University Wisconsin Press.

Beck, T.R. 1828. Annual Address Delivered before the Medical Society of the State of New-York. *New-York Medical & Physical Journal*, Jan/Feb/Mar 1828, 1–24.

Bell, D. 1999. The Power of Narrative. *Legal Studies Forum*, 23, 315–48.

Bell, P. 1985. Duchess of Letters (book review of West's novel *The Real Night*). *The New Republic*, April 1985, 33–60.

Bertomeu-Sánchez, J. 2006. Sense and Sensitivity: Mateu Orfila, the Marsh Test, and the Lafarge Affair, in *Chemistry, Medicine, and Crime: Mateu J.B. Orfila (1787–1853) and His Times*, edited by J. Bertomeu-Sánchez and A. Nieto-Galan. Sagamore Beach, MA: Science History Publications, 207–42.

Beyea, J. and Berger, D. 2001. Scientific Misconceptions Among *Daubert* Gatekeepers. The Need for Reform of Expert Review Procedures. *Law and Contemporary Problems*, 64, 327–72.

Bond, C. 2010. Laws of Race/Laws of Representation: The Construction of Race and Law in Contemporary America. *Texas Review of Entertainment and Sports*, 11, 219–65.

Borum, R. and Fulero, S.M. 1999. Empirical Research on the Insanity Defense and Attempted Reforms: Evidence Toward Informed Policy. *Law and Human Behavior*, 23, 117–35.

Boyesen, H. 1894. *A Commentary on the Works of Henrik Ibsen*. London: W. Heinemann.

Boz [Charles Dickens]. 1837. Full Report of the First Meeting of the Mudfog Association for the Advancement of Everything. *Bentley's Miscellany*, 2, 397–413.

Bradie, M. 1998. Models and Metaphors in Science: The Metaphorical Turn. *Proto Sociology*, 12, 305–18.

Burchell, K. 2007. Empiricist selves and contingent "others": the performative function of the discourse of scientists working in conditions of controversy. *Public Understanding of Science*, 16, 145–62.

Burdeau, E. 2006. The Writing of Crimes. *Cahiers Du Cinéma*, 610, 32–3 (March 2006). English translation by Sally Shafto available at http://www.cahiersducinema.com/article695.html.

Burney, I. 1999. A Poisoning of No Substance: The Trials of Medico-Legal Proof in Mid-Victorian England. *J. Brit. Stud.*, 30, 5–92.

Cajal, S. Ramón y. 2001. *Vacation Stories: Five Science Fiction Tales*. Translated by Laura Otis. Campagne, IL: University of Illinois Press.

California v. Sommer [2007]. Calif. Sup. Ct. for San Diego County, Case No. SCD195202.

Callebaut, W. 1993. *Taking the Naturalist Turn, or How Real Philosophy of Science is Done*. Chicago, IL: University Chicago Press.

Capote, T. 1965. *In Cold Blood: A True Account of a Multiple Murder and Its Consequences*. New York, NY: Random House.

Caudill, D. 2003. Advocacy, Witnesses, and the Limits of Scientific Knowledge: Is There an Ethical Duty to Evaluate Your Expert's Testimony? *Idaho Law Review*, 39, 341–56.

________. 2002a. Barely Opening, Then Slamming Shut, Science's "Black Box" in Law: A Response to Beecher-Monas's Heuristics. *Cardozo Law Review*, 23, 1795–810.

________. 2002b. Ethnography and the Idealized Accounts of Science in Law. *San Diego Law Review*, 39, 269–306.

________. 2002c. Give Me a Line in a U.S. Supreme Court Opinion or in Official Commentary to the Rules of Evidence for Admissibility of Experts in Court, and I Will Move the [Legal] World. *Houston Law Review*, 39, 437–46.

________. 2001. Law and Science: An Essay on Links and Socio-Natural Hybrids. *Syracuse Law Review*, 51, 841–62.

Caudill, D. and LaRue, L. 2006. *No Magic Wand: The Idealization of Science in Law*. Lanham, MD: Rowman & Littlefield.

Caudill, D. and Redding, R. 2000. Junk Philosophy of Science: The Paradox of Expertise and Interdisciplinarity in Federal Courts. *Washington and Lee Law Review*, 57, 685–766.

Ceccarelli, L. 2001. *Shaping Science with Rhetoric: The Cases of Dobzhansky, Schrodinger, and Wilson*. Chicago, IL: University of Chicago Press, p. 3.

Chaires, R. and Chilton, B. 2003. *Star Trek Visions of Law and Justice*. Dallas, TX: Adios Press.

Clark, W. 1995. Narratology and the History of Science. *Studies in the History and Philosophy of Science*, 26, 1–71.

Coley, N. 1998. Forensic Chemistry in 19th-century Britain. *Endeavor*, 22(4), 143–7.

Collins, H. and Evans, R. 2002. The Third Wave of Science Studies: Studies of Expertise and Experience. *Social Studies of Science*, 32(2), 235–96.

Cookson, S. 2009. The Real Lab Rats. *Financial Times*, 23 May. Available at http://www.ft.com/cms/s/2/72985c24-465d-11de-803f-00144 feabdc0.html#axzz18DPLiP36.

Cooper v. Carl E. Nelson & Co. [2000] 211 F.3d 1008, 1021 (7th Cir.).

Crowther, A. 2006. The Toxicology of Robert Christison: European Influences and British Practice in the Early Nineteenth Century, in *Chemistry, Medicine, and Crime: Mateu J.B. Orfila (1787–1853) and His Times*, edited by J. Bertomeu-Sánchez and A. Nieto-Galan. Sagamore Beach, MA: Science History Publications, 125–52.

Curry, A. 1988. *Poison Detection in Human Organs*. Springfield, IL: Charles C. Thomas Publisher.

Daubert v. Merrell Dow Pharmaceuticals, Inc. [1993] 509 U.S. 579.

Daubert v. Merrell Dow Pharmaceuticals [1995] 43 F.3d 1311 (9th Cir.).

Day, K. and Murphy, R. 2009. "Just Trying to Be Human in this Place": Storytelling and Film in the First Year Law School Classroom. *Stetson Law Review*, 39, 247–84.

Denvir, J. 1996. *Legal Reelism: Movies as Legal Texts*. Champagne, IL: University Illinois Press.

_______. 2003. What Movies Teach Law Students. *Picturing Justice: On-line Journal of Law and Popular Culture*, 25 August. Available at http://usfca.edu/ph/teach_denvir.htm.

DeVries, H. 1990. The Police Reporter at the Garden Party, in *Conversations with Tom Wolfe*, edited by D.M. Scura. Jackson, MS: University Press of Mississippi, 241–5.

Dobbin, S., et al. 2002. Applying Daubert: How Well Do Judges Understand Science and the Scientific Method? *Judicature*, 85, 244–7.

Dobbs, D. 2006. Trial and Error: The Scientific-Publishing System Does Little to Prevent Scientific Fraud. Is There a Better Way? *N.Y. Times Magazine*, 15 January, 18. Available at http://www.nytimes.com/2006/01/15/magazine/5wwln_idealab.html?_1=1.

Edmond, G. 2007. Supersizing Daubert: Science for Litigation and Its Implications for Legal Practice and Scientific Research. *Villanova Law Review*, 52, 857–924.

Elkins, J. n.d. The Legal Mind and the Lawyer Film. *Picturing Justice: The On-line Journal of Law & Popular Culture.* Available at http://www.usfca.edu/pj/mytake.htm.

Erin Brockovich (dir. Stephen Soderbergh, 2000).

Fabian, J. 1983. *Time and the Other: How Anthropology Makes Its Object*. New York, NY: Columbia University Press.

Fahnestock, J. 1998. Accommodating Science: The Rhetorical Life of Scientific Facts. *Written Communication*, 15, 330–50.

Faigman, D., et al. 1994. Check your Crystal Ball at the Courthouse Door, Please: Exploring the Past, Understanding the Present, and Worrying About the Future of Scientific Evidence. *Cardozo Law Review*, 15, 1799–836.

Faigman, D., et al. 1997. *Modern Scientific Evidence: The Law and Science of Expert Testimony*. Eagan, MN: Thompson West.

Faigman, D., Feinberg, S., and Stern, P. 2003. The Limits of the Polygraph. *Issues in Science and Technology*, 20(1), 40–46 (Fall 2003). Available at http://www.issues.org/20.1/faigman.html.

Faigman, D., Kaye, D., Saks, M. and Sanders, J. 2002. *Science in the Law: Social and Behavioral Science.* Eagan, MN: Thomson West.

Finn, M. 2003. *The Character of Credit: Personal Debt In English Culture, 1740–1914.* Cambridge: Cambridge University Press.

Fisher, J. 2008. *Forensics Under Fire: Are Bad Science and Dueling Experts Corrupting Criminal Justice?* Oxford: Kelly Elsevier Books.

Friedman, L. 1989. Law, Lawyers, and Popular Culture. *Yale Law Journal*, 98, 1579–606.

Frye v. United States [1923] 293 F. 1013 (D. C. Cir.).

Fuller, S. 2000. Why Science Studies Has Never Been Critical of Science: Some Recent Lessons on How to Be a Helpful Nuisance and a Harmless Radical. *Philosophy of the Social Sciences*, 30, 5–32.

Gattaca (dir. Andrew Niccol, 1997).

Gatowski, S., et al. 2001. Asking the Gatekeepers: A National Survey of Judges on Judging Expert Evidence in a Post-Daubert World. *Law and Human Behavior*, 25, 433–58.

Gemmette, E. ed. 1998. *Law in Literature: An Annotated Bibliography of Law-Related Works*. Troy, NY: Whitson Publishing Company, Inc.

Gerbner, G. 1987. Science on Television: How it Affects Public Conceptions. *Issues in Science and Technology*, 3, 109–15.
Gershman, B.L. 2008–2009. *Prosecutorial Misconduct*, 2nd edition. Eagan, MN: Thomson West.
Giannelli, P. 2003. Crime Labs Need Improvement. *Issues in Science and Technology*, 20(1), 55–8 (Fall). Available at http://www.issues.org/20.1/giannelli.html.
Gilbert, N. and Mulkay, M. 1984. *Opening Pandora's Box: A Sociological Analysis of Scientists' Discourse*. Cambridge: Cambridge University Press.
Glassy, M. 2005. *The Biology of Science Fiction Cinema*. Jefferson, NC: McFarland & Company.
Golan, T. 2004. *Laws of Men and Laws of Nature: The History of Scientific Expert Testimony in England and America*. Cambridge, MA: Harvard University Press.
Goldsmith, R. 1997. The Search for Arsenic, in *More Chemistry and Crime: From Marsh Arsenic Test to DNA Profile*, edited by S. Gerber and R. Saferstein. Oxford: Oxford University Press USA, 149–68.
Goldstein, R. 2001. *Properties of Light*. New York, NY: Houghton Mifflin.
Goldstein, T. 1985. *The News at Any Cost: How Journalists Compromise Their Ethics to Shape the News*. New York, NY: Simon & Schuster.
Goodman, A. 2006. *Intuition*. New York: Dial Press.
Gragson, G. and Gragson, T. Uncertain Science and the Sponsored-Research Process, in *Essays in the Study of Scientific Discourse: Methods, Practice, Pedagogy*, edited by J. Battalio. Stamford, CT: Ablex Publishing Corporation, 3–21.
Graves, H. 1998. Marbles, Dimples, Rubber Sheets, and Quantum Wells: The Role of Analogy in the Rhetoric of Science. *Rhetoric Society Quarterly*, 28(l), 25–48.
Green, E., et al. 2002. Jurors and Juries: A Review of the Field, in *Taking Psychology And Law Into the Twenty-First Century*, edited by J.R.P. Ogloff. New York, NY: Kluwer Academic/Plenum Publishers, 225–81.
Greenfield, S. et al. 2001. *Film and The Law*. London: Cavendish Publishing Ltd.
Grobel, L. 1985. *Conversations With Capote*. La Vergne, TN: Lightning Source, Inc.
Gross, A. 1990a. The Origin of Species: Evolutionary Taxonomy as an Example of the Rhetoric of Science, in *The Rhetorical Turn*, edited by H.W Simons. Chicago, IL: University of Chicago Press, 91–115.
_______. 1990b. *The Rhetoric of Science*. Cambridge, MA: Harvard University Press.
Gross, S. and Mnookin, J. 2003. Expert Information and Expert Evidence: A Preliminary Taxonomy. *Seton Hall Law Review*, 34, 141–90.
Gusfield, J. 1976. The Literary Rhetoric of Science: Comedy and Pathos of Drinking Driver Research. *American Sociological Review*, 41(l), 16–34.

Gwiasda, S. et al. 2000. Bibliography: Relations of Science to Literature and the Arts 1998. *Configurations*, 8, 429–62.

Haack, S. 2008. What's Wrong with Litigation Driven Science?: An Essay on Legal Epistemology. *Seton Hall Law Review*, 38, 1053–84.

Hacking, I. 2000. How Inevitable Are the Results of Successful Science? *Philosophy of Science*, 67, S58–S91.

Hamlin, C. 1986. Scientific Method and Expert Witnessing: Victorian Perspectives on a Modern Problem. *Social Studies of Science*, 16, 485–513.

Hans, V. 2007. Judges, Juries, and Scientific Evidence. *Journal of Law and Policy*, 16, 19–49.

Harris, T. 1987. *Courtroom's Finest Hour in American Cinema*. Metuchen, NJ: Scarecrow Press.

Harris, S. 1998. Thinking Locally, Acting Globally. *Configurations*, 6, 131–9.

Haynes, R. 1994. *From Faust to Strangelove: Representations of the Scientist in Western Literature*. Baltimore, MD: Johns Hopkins Press.

________. 2006. The Alchemist in Fiction: The Master Narrative. *Hyle – International Journal for the Philosophy of Chemistry*, 12, 5–29.

Hickock v. Crouse [1963] 372 U.S. 924; 344 F.2d at 96, 99.

Hickock v. Crouse [1964] 334 F.2d 95, 97 (10th Cir.).

Hickock v. Crouse [1965] 379 U.S. 982 (cert denied), rehearing denied 380 U.S. 928.

Hickock v. Hand [1962] 190 Kan. 224, 231, 373 P.2d 206, 213.

Hollander, R. 1991. Expert Claims and Social Decisions: Science, Politics, and Responsibility, in *Acceptable Evidence: Science and Values in Risk Management*, edited by D. Mayo and R. Hollander. Oxford: Oxford University Press, 160–76.

Hornby, R. 1981. *Patterns in Ibsen's Middle Plays*. Lewisburg, PA: Bucknell University Press.

Hough, G., III. 1975. How 'New'?, in *New Journalism*, edited by M. Fishwick. Bowling Green, OH: Bowling Green University Popular Press, 16–23. Available in *Journal of Popular Culture*, 9 114–21 (Summer 1975).

Hyland, K. 1998. Boosting, Hedging, and the Negotiation of Academic Knowledge, *Text*, 18, 349–82.

I am Sam (dir. Jessie Nelson, 2001).

Ibsen, H. 1999. *An Enemy of the People*. Cambridge, MA: Harvard University Press.

Irwin, A., et al. 1996. Science and Hell's Kitchen: The Local Understanding of Hazard Issues, in *Misunderstanding Science?: The Public Reconstruction of Science and Technology*, edited by A. Irwin and B. Wynne. Cambridge: Cambridge University Press, 47–64.

Jackson, S. 1829. Case of Supposed Poisoning with Arsenic. *American Journal of Medical Science*, 5, 237–61.

Jahn v. Equine Services PSC [2000], 233 F.3d 382, 391 (6th Cir.).

Jensen, V. 2005. Writing History: Capote's Novel has a Lasting Effect on Journalism. *Lawrence Journal-World*, April 3.

Johnson-McGrath, J. 1998. Witness for the Prosecution: Science versus Crime in Twentieth-Century America. *Legal Studies Forum*, 22, 1843–199.

Kallan, R. 1975. Entrance, in *New Journalism*, edited by M. Fishwick. Bowling Green, OH: Bowling Green University Popular Press, 8–15. Available in *Journal of Popular Culture*, 9, 106–13 (Summer 1975).

Kaye, D., et al. 2004. *The New Wigmore: A Treatise on Evidence, Expert Evidence* § 10.2, at 334. New York, NY: Aspen Publishing Company.

Kennedy, D. and Merrill, R. 2003. Assessing Forensic Science. *Issues in Science and Technology*, 20(1), 33–4 (Fall 2003). Available at http://www.issues.org/20.1/kennedy.html.

Kermode, M. 2006. Truman Capote, you've got a lot to answer for. *The Observer*, 15 January, 7. Available at http://film.guardian.co.uk/features/featurepages/0,1686611,00.html.

Kester, C. 1995. The Language of Law, the Sociology of Science, and the Troubles of Translation: Defining the Proper Role for Scientific Evidence of Causation. *Nebraska Law Review*, 74, 529–68.

Kirby, D. 2000. The New Eugenics in Cinema: Genetic Determinism and Gene Therapy in *Gattaca. Science Fiction Studies*, 27, part 2, no. 81, 193–215.

_______. 2003. Science Advisors, Representation, and Hollywood Films. *Molecular Interventions*, 3, 54–60.

_______. 2005. Hollywood Disaster Movies Can be Great for Science. *The Times*, 30 June, 12. Available at http://entertainment.timesonline.co.uk/article/0,14931-1673926,00.html.

Kitcher, P. 1998. A Plea for Science Studies, in *A House Built on Sand: Exposing Postmodern Myths About Science*, edited by Noretta Koertge. Oxford: Oxford University Press, 32–56.

Klein, P. 2006. Film *Capote* Raises Disturbing Ethical Questions. *Journalism Ethics for the Global Citizen.* January, 2006. Available at http://www.journalismethics.ca/book_reviews/capote/htm.

Kraus, E., Auer, C., and Mauer W. 2000. Introduction, in *Simulacrum America: The USA and the Popular Media*, edited by E. Kraus et al. Rochester, NY: Camden House, 1–20.

Kumho Tire Co. v. Carmichael [1999] 526 U.S. 137, 152.

Landsman, S. 1995. Of Witches, Madmen, and Products Liability: Historical Survey of the Use of Expert Testimony. *Behavioral Science and Law*, 13, 131–57.

__________. 1998. One Hundred Years of Rectitude: Medical Witnesses at the Old Bailey, 1717–1817. *Law and History Review*, 16, 445–94.

Laszlo, P. 2006. Self-Image of Chemists, 1950–2002. *Hyle – International Journal for the Philosophy of Chemistry*,12, 99–130.

Latour, B. 1987. *Science in Action.* Cambridge, MA: Harvard University Press.

_______. 1993. *We Have Never Been Modern*, trans, C. Porter. Cambridge, MA: Harvard University Press.

Lauzon v. Senco Products, Inc. [2001] 270 F.3d 681, 693 (8th Cir.).

Ledger, S. 1999. *Henrik Ibsen*. Plymouth: Northcote House.

Lee, Y.J. and Roth, W.M. 2004. Making a Scientist: Discursive "Doing" of Identity and Self-Presentation During Research Interviews. *5(1) Forum: Qualitative Social Research*, article 12. Available at http://www.qualitative-research.net/fqs-texte/1-04/1-04leeroth-e.htm.

Leitch, T. 2005. *Perry Mason*. Detroit, MI: Wayne State University Press.

Leiter, B. 1997. The Epistemology of Admissibility: Why Even Good Philosophy of Science Would Not Make for Good Philosophy of Evidence. *Brigham Young Law Review*, 803–20.

Lenoir, T. 1998. Inscription Practices and Materialities of Communication, in *Inscribing Science: Scientific Texts and the Materiality of Communication*, edited by T. Lenoir. Stanford: Stanford University Press, 1–19.

_______. 1999. Was the Last Turn the Right Turn? The Semiotic Turn and A.J. Greimas, in *The Science Studies Reader*, edited by M. Biagioli. New York, NY: Routledge, 290–301.

Levi, P. 1984. *The Periodic Table*. Raymond Rosenthal trans. New York, NY: Schocken Books.

Levidow, L. 2001. Precautionary Uncertainty: Regulating GM Crops in Europe. *Social Studies of Science*, 31, 842–74.

Little, G. 2006. Literature and Legal History: Analyzing Methodology. *Entertainment and Sports Law Journal*, 3, 1–12.

Littlefield, D. 2008. Case vs. Marine Widow is Dropped. *San Diego-Union Tribune*. 19 April, B1. Available at http.//news.topic.com/category/cynthia-sommer.

Locke, S. 2001. Sociology and the Public Understanding of Science: From Rationalization to Rhetoric. *British Journal of Sociology*, 52, 1–18.

_______. 2002. The Public Understanding of Science – A Rhetorical Invention. *Science, Technology, and Human Values*, 27, 87–111.

Lodge, D. 2001. *Thinks*. London: Secker & Warbug, 229.

Lubet, S. 1998. *Expert Testimony: A Guide for Expert Witnesses and the Lawyers Who Examine Them*. New York, NY: Louisville, CO: NITA Publications.

Lustre, A. 2001. Post-*Daubert* Standards for Admissibility of Scientific and Other Expert Evidence in State Courts. *American Law Reports*, 5th edition, 90, 453–545.

Lynch, M. and Cole, S. 2005. Science and Technology Studies on Trial: Dilemmas of Expertise. *Social Studies of Science*, 35, 269–311.

MacNeil, W. 2007. *Lex Populi: The Jurisprudence of Popular Culture*. Palo Alto, CA: Stanford University Press.

Mandel, G. et al. 2008. *The Cultural Cognition of Synthetic Biology Risks: A Preliminary Analysis*. Available at http://ssrn.com/abstract=1264804 (15 September 2008).

Manuta, D.M. 2005. A Counsulting Chemist's Perspectives. *Chemical and Engineering News*, February 21, 2005, 7.

Markey, Chief Judge Howard T. 1984. Jurisprudence or "Juriscience"? *William. & Mary Law Review*, 25, 525–44.

Mayo, D. 1991. Sociological Versus Metascientific Views of Risk Assessment, in *Acceptable Evidence: Science and Values in Risk Management*, edited by D. Mayo and R. Hollander. Oxford: Oxford University Press, 29–47.

McCloskey, D. 1991. The Essential Rhetoric of Law, Literature, and Liberty. *Critical Review*, 5, 203–23.

McKechnie, R. 1996. Insiders and Outsiders: Identifying Experts on Home Ground, in *Misunderstanding Science? The Public Reconstruction of Science and Technology*, edited by A. Irwin and B. Wynne. Cambridge: Cambridge University Press, 126–51.

Metabolife International, Inc. v. Wornick [2001] 264 F.3d 832, 843 (9th Cir.).

Michael, M. 2002. Comprehension, Apprehension, Prehension: Heterogeneity and the Public Understanding of Science. *Science, Technology, and Human Values*, 27, 357–78.

_______. 1996. Ignoring Science: Discourses of Ignorance in the Public Understanding of Science, in *Misunderstanding Science? The Public Reconstruction of Science and Technology*, edited by A. Irwin and B. Wynne. Cambridge: Cambridge University Press, 107–25.

Middleburg, R. 2008. Forensic Toxicology in the Fore … and Aft. *Forensic Magazine*, June/July. Available at http://www.forensicmag.com/print/207.

Miller, A. 1950. *An Enemy of the People* (adaptation of Ibsen's play). New York, NY: Penguin Books USA, Inc.

_______. 1989. Ibsen's Warning. *Index on Censorship*, Jul/Aug, 74–6.

Miller, P. n.d. "Infamous" Truman Capote in Cold Blooded Media Seduction. *WBAI Arts Magazine.* Available at http://www.wbai.org/index.php?options=com co ntent&task=view&id=9165&Itemid=125.

Mnookin, J. 2007. Idealizing Science and Demonizing Experts: An Intellectual History of Expert Evidence. *Villanova. Law Review*, 52, 763 802.

Moriarty, J.C. 2007. "Misconvictions," Science, and The Ministers of Justice. *Nebraska Law Review*, 86, 1–42.

Moriarty, J.C. and Saks, M.J. 2005. Forensic Science: Grand Goals, Tragic Flaws, and Judicial Gatekeeping. *Judge's Journal*, 44(5), 16–33.

Mulkay, M. 1979. *Science and the Sociology of Knowledge*. London: George Allen & Unwin.

Mulkay, M., Potter, J. and Yearley, S. 1983. Why an Analysis of Scientific Discourse is Needed, in *Science Observed: Perspectives on the Social Study of Science*, edited by K. Knorr-Cetina and M. Mulkay. London: Sage Publications, 171–203.

Music Box (dir. Costa-Gavras, 1989).

My Cousin Vinny (dir. Jonathan Lynn, 1992).

Myers, G. 1990. *Writing Biology.* Madison, WI: University Wisconsin Press.

Nacquet, A. 1884. *Legal Chemistry: A Guide to the Detection of Poisons, Examination of Tea, Stains, etc., as Applied to Chemical Jurisprudence* (J.P. Battershall translation with additions). New York, NY: D. Van Nostrand.
Nelson, J. 1998. *Tropes of Politics: Science, Theory, Rhetoric, Action.* Madison, WI: University of Wisconsin Press.
Nelson, W. 1964. The Changing Role of the Jury in the Nineteenth Century. *Yale Law Journal*, 74, 170–92.
Nesteruk, J. 1999. A New Narrative for Corporate Law. *Legal Studies Forum*, 23, 281–92.
Niyoki, S. 1980. Historic Development of Forensic Toxicology in America up to 1978. *American Journal of Forensic Medicine & Pathology*, 1, 251–8.
NMS Labs. 2007a. (Letter dated 8 March 2007 to Robert G. Udell, Esq., counsel for Cynthia Arlene Sommer).
NMS Labs. 2007b. (Letter dated 22 March 2007 to Robert Udell, Esq., counsel for Cynthia Arlene Sommer).
Note. 2002. *Harvard Law Review*, 115, 2349–56.
Olsen, E.C. and Czerkas, S.M. 1987. *Dinosaurs Past and Present.* Los Angeles, CA: Natural History Museum of Los Angeles County.
Orfila, M. 1849. On Poisoning by Arsenic, Antinomy and Copper. *British and Foreign Medical Review*, 11, 37–55.
_______. 1815. *Traité des Poisons Tirés des Règnes*, *Minéral*, *Vēgétal* et *Animal* ou *Toxicologie Général.* Paris: Cuchet.
Otis, L. 2001. Introduction, in Ramón y Cajal, S., *Vacation Stories: Five Science Fiction Tales.* Champagne, IL: University of Illinois Press, vii–xx.
Pencak, W. 1999. Lyres Against the Law: Orpheus as Cyberpunk Outlaw. *Legal Studies Forum*, 23, 293–313.
People's Motion to Dismiss. 2008. *People v. Sommer*, California Superior Court No. SCD195202, 17 April.
Peterfreund, S. 1990. Introduction, in *Literature and Science: Theory and Practice*, edited by S. Peterfreund. Boston, MA: Northeastern University Press, 3–13.
___________. 1987. Literature and Science: The Present State of the Field. *University of Hartford Studies in Literature*, 19, 25–36.
Pether, P. 2009. Language, in *Law and The Humanities: An Introduction*, edited by Sarat, Anderson, and Frank. Cambridge: Cambridge University Press, 315–38.
Plimpton, G. 1966. The Story Behind a Nonfiction Novel. *New York Times Book Review*, 16 January, 2–3, 38–43.
_________. 1997. *Truman Capote: In Which Various Friends, Enemies, Acquaintances and Detractors Recall His Turbulent Career.* New York, NY: Doubleday.
Posner, R. 1986. Law and Literature: A Relation Reargued. *Virginia Law Review*, 72, 1351–92.
________. 1989. The Depiction of Law in *The Bonfire of the Vanities*. 98 *Yale Law Journal*, 98, 1653–62.

Potter, J. 1996. *Representing Reality: Discourse, Rhetoric and Social Construction.* Thousand Oaks, CA: Sage Publications Ltd.

Prelli, L. 1989. *A Rhetoric of Science: Inventing Scientific Discourse.* Columbia, SC: University of South Carolina Press.

Presumed Innocent (dir. Alan J. Pakula, 1990).

Primal Fear (dir. Gregory Hoblit, 1995).

Pyrek, K. 2007. *Forensic Science Under Seige: The Challenges of Forensic Laboratories and the Medico-Legal Investigation System.* Oxford: Kelly Elsevier Books.

Ramón y Cajal, S. (See Cajal, S. Ramón y).

Reed, K. 1981. *Truman Capote.* Boston, MA: Twayne.

Reichman, A. 2007. The Production of Law (and Cinema), paper 1997, in *Bepress Legal Series.* Available at http://law.bepress.com/express/eps/1997, and in *Southern California Interdisciplinary Law Journal*, 17, 457–508.

Rincon, P. 2005. CSI Shows Give "Unrealistic Wiew." *BBC News*, 21 February. Available at http://news.bbc.co.uk/1/hi/sci/tech/4284335.stm.

Rip, A. 2003. Constructing Expertise: In a Third Wave of Science Studies? *Social Studies of Science*, 33(3), 419–34.

Ripley, G. and Dana, C. 1874. *The American Cyclopaedia: A Popular Dictionary of Current Knowledge.* Boston, MA: D. Appleton and Company.

Risinger, D. and Saks, M. 2003. A House with No Foundation: Forensic Science Needs to Build a Base of Rigorous Research to Establish Its Reliability. *Issues in Science and Technology*, 20(1), 35–9. Available at http://www.issues.org/20.1/risinger.html.

Rockwood, B. 1999. New Possibilities. *Legal Studies Forum*, 23, 167–279.

Rohn, J. 2010a. More Lab in the Library. *Nature*, 465, 265.

_____. 2010b. An Honest Look at Biotech. *The Scientist*, 24(12), 76.

_____. 2006. Experimental Fiction. *Nature*, 439, 269.

Roszak, T. 1974. The Monster and the Titan: Science, Knowledge, and Gnosis. *Daedalus*, 103(3), 17–32.

Rouse, J. 1996. *Engaging Science: How to Understand Its Practices Philosophically.* Ithaca, NY: Cornell University Press.

______. 1999. Understanding Scientific Practices: Cultural Studies of Science as a Philosophical Program, in *The Science Studies Reader*, edited by M. Biagioli. New York, NY: Routledge, 442–56.

Saks, M. 1987. Accuracy vs. Advocacy: Expert Testimony Before the Bench. *Technology Review*, Aug/Sept., 42–50.

_______. 2000. Banishing Ipse-Dixit: The Impact of Kumho Tire on Forensic Identification Science. *Washington and Lee Law Review*, 57, 879–900.

Salvador, W. 1901. *Alumni Register* (University of Pennsylvania), 5, 116–17.

Scharf, T. and Westcott, T., II. 1884. *History of Philadelphia.* Philadelphia, PA: L.H. Everts & Co.

Schuck, P. 1993. Multi-Culturalism Redux: Science, Law, and Politics. *Yale Law & Policy Review*, 11, 1–46.

Schummer, J. 2006. Historical Roots of the "Mad Scientist": Chemists in Nineteenth-century Literature. *AMBIX*, 53, 99–127.

Schwartz, M. and Thompson, M. 1990. *Divided We Stand: Redefining Politics, Technology, and Social Choice.* New York, NY: Harvester Wheatsheaf.

Serres, M. with Latour, B. 1990. *Conversations on Science, Culture, and Time* (Roxanne Lapidus trans.). Ann Arbor, MI: University Michigan Press.

Serres, M. 1987. *Statues*. Paris: François Bourin.

Shapiro and Associates. 2002. *Public Perception of Lawyers: Consumer Research Findings*. Chicago, IL: ABA Publications.

Sheffield, C. 2002. High Tech Futures: How 'Hard SF' Keeps the Science in Science Fiction. *Washington Post Book World*, 7 April, TO4.

Sherwin, R. 2006. Introduction, in *Popular Culture and Law*, edited by R. Sherwin. Aldershot: Ashgate Publishing, xi–xxii.

Shelley, M. 1818. *Frankenstein*. London: George Routledge & Sons.

Sheppard, R.Z. 1987. The Haves and the Have-Mores. *Time*, 9 November, 101.

Silverman, D. 2001. *Interpreting Qualitative Data: Methods For Analyzing Talk, Text and Interaction*. London: Sage Publications Ltd.

Simons, H. 1993. The Rhetoric of the Scientific Research Report: 'Drug-pushing' in a Medical Journal Article, in *The Recovery of Rhetoric: Persuasive Discourse and Disciplinarity in the Human Sciences*, edited by R.H. Roberts and J.M.M. Good. Charlottesville, VA: University Press of Virginia, 148–63.

Smith, P. 2005. An Outspoken Critic: Former Prosecutor Says Capote Misrepresented Him. *Lawrence Journal-World*, 5 April. Available at http://www2.ljworld.com/news/2005/apr/05/an_outspoken_critic/.

Spokes, S. 1937. A Case of Circumstantial Evidence. *Sussex County Magazine*, Jan.–Dec., 118–22.

Spurrill, E.G. n.d. Truth, Better Than Fiction: How *In Cold Fact* by Phillip K. Tompkins changed my opinion of *In Cold Blood* by Truman Capote. *Authors' Den*. Available at http://authorsden.com/visit/viewArticle.asp?id=4155.

State v. Boan [1984] 235 Kan. 800, 809, 686 P.2d 160.

State v. Hickock and Smith [1961], 188 Kan. 473, 363 P.2d 541, appeal dismissed 373 U.S. 574 (1965).

Stewart, J. 1988. Science Shops in France; a Personal View. *Science as Culture*, 2, 52–74.

Sundby, S. 1997. The Jury as Critic: An Empirical Look at How Capital Juries Perceive Expert and Lay Testimony. *Virginia Law Review*, 83, 1109–18.

Suppe, F. 1998. The Structure of a Scientific Paper. *Philosophy of Science*, 65, 381–405.

Suspect (dir. Peter Yates, 1987).

Taylor, A.S. 1873. I *The Principles and Practice of Medical Jurisprudence*. London: Churchill.

Taylor, C. 1996. *Defining Science: A Rhetoric of Demarcation.* Madison, WI: University Wisconsin Press.

________. 1998a. Feuding Communities and the Feudalism of Science: Democratizing the Community and/of Science, in *Rhetoric and Community: Studies in Unity and Fragmentation*, edited by J. Hogan. Columbia, SC: University of South Carolina Press, 284–91.

________. 1998b. Science as Cultural Practice: A Rhetorical Perspective, in *Essays in the Study of Scientific Discourse: Methods, Practice, and Pedagogy*, edited by J. Battalio. Stamford, CT: Ablex Publishing Corporation, 89–101.

The Verdict (dir. Sydney Lumet, 1982).

Thornburgh, D. 1998. Junk Science – the Lawyer's Ethical Responsibilities. *Fordham Urban Law Journal*, 25, 449–69.

Toburen, A. 2002. Science Movies: Always Science Fiction? *Why Files*, 11 January, 1–4. Available at http://whyfiles.org/147sci_in_film/.

Tompkins, P. 1966. In Cold Fact. *Esquire*, June 1966, 125, 127, 166–71.

Toumey, C.P. 1992. The Moral Character of Mad Scientists: A Cultural Critique of Science. *Science, Technology & Human Values*, 17, 411–37.

Traweek, S. 1993. An Introduction to Cultural and Social Studies of Sciences and Technologies. *Culture, Medicine, and Psychiatry*, 17, 3–25.

Trilling, D. 1955. A Symbol of Reason. *N.Y. Times*, 3 March, BR3.

Tudor, A. 1989. *Monsters and Mad Scientists: A Cultural History of the Horror Movie*. Cambridge, MA: Blackwell.

Tynan, K. 1966. Review of In Cold Blood. *London Sunday Observer Weekend Review*, 13 March, 1.

US v. Havvard [2001] 260 F.3d 597 (7th Cir.).

Vigilante, R. 1987. The Truth About Tom Wolfe (book review of *The Bonfire of the Vanities*). *National Review*, 18 December, 46–9.

Wall Street Journal. 2010. Ag Department Uproots Science (editorial). 27 Dec. 2010, A16.

War Games (dir. John Badham, 1983).

Ward, I. 1998. Literature and the Legal Imagination. *Ireland Legal Quarterly*, 49, 167–79.

Ward, T. 2005. A Mania for Suspicion: Poisoning, Science, and the Law, in *Criminal Conversations: Victorian Crimes, Social Panic, and Moral Outrage*, edited by J. Rowbotham and K. Stevenson. Columbus, OH: Ohio State University Press, 140–56.

Watson, K. 2004. *Poisoned Lives: English Poisoners and Their Victims*. London: Hambledon and London.

________. 2006. Criminal Poisoning in England and the Origins of the Marsh Test for Arsenic, in *Chemistry, Medicine, and Crime: M.B. Orfila (1789–1853) and His Times*, edited by J. Bertomeu-Sánchez and A. Nieto-Galan, 2006). Sagamore Beach, MA: Science History Publications, 183–206.

Weingart, P. 2006. Chemists and the Craft in Fiction Film. Hyle – *International Journal for the Philosophy of Chemistry*, 12, 31–44.

Weinstein, J. 1986. Improving Expert Testimony. *University of Richmond Law Review*, 20, 473–97.

Weisberg, R. 1992. *Poethics: and Other Strategies of Law and Literature*. New York, NY: Columbia University Press.

Wells, D. 1854. Interesting Case of Medical Jurisprudence – Poisoning by Aconite. *Boston Medical & Surgical Journal*, 50(15), 289–304.

Wells, H.G. 1967. *The Island of Doctor Moreau*. New York, NY: Penguin Young Readers Group.

West, R. 1966. A Grave and Reverend Book (review of *In Cold Blood*). *Harper's Magazine*, February, 108–114.

_______. 1947. *The Meaning of Treason*. New York, NY: Viking Press.

_______. 1955. Mr. Setty and Mr. Hume, in *A Train of Powder*. New York, NY: Viking Press, 165–232.

Willing, R. 2004. 'CSI Effect' has Juries Wanting More Evidence. *USA Today*, 5 August, A01. Available at http://usatoday.com/news/nation/2004-08-05-csi-effect_x.htm.

Wright, S. 2006. *The Amalgamation Polka*. New York, NY: Vintage Books.

Wynne, B. 1996. Misunderstood Misunderstandings: Social Identities and Public Uptake of Science, in *Misunderstanding Science? The Public Reconstruction of Science and Technology*, edited by A. Irwin and B. Wynne. Cambridge: Cambridge University Press, 19–46.

Zizek, S. 2002. Lacan Between Cultural Studies and Cognitivism, in *Lacan and Science*, edited by J. Glynos and Y. Stavrakakis. London: Karnac Books, 291–320.

Index

For Product Safety Concerns and Information please contact our EU
representative GPSR@taylorandfrancis.com
Taylor & Francis Verlag GmbH, Kaufingerstraße 24, 80331 München, Germany

www.ingramcontent.com/pod-product-compliance
Ingram Content Group UK Ltd.
Pitfield, Milton Keynes, MK11 3LW, UK
UKHW011018180926
475701UK00004B/812
9781138261365